Also by Cynthia Ozick

The Puttermesser Papers

Fame & Folly

The Shawl

Metaphor & Memory

The Messiah of Stockholm

The Cannibal Galaxy

Art & Ardor

Levitation: Five Fictions

Bloodshed and Three Novellas

The Pagan Rabbi and Other Stories

Trust

Quarrel & Quandary

Quarrel & Quandary

ESSAYS BY

Cynthia Ozick

ALFRED A. KNOPF   NEW YORK   2000

The essays in this collection originally appeared, in whole or in
part, in the following publications: *American Scholar, Atlantic
Monthly, Borders, Commentary, Expressen* (Stockholm),
*House & Garden, Los Angeles Times Book Review, The
New Republic, The New York Times, The New York Times
Magazine, The New Yorker,* and *The Yale Review.*

Grateful acknowledgment is made to the following for
permission to reprint previously published material:
Random House, Inc.: Four lines from "The More Loving
One" from *W. H. Auden: Collected Poems* by W. H. Auden.
Copyright © 1976 by Edward Mendelson, William
Meredith, and Monroe K. Spears, Executors of the Estate of
W. H. Auden. Reprinted by permission of Random House, Inc.
Charles Wright: Eight lines from poem by Charles
Wright. Reprinted by permission of the author.

Library of Congress Cataloging-in-Publication Data
Ozick, Cynthia.
Quarrel & quandary : essays / Cynthia Ozick.—1st ed.
p.   cm.
ISBN 0-375-41061-9 (alk. paper)
1. Literature—History and criticism.   I. Title: Quarrel & quandary.   II. Title.

PN511 .O95 2000
814'.54—dc21   99-089889

To

Martin Baron

Contents

Forethoughts

We make out of the quarrel with others, rhetoric,
but out of the quarrel with ourselves, poetry.
—W. B. Yeats

"But you *are* engagé," the famous and energetic man who four years ago directed my play remarked the other day. I say "my play," and not "a play of mine," which may suggest more than one, because it is the only work for the theater I have ever written; I feel certain I will never write another. I had not seen the director since the play closed, and his comment—that once-faddish, Sartre-sounding word—startled me. My one play had, in fact, been political, even polemical; it was about Holocaust denial. And though I had always longed to try my hand at drama, I had supposed it would find its shape, if the time ever came, in something literary or satiric, or both; my secret mnemonic model was Simon Gray's frivolously melancholic *The Common Pursuit*, which had, decades ago, enthralled me. So I was surprised when a congeries of circumstances, not all of my own manufacture, resulted in a play that was indisputably "engagé." I had been driven to it like a wheel the spokes of which were being nailed into place, even while it ran, by mechanics in unfamiliar uniform.

I mean by all this that I resist the political, and am reluctant to take on its spots and stripes: the focus and deliberateness of political engagement, its judgments and its zeal, are so much the opposite of loafing and inviting one's soul. This collection, for instance, includes an essay on essays, wherein the form of the

essay is defined, and defended, as follows: "If there is information in an essay, it is by-the-by, and if there is an opinion in
it, you need not trust it for the long run. A genuine essay has
no educational, polemical, or sociopolitical use." This was only
the latest in a string of similar formulations—or call them
wardings-off; what was being warded off was any tincture of the
topical or the tendentious. In 1983, in a foreword to my first
non-fiction collection, I wrote, comparing essays to stories,
"Sometimes even an essay can invent, burn, guess, try out, hur-
tle forward, succumb to that flood of sign and nuance that adds
up to intuition, disclosure, discovery. The only non-fiction worth
writing—at least for me—lacks the summarizing gift, is heir to
nothing, and sets out with empty pockets from scratch." In a
1988 preface, this time dubbed a "forewarning," I continued
along the same line, or tightrope: "Nearly every essay, like every
story, is an experiment, not a credo. What I am repudiating," I
persisted, "is the inference that a handful of essays is equal to a
Weltanschauung; that an essay is generally anything more than
simply another fiction—a short story told in the form of an
argument, or a history, or even (once in a very great while) an
illumination. But never a tenet."

Can I make that stick here? Or, rather, can I claim that I have
stuck to this credo-contra-credos? Or have I, despite these
defensive and sometimes slippery declarations of resistance,
fallen, after all, into the distinctly educational, polemical, and
sociopolitical? How can I deny that I have willfully entered the
lists of tenet and exigency in writing here on Anne Frank; or,
contemplating the rights of history, on so-called Holocaust fiction; or on the responsibility of public intellectuals; or on Dostoyevsky's Unabomber; or on Central European politics and
policies, ancient and modern, as a framework for Kafka's familial
and personal history?

George Orwell, in "Why I Write," asserts that "the opinion

that art should have nothing to do with politics is itself a political attitude." There are times when one is tempted to agree with him, and in my discussion of E. M. Forster's views on art in the terrible year of 1941, I do mainly agree—or, in Forster's own formula ("Two Cheers for Democracy" is one of his celebrated phrases), I am willing to give the idea two cheers at least. Yet inserting politics into literature has, as we have seen, led to the extremist (or absurdist) notion that Jane Austen, for instance, is tainted with colonialism and slave-holding because Sir Thomas Bertram in *Mansfield Park* owns plantations in eighteenth-century Antigua. This kind of thinking fits nicely with James Thurber's tale of the bear who leaned so far backward that he fell on his face. It asks a novel of country-house manners to become a tract on British imperialism. Then must the soldiers and sailors in Jane Austen's fiction supply the occasion for a discourse on the Napoleonic Wars, or may they be left to their romantic employments in the minds of Austen's marriageable young ladies? (It is politics, of course, that accounts for the presence of those soldiers and sailors.) "No book is genuinely free from political bias," Orwell plausibly remarks—which is different from saying that every book ought to be politically acceptable to contemporary sensibilities. If that were our objective, then scores of European classics, beginning with Chaucer's "The Prioress's Tale"—the theme of which is responsible for centuries of calumny and bloodshed—would have to be thrown out with the bath water. (Which is what some readers of "Who Owns Anne Frank?" concluded I was seriously recommending for the *Diary* in the closing paragraph of that essay; these same readers may possibly believe that Dean Swift meant it when he suggested, as a way of ameliorating famine in Ireland, that the Irish babies be eaten.) The writer's subject matter, Orwell goes on, "will be determined by the age he lives in—at least that is true in tumultuous, revolutionary ages like our own." If Orwell is completely right, then both Jane Austen and E. M. Forster in 1941 (he was speaking at a writers' conference) are completely wrong. She declined to engage with colonialism, slavery, and the Napoleonic upheavals; he declined to engage with Hitler, anti-Semitism, and the German upheavals. Both were determined to be undetermined by the politics of the age they lived in. (And yet Forster, in 1924, had already published *A Passage to India*, arguing against Britain as a colonial power.) If I feel less critical of Austen than of Forster (and I do), it is not only because there is a difference between a novel and a speech, but also because undoubtedly I am, as Orwell insists, determined by my own tumultuous age. Never mind that we are launched now into the twenty-first century; as my essay on the contentions of history and imagination may signify, the twentieth is not yet done with us, nor we with it.

The central question, perhaps, is this: is politics a distraction from art, or is it how we pay attention to the life that gives rise to art? And might not the answer be: both, depending on the issues and the times? A reflection on a ladle in a kitchen drawer can outweigh what the President is up to when what the President is up to is too trivial to bear serious contemplation. The essential point has to do with the idea of the ephemeral. History is and is not ephemeral; situations and events evaporate, but their moral and intellectual residue does not. A century afterward, contemporary incarnations of Dreyfusards and anti-Dreyfusards are plainly recognizable. In a post-theological era, a romantic paganism (sometimes labeled "spirituality") freely roams. What Saul Bellow calls "the oceanic proliferating complexity of things" sweeps the mind away from concentration. Concentration on what? On the non-transient. And it is on that negative ground that I set my purpose.

In a recent issue of one of those Internet magazines (I read it in the paper version), a pair of reviewers in e-mail dialogue faulted an esteemed young critic of earned authority for writing about the old moderns—Chekhov, Flaubert, Mann, Woolf—as if to say that ripeness isn't all it's cracked up to be. (They were this-generation reviewers, and appeared to regard the critic as a traitor to his cohort.) What was clearly in play was the journalistic conviction—a kind of noose—that there is only so much space on a page (even on a cybernetic page), so it had better be filled up with Now: Now being the politics of the current literary marketplace. Generations, yours and mine, are broader and roomier and more flexible than that. Commenting on the beautiful heads of unschooled TV anchormen, Bellow notes, "These crowns of hair contribute charm and dignity but perhaps also oppress the brain with their weight." Journalism is a necessity, but it is not a permanence. When I hear someone (seventy-plus or twenty-something) utter "my generation," I know I am in the vicinity of a light mind. This is not what Orwell intended when he spoke of being determined by the turbulence of one's own time. When we allude to "our age," either we include our predecessors and their travail (and also their bold genius) or we show ourselves to be minor in brain and intuition.

Two cheers, then—when there is no choice—for being engagé; but three cheers and more for that other bravery, the literary essay, and for memory's mooning and maundering, and for losing one's way in the bliss of American prose, and finding one's way, too, when politics is slumbering, in the surprising atlas of all that is not benign, yet (somehow, sometimes) stirring.

June 1999

Quarrel & Quandary

Dostoyevsky's Unabomber

Soon after dawn on a very cold winter morning in 1849, fifteen Russian criminals, in groups of three, were led before a firing squad. They were all insurgents against the despotism of Czar Nicholas I. They were mostly educated men, idealists in pursuit of a just society. They felt no remorse. Several were professed atheists. All were radicals. A priest carrying a cross and a Bible accompanied them. The first three were handed white gowns and shapeless caps and ordered to put these on; then they were tied to posts. The rest waited their turn. Each man in his own way prepared to die. The sun was beginning to brighten; the firing squad took aim. At just that moment there was a signal—a roll of drums—and the rifles were lowered. A galloping horseman announced a reprieve. Although the condemned were unaware of it, the execution was staged, and the reprieve was designed to demonstrate the merciful heart of the Czar. Instead of being shot, the criminals were to be transported in shackles to a Siberian penal colony.

One of the men went permanently mad. Another, fifteen years afterward, wrote *Crime and Punishment,* an impassioned assault on exactly the kind of radical faith that had brought its author to face the Czar's riflemen that day. It was a work almost in the nature of double jeopardy: as if Fyodor Dostoyevsky in middle age—a defender of the Czar, the enemy of revolutionary socialism—were convicting and punishing his younger self yet again for the theories the mature novelist had come to abhor.

2.

A new type of crime is on the American mind—foreign, remote, metaphysical, even literary; and radically different from what we are used to. Street crime, drunken crime, drug-inspired crime, crimes of passion, greed, revenge, crimes against children, gangster crime, white-collar crime, break-ins, car thefts, holdups, shootings—these are familiar, and to a degree nearly expected. They shake us up without disorienting us. They belong to our civilization; they are the darker signals of home. "Our" crime has usually been local—the stalker, the burglar, the mugger lurking in a doorway. Even Jeffrey Dahmer, the cannibal sadist who kept boys' body parts in his kitchen refrigerator, is not so very anomalous in the context of what can happen in ordinary neighborhoods—a little girl imprisoned in an underground cage; children tormented, starved, beaten to death; newborns bludgeoned; battered women, slain wives, mutilated husbands. Domesticity gone awry.

All that is recognizable and homespun. What feels alien to America is the philosophical criminal of exceptional intelligence and humanitarian purpose who is driven to commit murder out of an uncompromising idealism. Such a type has always seemed a literary construct of a particular European political coloration (*The Secret Agent, The Princess Casamassima*), or else has hinted at ideologies so removed from tame Republicans and Democrats as to be literally outlandish. Then came the mysterious depredations of the Unabomber. Until the melodramatic publication of his manifesto in major newspapers, the Unabomber remained an unpredictable riddle, unfathomable, sans name or habitation. In garrulous print his credo revealed him to be a visionary. His dream was of a green and pleasant land liberated from the curse of technological proliferation. The technical élites were his targets: computer wizards like Professor David Gelernter of Yale, a thinker in pursuit of artificial intelligence. Maimed by a package bomb, Gelernter escaped death; others did not.

In the storm of interpretation that followed the Unabomber's public declaration of principles, he was often mistaken for a kind of contemporary Luddite. This was a serious misnomer. The nineteenth-century Luddites were hand weavers who rioted against the introduction of mechanical looms in England's textile industry; they smashed the machines to protect their livelihoods. They were not out to kill, nor did they promulgate romantic theories about the wholesome superiority of hand looms. They were selfish, ruthlessly pragmatic, and societally unreasonable. By contrast, Theodore Kaczynski—the Unabomber—is above all a calculating social reasoner and messianic utopian. His crimes, for which he was found guilty as charged, were intended to restore us to cities and landscapes clear of digital complexities; he meant to clean the American slate of its accumulated techno-structural smudges. At the same time, we can acknowledge him to have been selfless and pure, loyal and empathic, the sort of man who befriends, without condescension, an uneducated and impoverished Mexican laborer. It is easy to think of the Unabomber, living out his principles in his pollution-free mountain cabin, as a Thoreauvian philosopher of advanced environmentalism. The philosopher is one with the murderer. The Napoleonic world-improver is one with the humble hermit of the wilderness.

In the Unabomber, America has at last brought forth its own Raskolnikov—the appealing, appalling, and disturbingly visionary murderer of *Crime and Punishment*, Dostoyevsky's masterwork of 1866. But the Unabomber is not the only ideological criminal (though he may be the most intellectual) to burst out of remoteness and fantasy onto unsuspecting native grounds. It was a political conviction rooted in anti-government ideas of liberty suppressed that fueled the deadly bombing of a Federal building in Oklahoma City. God's will directed the bombing of the World Trade Center, and the Muslim zealots who devised the means are world-improvers obedient to the highest good; so are the bombers of abortion clinics. The Weathermen of the sixties, who bombed banks and shot police in order to release "Amerika" from the tyranny of a democratic polity, are close ideological cousins of the Russian nihilists who agitated against Alexander II, the liberalizing Czar of a century before. That celebrated nineteen-sixties mantra—to make an omelet you need to break eggs—had its origin not in an affinity for violence, but in the mouth-watering lure of the humanitarian omelet. It was only the gastronomic image that was novel. In the Russian sixties, one hundred years earlier—in 1861, the very year Alexander II freed the serfs—a radical young critic named Dimitry Pisarev called for striking "right and left" and announced, "What resists the blow is worth keeping; what flies to pieces is rubbish." Here was the altruistic bomber's dogma, proclaimed in the pages of a literary journal—and long before *The New York Review of Books* published on its front cover a diagram of how to construct a Molotov cocktail.

Like the Unabomber, Raskolnikov is an intellectual who publishes a notorious essay expounding his ideas about men and society. Both are obscure loners. Both are alienated from a concerned and affectionate family. Both are tender toward outcasts and the needy. Both are élitists. Both are idealists. Both are murderers. Contemporary America, it seems, has finally caught up with czarist Russia's most argumentative novelist.

And in *Crime and Punishment* Dostoyevsky was feverishly pursuing an argument. It was an argument against the radicals who were dominant among Russian intellectuals in the eighteen-sixties, many of them espousing nihilist views. In the universities especially, revolutionary commotion was on the rise. Yet there was an incongruity in the timing of all these calls for violent subversion. St. Petersburg was no longer the seat of the old Czar of the repressive eighteen-forties, the tyrannical Nicholas I, against whose cruelties convulsive outrage might be justly presumed. Paradoxically, under that grim reign even the most fiery radicals were at heart gradualists who modeled their hopes on Western reformist ideas. By the incendiary sixties, the throne was held by Nicholas's moderate son and successor, whose numerous democratic initiatives looked to be nudging Russia toward something that might eventually resemble a constitutional monarchy. The younger revolutionary theorists would have none of it. It was incomplete; it was too slow. Liberalism, they roared, was the enemy of revolution, and would impede a more definitive razing of evil.

The first installments of *Crime and Punishment* had just begun to appear in *The Russian Messenger*, a Slavophile periodical, when a student revolutionary made an attempt on the life of the Czar as he was leaving the gardens of the Winter Palace to enter his carriage. The government responded with a draconian crackdown on the radicals. "You know," Dostoyevsky wrote cuttingly to his publisher in the wake of these events, "they are completely convinced that on a *tabula rasa* they will immediately construct a paradise." But he went on to sympathize with "our poor little defenseless boys and girls" and "their enthusiasm for the good and their purity of heart." So many "have become nihilists so purely, so unselfishly, in the name of honor, truth, and genuine usefulness! You know they are helpless against these stupidities, and take them for perfection." And though in the same letter he spoke of "the powerful, extraordinary, sacred union of the Czar with the people," he objected to the increase in repression. "But how can nihilism be fought without freedom of speech?" he asked.

This mixture of contempt for the radicals and solicitude for their misguided, perplexed, and perplexing humanity led to the fashioning of Raskolnikov. Pisarev striking right and left was one ingredient. Another was the appeal of self-sacrificial idealism. And a third was the literary mode through which Dostoyevsky combined and refined the tangled elements of passion, brutishness, monomaniacal principle, mental chaos, candor, mockery, fury, compassion, generosity—and two brutal ax-murders. All these contradictory elements course through Raskolnikov with nearly a Joycean effect; but if stream of consciousness flows mutely and uninterruptedly, assimilating the outer world into the inner, Raskolnikov's mind—and Dostoyevsky's method—is zigzag and bumpy, given to rebellious and unaccountable alterations of purpose. Raskolnikov is without restraint—not only as an angry character in a novel, but as a reflection of Dostoyevsky himself, who was out to expose the entire spectrum of radical thought engulfing the writers and thinkers of St. Petersburg.

This may be why Raskolnikov is made to rush dizzyingly from impulse to impulse, from kindliness to withdrawal to lashing out, and from one underlying motive to another—a disorderliness at war with his half-buried and equivocal conscience. Only at the start is he seen, briefly, to be deliberate and in control. Detached, reasoning it out, Raskolnikov robs and murders a pawnbroker whom he has come to loathe, an unpleasant and predatory old woman alone and helpless in her flat. He hammers her repeatedly with the heavy handle of an ax:

Her thin hair, pale and streaked with gray, was thickly greased as usual, plaited into a ratty braid and tucked under

a piece of horn comb that stuck up at the back of her head . . .
he struck her again and yet again with all his strength, both
times with the butt-end, both times on the crown of the
head. Blood poured out as from an overturned glass.

Unexpectedly, the old woman's simple-minded sister just then
enters the flat; she is disposed of even more horribly: "The blow
landed directly on the skull, with the sharp edge, and immediately split the whole upper part of the forehead, almost to the
crown."

The second slaying is an unforeseen by-product of the first.
The first is the rational consequence of forethought. What is the
nature—the thesis—of this forethought? Shortly before the
murder, Raskolnikov overhears a student in a tavern speculating
about the pawnbroker: she is "rich as a Jew," and has willed all
her money to the Church. "A hundred, a thousand good deeds
and undertakings . . . could be arranged and set going by the
money that old woman has doomed to the monastery!" exclaims
the student.

Hundreds, maybe thousands of lives put right; dozens of
families saved from destitution, from decay, from ruin, from
depravity, from the venereal hospitals—all on her money.
Kill her and take her money, so that afterwards with its help
you can devote yourself to the service of all mankind and
the common cause. . . . One death for hundreds of lives—it's
simple arithmetic! And what does the life of this stupid, consumptive, and wicked old crone mean in the general balance? No more than the life of a louse, a cockroach.

Startled by this polemic, Raskolnikov admits to himself that
"*exactly the same thoughts* had just been conceived in his own
head"—though not as harmless theoretical bombast.

The theory in Raskolnikov's head—Benthamite utilitarianism, the greatest good for the greatest number, with its calibrated notions of what is useful and what is expendable—had been current for at least a decade among the Westernizing majority of the Russian intelligentsia, especially the literati of the capital. In supplying Bentham with an ax, Dostoyevsky thought to carry out the intoxications of the utilitarian doctrine as far as its principles would go: brutality and bloodletting would reveal the poisonous fruit of a political philosophy based on reason alone.

A fiercely sardonic repudiation of that philosophy—some of it in the vocabulary of contemporary American controversy—is entrusted to Raskolnikov's affectionate and loyal comrade, Razumikhin:

> It started with the views of the socialists. . . . Crime is a protest against the abnormality of the social set-up—that alone and nothing more, no other causes are admitted—but nothing! . . . With them one is always a "victim of the environment"—and nothing else! . . . If society itself is normally set up, all crimes will at once disappear, because there will be no reason for protesting. . . . Nature isn't taken into account, nature is driven out, nature is not supposed to be! . . . On the contrary, a social system, coming out of some mathematical head, will at once organize the whole of mankind and instantly make it righteous and sinless. . . . And it turns out in the end that they've reduced everything to mere brickwork and the layout of corridors and rooms in a phalanstery!

The phalanstery, a cooperative commune, was the brainchild of Charles Fourier, who, along with the political theorist Saint-Simon (and well before Marx), was an enduring influence on the Francophile Russian radical intelligentsia. But Razumikhin's outcry against the utopian socialists who idealize the life of the commune and fantasize universal harmony is no more than a satiric rap on the knuckles. Dostoyevsky is after a bloodier and more threatening vision—nihilism in its hideously perfected form. This is the ideological cloak he next throws over Raskolnikov; it is Raskolnikov's manifesto as it appears in his article. The "extraordinary man," Raskolnikov declaims, has the right to "step over certain obstacles" in order to fulfill a mission that is "salutary for the whole of mankind."

> In my opinion, if, as the result of certain combinations, Kepler's or Newton's discoveries could become known to people in no other way than by sacrificing the lives of one, or ten, or a hundred or more people who were hindering the discovery, or standing as an obstacle in its path, then Newton would have the right, and it would even be his duty ... *to remove* those ten or a hundred people, in order to make his discoveries known to all mankind.

Every lawgiver or founder of a new idea, he goes on, has always been a criminal—"all of them to a man . . . from the fact alone that in giving a new law they thereby violated the old one . . . and they certainly did not stop at shedding blood either, if it happened that blood . . . could help them." Such extraordinary men—Lycurgus, Solon, Napoleon—call for "the destruction of the present in the name of the better," and will lead the world toward a new Jerusalem.

To which Razumikhin, recoiling, responds: "You do finally permit bloodshed *in all conscience.*" And just here, in the turbulence of Razumikhin's revelation—and prefiguring Sakharov, Solzhenitsyn, and Sharansky—Dostoyevsky makes his case for the dismantling of the Soviet state half a century before the revolutionary convulsion that brought it into being.

3.

Yet the mammoth irony of Dostoyevsky's life remains: the writer who excoriated the radical theorists, who despised the nihilist revolutionaries, who wrote novel after novel to defy them, once belonged to their company.

It is easy to dislike him, and not because the spectacle of a self-accusing apostate shocks. He ended as a Slavophile religious believer; but in his twenties he was what he bitterly came to scorn—a Westernizing Russian liberal. Nevertheless a certain nasty consistency ruled. At all times he was bigoted and xenophobic: he had an irrational hatred of Germans and Poles, and his novels are speckled with anti-Semitism. He attacked Roman Catholicism as the temporal legacy of a pagan empire, while extolling Russian Orthodoxy. He was an obsessive and deluded gambler scheming to strike it rich at the snap of a finger: he played madly at the roulette tables of Europe, and repeatedly reduced himself and his pregnant young second wife to actual privation. Escaping debtors' prison in Russia, he was compelled for years to wander homelessly and wretchedly through Germany and Switzerland. In Wiesbaden he borrowed fifty thalers from Turgenev and took ten years to repay him. He held the rigidly exclusionary blood-and-soil tenet that the future of civilization lay with Russia alone. He was seriously superstitious and had a silly trust in omens and dreams. He was irritable, sometimes volcanically so, and inordinately vain. And if all these self-inflicted debilities of character were not ugly enough, he suffered from a catastrophic innate debility: he was subject, without warning, to horrifying epileptic seizures in a period when there were no medical controls.

Though not quite without warning. Dostoyevsky's fits were heralded by a curious surge of ecstasy—an "aura" indistinguishable from religious exaltation. He underwent his first seizure, he reported, on Easter morning in 1865, when he was forty-four years old: "Heaven had come down to earth and swallowed me. I really grasped God and was penetrated by Him." But there may have been unidentified earlier attacks, different in kind. At the age of ten he experienced an auditory hallucination; he thought he heard a voice cry "A wolf is on the loose!" and was comforted by a kindly serf who belonged to his father.

Later fits uniformly triggered the divine penumbra. He was well prepared for it. From childhood he had been saturated in a narrow household piety not unlike the unquestioning devoutness of the illiterate Russian peasant. Prayers were recited before icons; a clergyman came to give lessons. The Gospels were read, and the *Acta Martyrum*—the lives of the saints—with their peculiarly Russian emphasis on passive suffering. No Sunday or religious holiday went unobserved, on the day itself and at vespers the evening before. Rituals were punctiliously kept up. Dostoyevsky's father, a former army doctor on the staff of a hospital for the poor outside Moscow, frequently led his family on excursions to the great onion-domed Kremlin cathedrals, where religion and nationalism were inseparable. Every spring, Dostoyevsky's mother took the children on a pilgrimage to the Monastery of St. Sergey, sixty miles from Moscow, where they knelt among mobs of the faithful before an imposing silver reliquary said to contain the saint's miraculous remains. None of this was typical of the Russian gentry of the time. Neither Tolstoy nor Turgenev had such an upbringing. Joseph Frank, Dostoyevsky's superb and exhaustive biographer, explains why. "Most upper-class Russians," he recounts, "would have shared the attitude exemplified in Herzen's anecdote about his host at a dinner party who, when asked whether he was serving Lenten dishes out of personal conviction, replied that it was 'simply and solely for the sake of the servants.' "

There is speculation that Dostoyevsky's father may himself have had a mild form of epilepsy: he was gloomy, moody, and unpredictably explosive, a martinet who drank too much and imposed his will on everyone around him. In his youth he had completed his studies at a seminary for non-monastic clergy, a low caste, but went on instead to pursue medicine, and eventually elevated himself to the status of the minor nobility. His salary was insufficient and the family was not well off, despite the doctor's inheritance of a small and scrubby estate, along with its "baptized property"—the serfs attached to the land. When Dostoyevsky was sixteen, his father dispatched him and his older brother Mikhail, both of whom had literary ambitions, to the Academy of Military Engineers in St. Petersburg, in preparation for government careers. But the doctor's plan for his sons came to nothing. Less than two years later, in a season of drought, bad crops, and peasant resentment, Dostoyevsky was informed that his father had been found dead on the estate, presumably strangled by his serfs. Killings of this kind were not uncommon. In a famous letter to Gogol (the very letter that would ultimately send Dostoyevsky before the firing squad), the radical critic Vissarion Belinsky wrote that the Czar was "well aware of what landowners do with their peasants and how many throats of the former are cut every year by the latter."

Freed from engineering (and from a despotic father), Dostoyevsky went flying into the heart of St. Petersburg's literary life. It was the hugely influential Belinsky who catapulted him there. Dostoyevsky's first novel, *Poor Folk*—inspired by the social realism of Balzac, Victor Hugo, and George Sand, and published in 1846—was just the sort of fiction Belinsky was eager to promote. "Think of it," he cried, "it's the first attempt at a social novel we've had." Belinsky was a volatile man of movements—movements he usually set off himself. He was also quickly excitable: he had leaped from art-for-art's-sake to a kind of messianic socialism (with Jesus as chief socialist) to blatant atheism. In literature he espoused an ardent naturalism, and saw Dostoyevsky as its avatar. He instantly proclaimed the new writer to be a genius, made him famous overnight, and admitted him, at twenty-four, into St. Petersburg's most coveted intellectual circle, Belinsky's own "pléiade." Turgenev was already a member. The talk was socialist and fervent, touching on truth and justice, science and atheism, and, most heatedly, on the freeing of the serfs. Here Christianity was not much more than a historical metaphor, a view Dostoyevsky only briefly entered into; but he was fiery on the issue of human chattel.

Success went to his head. "Everywhere an unbelievable esteem, a passionate curiosity about me," he bragged to his brother. "Everyone considers me some sort of prodigy. . . . I am now almost drunk with my own glory." The pléiade responded to this posturing at first with annoyance and then with rough ribbing. Belinsky kept out of it, but Turgenev took off after the young prodigy with a scathing parody. Dostoyevsky walked out, humiliated and enraged, and never returned. "They are all scoundrels and eaten up with envy," he fumed. He soon gravitated to another socialist discussion group, which met on Friday nights at the home of Mikhail Petrashevsky, a twenty-six-year-old aristocrat. Petrashevsky had accumulated a massive library of political works forbidden by the censors, and was even less tolerant of Christianity than the pléiade: for him Jesus was "the well-known demagogue." To improve the miserable living conditions of the peasants on his land, Petrashevsky had a commodious communal dormitory built for them, with every amenity provided. They all moved in, and the next day burned down the master's paternalistic utopia. Undaunted, Petrashevsky continued to propagandize for his ideas: the end of serfdom and censorship, and the reform of the courts. His commitment was to gradualism, but certain more impatient members of the Petrashevsky circle quietly formed a secret society dedicated to an immediate and deeply perilous activism.

It was with these that Dostoyevsky aligned himself; he joined a scheme to print and disseminate the explosive manifesto in the form of the letter to Gogol, which Belinsky had composed a year or so earlier, protesting the enslavement of the peasants. Russia, Belinsky wrote, "presents the dire spectacle of a country where men traffic in men, without ever having the excuse so insidiously exploited by the American plantation owners who claim that the Negro is not a man." Dostoyevsky gave an impressive reading of this document at one of Petrashevsky's Friday nights. His audience erupted into an uproar; there were yells of "That's it! That's it!" A government spy, unrecognized, took notes, and at four in the morning Dostoyevsky's bedroom was invaded by the Czar's secret police. He was arrested as a revolutionary conspirator; he was twenty-seven years old.

Nicholas I took a malicious interest in the punishment for this crime against the state—the Czar *was* the state—and personally ordered the mock execution, the last-minute reprieve, the transport to Siberia. Dostoyevsky's sentence was originally eight years; he served four at forced labor in a prison camp at Omsk and the rest in an army regiment. In Siberia, after his release from the camp, he married for the first time—a tumultuous widow with worsening tuberculosis. His own affliction worsened; seizure followed on seizure. For the remainder of his life he would not be free of the anguish of fits. He feared he would die while in their grip.

The moment of cataclysmic terror before the firing squad never left him. He was not so much altered as strangely—almost mystically—restored: restored to what he had felt as a child, kneeling with his mother at the reliquary of St. Sergey. He spoke circumspectly of "the regeneration of my convictions." The only constant was his hatred of the institution of serfdom—but to hate serfdom was not to love peasants, and when he began to live among peasant convicts (political prisoners were not separated from the others), he found them degraded and savage, with a malignant hostility toward the gentry thrown into their midst. The agonies of hard labor, the filth, the chains, the enmity, the illicit drunkenness, his own nervous disorders—all these assailed him, and he suffered in captivity from a despondency nearly beyond endurance.

And then—in a metamorphosis akin to the Ancient Mariner's sudden love for the repulsive creatures of the sea—he was struck by what can only be called a conversion experience. In the twisted and branded faces of the peasant convicts—men much like those who may have murdered his father—he saw a divine illumination; he saw the true Russia; he saw beauty; he saw the kind-hearted serf who had consoled him when the imaginary wolf pursued. Their instinctive piety was his. Their soil-rootedness became a precept. He struggled to distinguish between one criminal motive and another: from the viewpoint of a serf, was a crime against a hardened master really a crime? Under the tatters of barbarism, he perceived the image of God.

The collective routine of the stockade drove him further and further from the socialist dream of communal living. "To be alone is a normal need," he railed. "Otherwise, *in this enforced communism one turns into a hater of mankind.*" And at the same time he began to discover in the despised and brutalized lives of the peasant convicts a shadow of the redemptive suffering that is the Christian paradigm. More and more he inclined toward the traditional Orthodoxy of his upbringing. He fought doubt with passionate unreason: "If someone proved to me that Christ is outside the truth, then I should prefer to remain with Christ than with the truth." This set him against his old associates, both radicals and liberals. It set him against Petrashevsky and Belinsky, whose highest aspiration had been a constitutional republic in league with a visionary ethical socialism. It set him against illustrious literary moderates and Westernizers like Turgenev and Alexander Herzen. Emerging from his Siberian ordeal, he thundered against "the scurvy Russian liberalism propagated by good-for-nothings." Years later, when Belinsky was dead, Dostoyevsky was still sneering at "shitheads like the dung-beetle Belinsky," whom he would not forgive because "that man reviled Christ to me in the foulest language."

The culmination of these renunciations was a white-hot abomination of radicalism in all its forms—from the Western-influenced gentry-theorists of the eighteen-forties to the renegade *raskolniki* (dissenters) who burst into nihilism in the sixties, when student revolutionaries radicalized the universities. With his brother Mikhail, Dostoyevsky founded *Vremya (Time)*, a literary-political periodical intended to combat the socialist radicals. Their immediate target was *The Contemporary*, an opposing polemical journal; it was in the arena of the monthlies that the ideological fires, under literary cover to distract the censors, smoldered. Though *Vremya* was a success, a misunderstanding led the censorship to close it down. Soon afterward, Dostoyevsky's wife died of consumption; then Mikhail collapsed and died. The grieving Dostoyevsky attempted to revive the magazine under another name, but in the absence of his brother's business management he fell into serious debt, went bankrupt, and in 1867 fled to the hated West to escape his creditors.

With him went Anna, the worshipful young stenographer to whom he had begun to dictate his work, and whom he shortly married. Four enforced years abroad took on the half-mad, hallucinatory frenzy of scenes in his own novels: he gambled and lost, gambled and wrote, pawned his wife's rings and gambled and lost and wrote. His work was appearing regularly in the reactionary *Russian Messenger*. Dostoyevsky had now altogether gone over to the other side. "All those trashy little liberals and progressives," he mocked, "find their greatest pleasure and satisfaction in criticizing Russia . . . everything of the slightest originality in Russia [is] hateful to them." It was on this issue that he broke with Turgenev, to whom words like "folk" and "glory" smelled of blood. Turgenev, for his part, thought Dostoyevsky insane. And yet it was Turgenev's *Fathers and Sons*, with its ambiguous portrait of a scoffing nihilist, that was Raskolnikov's sensational precursor.

Turgenev's novel was dedicated to Belinsky. Dostoyevsky broke with Belinsky, he broke with Turgenev, he broke with Petrashevsky, he broke with Herzen—not only because of their liberalism, but because he believed that they did not love Russia enough. To love Russia was to love the Czar and the debased peasant (who, debased by the Czar, also loved the Czar); it was to see human suffering as holy and the peasant as holy; it was to exalt the *obshchina*, the Russian village commune, while condemning the French philosophic cooperative; it was to love the Russian Church largely through the vilification of all other churches; it was to press for the love of God with a hateful ferocity.

Joseph Frank seems certain that Dostoyevsky's conversion "should not be seen as that of a strayed ex-believer returning to Christ," since he had "always remained in some sense a Christian." But the suggestion of a continuum of sensibility may be even stronger than that. After a plunge into the period's dominant cultural milieu, the son of an authoritarian father—

authoritarian personally, religiously, nationally—returns to the father. It is common enough that an intellectual progression will lead to a recovery of the voices around the cradle.

In January of 1881, Dostoyevsky, now an honored literary eminence more celebrated than Turgenev, died of a hemorrhage of the throat. Two months later, Czar Alexander II—Russia's earnest liberalizer and liberator—was assassinated. From the last half of the nineteenth century until the Bolshevik defeat of the liberal Kerensky government in the second decade of the twentieth, revolution continued to overcome reform. In this guise— injury for the sake of an ideal—Raskolnikov lives on. For seventy years he was victorious in Russia. And even now, after the death of the Soviet Union, auguring no one knows what, his retributive figure roves the earth. If he is currently mute in Russia, he remains restive in Northern Ireland, and loud in the Middle East; he has migrated to America. He survives in the violence of humanitarian visionaries who would seize their utopias via ax, Molotov cocktail, or innocent-looking packages sent through the mail.

4.

Raskolnikov as monster of ruination, reason's avenging angel: here speaks the ideologue Dostoyevsky, scourge of the radicals. But this single clangorous note will not hold. Dostoyevsky the novelist tends toward orchestration and multiplicity. Might there be other reasons for the murder of the old woman? Raskolnikov has already been supplied with messianic utilitarianism, a Western import, carried to its logical and lethal end. On second thought (Dostoyevsky's second thought), the killing may have a different and simpler source—family solidarity. A university dropout, unable to meet his tuition payments, Raskol-

nikov, alienated and desperate, has been guiltily taking money
from his adoring mother and sister in the provinces. At home
there is crisis: Dunya, his sister, has been expelled from her position as governess in the Svidrigailov household, where the
debauched husband and father had been making lecherous
advances. To elude disgrace and to ease her family's poverty—
but chiefly to secure a backer for her brother's career—Dunya
becomes engaged to a rich and contemptible St. Petersburg
bureaucrat. In this version of Raskolnikov's intent, it is to save
his sister from a self-sacrificial marriage that he robs the old
woman and pounds her to death.

Dostoyevsky will hurry the stealing-for-sustenance thesis out
of sight quickly enough. As a motive, it is too narrow for his
larger purpose, and by the close of the novel it seems almost forgotten, and surely marginal—not only because Raskolnikov
hides the stolen money and valuables and never touches them
again, but because such an obvious material reason is less shat-
tering than what Dostoyevsky will soon disclose. He will goad
Raskolnikov to a tempestuousness even past nihilism. Past
nihilism lies pure violence—violence for is own sake, without
the vindication of a superior future. The business of revolution is
only to demolish, the anarchist theorist and agitator Mikhail
Bakunin once declared. But in Raskolnikov's newest stand, not
even this extremist position is enough:

> Then I realized . . . that power is given only to the one who
> dares to reach down and take it. Here there is one thing, one
> thing only: one has only to dare! . . . I wanted to *dare,* and I
> killed . . . that's the whole reason! . . . I wanted to kill without
> casuistry . . . to kill for myself, for myself alone! I didn't
> want to lie about it even to myself! It was not to help my
> mother that I killed—nonsense! I did not kill so that, having
> obtained means and power, I could become a benefactor of
> mankind. Nonsense! . . . And it was not money above all

that I wanted when I killed . . . I wanted to find out then, and
find out quickly, whether I was a louse like all the rest, or a
man? . . . Would I dare to reach down and take, or not?

A rapid shuttling of motives, one overtaking the other: family
reasons, societal reasons, altruism, utilitarianism, socialism, nihilism, Napoleonic raw domination. Generations of readers have
been mystified by this plethora of incitements and explanations.
Why so many? One critic, the Russian Formalist Mikhail
Bakhtin, analyzing Dostoyevsky's frequent ellipses and the
back-and-forth interior dialogue of characters disputing with
themselves—each encompassing multiple points of view—
concludes that Dostoyevsky was the inventor of a new "multi-
voice" genre, which Bakhtin calls the "polyphonic novel." Some
simply assume that Dostoyevsky changed his mind as he went
along, and since he was unable to revise what was already in
print—the novel appeared in installments written against deadlines—he was compelled to stitch up the loose ends afterward as
best he could. (This sounds plausible enough; if true, it would
leave most serious Dostoyevsky scholars of the last century with
egg on their faces.)

A British academic, A. D. Nuttall, offers a psychiatric solution:
Raskolnikov is in a state of self-hypnotic schizophrenia. Walter
Kaufmann invokes existentialism, drawing Dostoyevsky into
Nietzsche's and Kierkegaard's web. Freud speculates that Dostoyevsky expresses "sympathy by identification" with criminals
as a result of an Oedipal revolt against his father. Harold Bloom,
sailing over Raskolnikov's inconsistencies, sees in him an apoca-
lyptic figure, "a powerful representative of the will demonized
by its own strength." "The best of all murder stories," says
Bloom, "*Crime and Punishment* seems to me beyond praise and
beyond affection." For Vladimir Nabokov, on the other hand, the
novel is beyond contempt; he knew even in his teens that it was

"long-winded, terribly sentimental, and badly written." Dostoyevsky is "mediocre," and his "gallery of characters consists almost exclusively of neurotics and lunatics." As for Dostoyevsky's religion, it is a "special lurid brand of the Christian faith." "I am very eager to debunk Dostoyevsky," Nabokov assures us.

Is this a case of the blind men and the elephant? Or the novel as Rorschach test? There is something indeterminate in all these tumbling alternatives—in Raskolnikov's changing theories, in the critics' clashing responses. Still, all of them taken together make plain what it is that Dostoyevsky's novel turns out not to be. It is not, after all, a singlemindedly polemical tract fulminating against every nineteenth-century radical movement in sight—though parts may pass for that. It is not a detective thriller, despite its introduction of Porfiry, a crafty, nimble-tongued, penetratingly intuitive police investigator. It is not a social protest novel, even if it retains clear vestiges of an abandoned earlier work on alcoholism and poverty in the forlorn Marmeladovs, whom Raskolnikov befriends: drunken husband, unbalanced tubercular wife, daughter driven to prostitution.

And it is not even much of what it has often been praised for being: a "psychological" novel—notwithstanding a startling stab, now and then, into the marrow of a mind. George Eliot is what we mean, in literature, by psychological; among the moderns, Proust, Joyce, James. Dostoyevsky is not psychological in the sense of understanding and portraying familiar human nature. *Crime and Punishment* is in exile from human nature— like the deeply eccentric *Notes from Underground*, which precedes it by a year. The underground man, Raskolnikov's indispensable foreshadower, his very embryo, revels in the corrupt will to seek out extreme and horrible acts, which gladden him with their "shameful accursed sweetness." But Raskolnikov will in time feel suffocated by the mental anguish that dogs

his crime. Suspicions close in on him; a room in a police station seems no bigger than a cupboard. And soon suffering crimi-
nality will put on the radiant robes of transcendence. Led by
the saintly Sonya Marmeladova, who has turned harlot to support her destitute family, Raskolnikov looks at last to God.
The nihilist, the insolent Napoleon, is all at once redeemed—
implausibly, abruptly—by a single recitation from the Gospels,
and goes off, docile and remorseful, to serve out his sentence in
Siberia.

Nabokov gleefully derides Dostoyevsky's sentimental con-
ventions: "I do not like this trick his characters have of 'sinning
their way to Jesus.' " Ridiculing Raskolnikov's impetuous "spiritual regeneration," Nabokov concedes that "the love of a noble
prostitute . . . did not seem as incredibly banal in 1866 . . . as it
does now when noble prostitutes are apt to be received a little
cynically." Yet the doctrine of redemption through suffering
came to be the bulwark of Dostoyevsky's credo. He believed
in spiritual salvation. He had been intimate with thieves and
cutthroats; he had lived among criminals. He had himself been
punished as a criminal. Even as he was writing *Crime and Punishment,* he was under the continuing surveillance of the secret
police.

The secret police, however, are not this novel's secret. Neither
are the ukases and explosives of that Czarist twilight. Murder
and degradation; perversity, distortion, paralysis, abnormal exci-
tation, lightning conversion; dive after dive into fits of madness
(Raskolnikov, his mother, Svidrigailov, Katerina Marmeladova);
a great imperial city wintry in tone, huddled, frozen in place,
closeted, all in the heart of summertime—these are not the
usual characteristics of a work dedicated to political repudiations.
Crime and Punishment is something else, something beyond
what Dostoyevsky may have plotted and what the scholars
habitually attend to. Its strangeness is that of a galloping cen-

taur pulling a droshky crowded with groaning souls; or else it is a kaleidoscopic phantasmagoria, confined, churning, stuttering. St. Petersburg itself has the enclosed yet chaotic quality of a perpetual dusk, a town of riverbank and sky, taverns, tiny apartments cut up into rented cabins and cells, mazy alleys, narrow stairways, drunks, beggars, peddlers, bedraggled students, street musicians, whores—all darkened and smudged, as if the whole of the city were buried in a cellar, or in hell.

This irresistible deformation of commonly predictable experience is what fires Dostoyevsky's genius. Nabokov dislikes that genius (I dislike it too) because its language is a wilderness and there are woeful pockets of obscurantist venom at its center. But in the end *Crime and Punishment* is anything but a manifesto. Citizenly rebuttal is far from its delirious art. In the fever of his imagining, it is not the radicals Dostoyevsky finally rebukes, but the Devil himself, the master of sin, an unconquerable principality pitted against God.

The Posthumous Sublime

There is almost no clarifying publisher's apparatus surrounding *The Emigrants,* W. G. Sebald's restless, melancholy, and (I am almost sorry to say) sublime narrative quartet. One is compelled—ludicrously, clumsily—to settle for that hapless term (what *is* a "narrative quartet"?) because the very identity of this work remains murky. Which parts of it are memoir, which fiction—and ought it to matter? As for external facticity, we learn from the copyright page that the original German publication date is 1993, and that the initials W.G. represent Winfried Georg. A meager paragraph supplies a handful of biographical notes: the author was born in Wartach im Allgäu, Germany; he studied German literature in Freiburg (where, one recalls, Heidegger's influence extended well into the nineteen-seventies), and later in Francophone Switzerland and in Manchester, England, where he began a career in British university teaching. Two dates stand out: Sebald's birth in 1944, an appalling year for all of Europe, and for European Jews a death's-head year; and 1970, when, at the age of twenty-six, Sebald left his native Germany and moved permanently to England.

It cannot be inappropriate to speculate why. One can imagine that in 1966, during the high period of Germany's "economic miracle," when Sebald was (as that meagerly informative paragraph tells us) a very young assistant lecturer at the University of Manchester—a city then mostly impoverished and in decline—he may have encountered a romantic attachment that finally lured him back to Britain; or else he came to the explicit determination, with or without any romantic attachment (yet he may, in fact, have fallen in love with the pathos of soot-blackened Manchester), that he would anyhow avoid the life of a contemporary German. "The life of a contemporary German": I observe, though from a non-visitor's distance, and at so great a remove now from those twelve years of intoxicated popular zeal for Nazism, that such a life is somehow still touched with a smudge, or taint, of the old shameful history; and that the smudge, or taint—or call it, rather, the little tic of self-consciousness—is there all the same, whether it is regretted or repudiated, examined or ignored, forgotten or relegated to a principled indifference. Even the youngest Germans traveling abroad—especially in New York—know what it is to be made to face, willy-nilly, a history of national crime, however long receded and repented.

For a German citizen to live with 1944 as a birth date is reminder enough. Mengele stood that year on the ramp at Auschwitz, lifting the omnipotent gloved hand that dissolved Jewish families: mothers, babies, and the old to the chimneys, the rest to the slave labor that temporarily forestalled death. —Ah, and it is sentences like this last one that present-day Germans, thriving in a democratic Western polity, resent and decry. A German professor of comparative literature accused me not long ago—because of a sentence like that—of owning a fossilized mind, of being unable to recognize that a nation "develops and moves on." Max Ferber, the painter-protagonist of the final tale in Sebald's quartet, might also earn that professor's fury. "To me, you see," Sebald quotes Ferber, "Germany is a country frozen in the past, destroyed, a curiously extraterritorial place." It is just this extraterritorialism—this ineradicable, inescapable,

ever-recurring, hideously retrievable 1944—that Sebald investi-
gates, though veiled and at a slant, in *The Emigrants*. And it was,
I suspect, not the democratic Germany of the economic miracle
from which Sebald emigrated in 1970; it may have been, after
all, the horribly frozen year of his birth that he meant to leave
behind.

That he did not relinquish his native language or its literature
goes without saying; and we are indebted to Michael Hulse,
Sebald's translator (himself a poet), for allowing us to see,
through the stained glass of his consummate Englishing, what
must surely be the most delicately powerful German prose since
Thomas Mann. Or, on second thought, perhaps not Mann really,
despite a common attraction to the history-soaked. Mann on
occasion can be as heavily ornate as those carved mahogany
sideboards and wardrobes—vestiges of proper German domesticity abandoned by the fleeing Jews—which are currently
reported to add a certain glamorous middle-thirties tone to
today's fashionable Berlin apartments. Sebald is more translucent than Mann; he writes as Turner paints: "To the south, lofty
Mount Spathi, two thousand meters high, towered above the
plateau, like a mirage above the flood of light. The fields of pota-
toes and vegetables across the broad valley floor, the orchards
and clumps of other trees, and the untilled land, were awash
with green upon green, studded with the hundreds of white sails
of wind pumps." Notably, this is not a landscape viewed by a
fresh and naked eye. It is, in fact, a verbal rendering of an old
photograph—a slide shown by a projector on a screen.

An obsession with old photographs is what separates Sebald
from traces of Mann, from Turner's hallucinatory mists, from
the winding reflections of Proust (to whom, in his freely searching musings and paragraphs wheeling cumulatively over pages,
Sebald has been rightly and repeatedly compared), and even
from the elusively reappearing shade of Nabokov. The four nar-

ratives recounted in *The Emigrants* are each accompanied by superannuated poses captured by obsolete cameras; in their fierce time-bound isolations they suggest nothing so much as Diane Arbus. Wittingly or not, Sebald evokes Henry James besides, partly for his theme of expatriation, and partly on account of the mysterious stillness inherent in photography's icy precision. In the 1909 New York Edition of his work, James eschewed illustration, that nineteenth-century standby, and turned instead to the unsentimental fixity of photography's Time and Place, or Place-in-Time. In Sebald's choosing to incorporate so many photos (I count eighty-six in 237 pages of text)—houses, streets, cars, headstones, cobblestones, motionless schoolchildren, mountain crevasses, country roads, posters, roofs, steeples, hotel postcards, bridges, tenements, grand and simple rooms, overgrown gardens—he, like James with his 1909 frontispieces, is acknowledging the uncanny ache that cries out from the silence of solid things. These odd old pictures attach to Sebald's voice like an echo that cannot be heard, no matter how hard one strains; they lie in the crevices of print with a terrible helplessness—deaf-mutes without the capacity to sign.

The heard language of these four stories—memories personal, borrowed, invented—is, as I noted earlier, sublime; and I wish it were not—or, if that is not altogether true, I admit to being disconcerted by a grieving that has been made beautiful. Grief, absence, loss, longing, wandering, exile, homesickness—these have been made millennially, sadly beautiful since the *Odyssey,* since the *Aeneid,* since Dante ("You shall come to know how salt is the taste of another's bread"); and, more venerably still, since the Psalmist's song by the waters of Babylon. Nostalgia is itself a lovely and piercing word, and even more so is the German *Heimweh,* "home-ache." It is art's sacred ancient trick to beautify pain, to romanticize the shadows of the irretrievable. "O lost, and by the wind grieved, ghost, come back again"—Thomas Wolfe, too much scorned for boyishness, tolls that bell as mournfully as anyone; but it is an American tolling, not a German one. Sebald's mourning bell is German, unmistakably German; when it tolls the hour, it is almost always 1944. And if I regret the bittersweet sublime Turner-like wash of Beauty that shimmers over the whole of this volume, it is because sublime grieving is a category of yearning, fit for that which is irretrievable. But 1944 is always, always retrievable. There stands Mengele on the ramp, forever lifting his gloved hand; and there, sent off to the left and the right, are the Jews, going to the left and the right forever. Nor is this any intimation of Keats's urn—there are human ashes in it. The posthumous sublime is discordant; an oxymoron. Adorno told us this long ago: after Auschwitz, no more poetry. We resist such a dictum; the Psalmist by the waters of Babylon resisted it; the poet Paul Célan resisted it; Sebald resists it. It is perhaps natural to resist it.

So, in language sublime, Sebald is haunted by Jewish ghosts— Europe's phantoms: the absent Jews, the deported, the gassed, the suffering, the hidden, the fled. There is a not-to-be-overlooked irony (a fossilized irony, my professor-critic might call it) in Sebald's having been awarded the Berlin Literature Prize—Berlin, the native city of Gershom (né Gerhardt) Scholem, who wrote definitively about the one-sided infatuation of Jews in love with high German culture and with the *Vaterland* itself. The Jewish passion for Germany was never reciprocated—until now. Sebald returns that Jewish attachment, although tragically: he is too late for reciprocity. The Jews he searches for are either stricken escapees or smoke. Like all ghosts, they need to be conjured.

Or, if not conjured, then come upon by degrees, gradually, incrementally, in hints and echoes. Sebald allows himself to discover his ghosts almost stealthily, with a dawning notion of who they really are. It is as if he is intruding on them, and so he is cautious, gentle, wavering at the outer margins of the strange places he finds them in. In "Dr. Henry Selwyn," as the first narrative is called, the young Sebald and his wife drive out into the English countryside to rent a flat in a wing of an overgrown mansion surrounded by a neglected garden and a park of looming trees. The house seems deserted. Tentatively, they venture onto the grounds and stumble unexpectedly on a white-haired, talkative old man who describes himself as "a dweller in the garden, a kind of ornamental hermit." By the time we arrive at the end of this faintly Gothic episode, however, we have learned that Dr. Henry Selwyn was once a *cheder-yingl*—a Jewish schoolchild—named Hersch Seweryn in a village near Grodno in Lithuania. When he was seven years old, his family, including his sisters Gita and Raya, set out for America, like thousands of other impoverished shtetl Jews at the beginning of the century; but "in fact, as we learnt some time later to our dismay (the ship having long since cast off again), we had gone ashore in London." The boy begins his English education in Whitechapel in the Jewish East End, and eventually wins a scholarship to Cambridge to study medicine. Then, like a proper member of his adopted milieu, he heads for the Continent for advanced training, where he becomes enamored—again like a proper Englishman—with a Swiss Alpine guide named Johannes Naegeli. Naegeli tumbles into a crevasse and is killed; Dr. Selwyn returns home to serve in the Great War and in India. Later he marries a Swiss heiress who owns houses in England and lets flats. He has now completed the trajectory from Hersch Seweryn to Dr. Henry Selwyn. But one day, when the word "homesick" flies up out of a melancholy conversation with Sebald, Selwyn tells the story of his childhood as a Jewish immigrant.

The American term is immigrant, not emigrant, and for good reason, America being the famous recipient of newcomers: more come in than ever go out. Our expatriates tend to be artists,

often writers: hence that illustrious row of highly polished run-
aways, James, Eliot, Pound, Wharton, Gertrude Stein, Hemingway. But an expatriate, a willing (sometimes temporary) seeker,
is not yet an emigrant. And an emigrant is not a refugee. A
cheder-yingl from a shtetl near Grodno in a place and period not
kind to Jews is likely to feel himself closer to being a refugee
than an emigrant: our familiar steerage image expresses it best.
Sebald, of course, knows this, and introduces Dr. Selwyn as a
type of foreshadowing. Displaced and homesick in old age for
the child he once was (or in despair over the man he has
become), Dr. Selwyn commits suicide. And on a visit to Switzerland in 1986, Sebald reads in a Lausanne newspaper that
Johannes Naegeli's body has been found frozen in a glacier
seventy-two years after his fall. "And so they are ever returning
to us, the dead," Sebald writes.

But of exactly what is Dr. Selwyn a foreshadowing? The second account, entitled "Paul Bereyter," is a portrait of a German
primary-school teacher—Sebald's own teacher in the fifties,
"who spent at least a quarter of all his lessons on teaching us
things that were not on the syllabus." Original, inventive, a
lover of music, a scorner of catechism and priests, an explorer, a
whistler, a walker ("the very image . . . of the German *Wander-
vogel* hiking movement, which must have had a lasting influence on him from his youth"), Paul Bereyter is nevertheless a
lonely and increasingly aberrant figure. In the thirties he had
come out of a teachers' training college (here a grim photo of the
solemn graduates, in their school ties and rather silly caps) and
taught school until 1935, when he was dismissed for being a
quarter-Jew. The next year his father, who owned a small department store, died in a mood of anguish over Nazi pogroms in his
native Gunzenhausen, where there had been a thriving Jewish
population. After the elder Bereyter's death, the business was

confiscated; his widow succumbed to depression and a fatal dete-rioration. Paul's sweetheart, who had journeyed from Vienna to visit him just before he took up his first teaching post, was also lost to him: deported, it was presumed afterward, to Theresien-stadt. Stripped of father, mother, inheritance, work, and love, Paul fled to tutor in France for a time, but in 1939 drifted back to Germany, where, though only three-quarters Aryan, he was unaccountably conscripted. For six years he served in the motor-ized artillery all over Nazi-occupied Europe. At the war's end he returned to teach village boys, one of whom was Sebald.

As Sebald slowly elicits his old teacher's footprints from interviews, reconstructed hints, and the flickering lantern of his own searching language, Paul Bereyter turns out to be that rare and mysterious figure: an interior refugee (and this despite his part in the German military machine)—or call it, as Sebald might, an internal emigrant. After giving up teaching—the boys he had once felt affection for he now began to see as "contemptible and repulsive creatures"—he both lived in and departed from German society, inevitably drawn back to it, and just as inevitably repelled. All his adult life, Sebald discovers, Paul Bereyter had been interested in railways. (The text is now interrupted by what appears to be Paul's own sketch of the local *Bahnhof*, or train station, with the inscription *So ist es seit dem 4.10.49:* This is how it has looked since the fourth of October 1949.) On the blackboard he draws "stations, tracks, goods depots, and signal boxes" for the boys to reproduce in their note-books. He keeps a model train set on a card table in his flat. He obsesses about timetables. Later, though his eyesight is troubled by cataracts, he reads demonically—almost exclusively the works of suicides, among them Wittgenstein, Benjamin, Klaus Mann, Koestler, Zweig, Tucholsky. He copies out, in shorthand, hundreds of their pages. And finally, on a mild winter afternoon, he puts on a windbreaker that he has not worn since his early teaching days forty years before, and goes out to stretch himself across the train tracks, awaiting his own (as it were) deportation. Years after this event, looking through Paul's photo album with its record of childhood and family life, Sebald again reflects: "it truly seemed to me, and still does, as if the dead were coming back"—but now he adds, "or as if we were on the point of joining them."

Two tales, two suicides. Yet suicide is hardly the most desolating loss in Sebald's broader scheme of losses. And since he comes at things aslant, his next and longest account, the history of his aunts and uncles and their emigration to the United States in the twenties—a period of extreme unemployment in Germany—is at first something of a conundrum. Where, one muses, are those glimmers of the Jewish ghosts of Germany, or any inkling of entanglement with Jews at all? And why, among these steadily rising German-American burghers, should there be? Aunt Fini and Aunt Lini and Uncle Kasimir, Aunt Theres and Cousin Flossie, "who later became a secretary in Tucson, Arizona, and learnt to belly dance when she was in her fifties"—these are garden-variety acculturating American immigrants; we know them; we know the smells of their kitchens; they are our neighbors. (They were certainly mine in my North Bronx childhood.) The geography is familiar—a photo of a family dinner in a recognizable Bronx apartment (sconces on the wall, steam-heat radiators); then the upwardly mobile move to Mamaroneck, in Westchester; then the retirement community in New Jersey. To get to Fini and Kasimir, drive south from Newark on the Jersey Turnpike and head for Lakehurst and the Garden State. In search of Uncle Adelwarth in his last years: Route 17, Monticello, Hurleyville, Oswego, Ithaca. There are no ghosts in these parts. It is, all of it, plain-hearted America.

But turn the page: here are the ghosts. A photo of Uncle

Kasimir as a young man, soon after his apprenticeship as a tin-smith. It is 1928, and only once in that terrible year, Kasimir recounts, did he get work, "when they were putting a new cop-per roof on the synagogue in Augsburg." In the photo Kasimir and six other metal workers are sitting at the top of the curve of a great dome. Behind them, crowning the dome, are three large sculptures of the six-pointed Star of David. "The Jews of Augs-burg," explains Kasimir, "had donated the old copper roof for the war effort during the First World War, and it wasn't till '28 that they had the money for a new roof." Sebald offers no comment concerning the fate of those patriotic Jews and their synagogue a decade on, in 1938, in the fiery hours of the Nazis' so-called *Kristallnacht*. But Kasimir and the half-dozen tinsmiths perched against a cluster of Jewish stars leave a silent mark in Sebald's prose: what once was is no more.

After the roofing job in Augsburg, Kasimir followed Fini and Theres to New York. They had been preceded by their legendary Uncle Ambros Adelwarth, who was already established as a majordomo on the Long Island estate of the Solomons family, where he was in particular charge of Cosmo Solomons, the son and heir. Adelwarth helped place Fini as a governess with the Seligmans in Port Washington, and Theres as a lady's maid to a Mrs. Wallerstein, whose husband was from Ulm in Germany. Kasimir, meanwhile, was renting a room on the Lower East Side from a Mrs. Litwak, who made paper flowers and sewed for a liv-ing. In the autumn succahs sprouted on all the fire escapes. At first Kasimir was employed by the Seckler and Margarethen Soda and Seltzer Works; Seckler was a German Jew from Brünn, who recommended Kasimir as a metal worker for the new yeshiva on Amsterdam Avenue. "The very next day," says Kasimir, "I was up on the top of the tower, just as I had been on the Augsburg Synagogue, only much higher."

So the immigrants, German and Jewish, mingle in America

much as Germans and Jews once mingled in Germany, in lives at least superficially entwined. (One difference being that after the first immigrant generation the German-Americans would not be likely to continue as tinsmiths, just as Mrs. Litwak's progeny would hardly expect to take in sewing. The greater likelihood is that a Litwak daughter is belly-dancing beside Flossie in Tucson.) And if Sebald means for us to feel through its American parallel how this ordinariness, this matter-of-factness, of German-Jewish coexistence was brutally ruptured in Germany, then he has succeeded in calling up his most fearful phantoms. Yet his narrative continues as impregnable here as polished copper, evading conclusions of any kind. Even the remarkably stoic tale of Ambros Adelwarth, born in 1896, is left to speak for itself—Adelwarth who, traveling as valet and protector and probably lover of mad young Cosmo Solomons, dutifully frequented the polo grounds of Saratoga Springs and Palm Beach, and the casinos of Monte Carlo and Deauville, and saw Paris and Venice and Constantinople and the deserts on the way to Jerusalem. Growing steadily madder, Cosmo tried to hang himself and at last succumbed to catatonic dementia. Uncle Adelwarth was obliged to commit him to a sanatorium in Ithaca, New York, where Cosmo died—the same sanatorium to which Adelwarth, with all the discipline of a lifetime, and in a strange act of replication, later delivered himself to paralysis and death.

The yeshiva on Amsterdam Avenue, the Solomons, Seligmans, Wallersteins, Mrs. Litwak and the succahs on the Lower East Side—this is how Sebald chooses to shape the story of the emigration to America of his Catholic German relations. It is as if the fervor of Uncle Adelwarth's faithful attachment to Cosmo Solomons were somehow a repudiation of Gershom Scholem's thesis of unrequited Jewish devotion; as if Sebald were casting a posthumous spell to undo that thesis.

And now on to Max Ferber, Sebald's final guide to the deeps. Ferber was a painter Sebald got to know—"befriended" is too implicated a term for that early stage—when the twenty-two-year-old Sebald came to study and teach in Manchester, an industrially ailing city studded with mainly defunct chimneys, the erstwhile black fumes of which still coated every civic brick. That was in 1966; my own first glimpse of Manchester was nine years before, and I marveled then that an entire metropolis should be so amazingly, universally charred, as if brushed by a passing conflagration. (Later Sebald will tell us that in its bustling heyday Lodz, in Poland—the site of the Lodz Ghetto, a notorious Nazi vestibule for deportation—was dubbed the Polish Manchester, at a time when Manchester too was booming and both cities had flourishing Jewish populations.) At eighteen Ferber arrived in Manchester to study art and thereafter rarely left. It was the thousands of Manchester smokestacks, he confided to the newcomer Sebald, that prompted his belief that "I had found my destiny." "I am here," he said, "to serve under the chimney." In those early days Ferber's studio, as Sebald describes it, resembled an ash pit: "When I watched Ferber working on one of his portrait studies over a number of weeks, I often thought that his prime concern was to increase the dust . . . that process of drawing and shading [with charcoal sticks] on the thick, leathery paper, as well as the concomitant business of constantly erasing what he had drawn with a woollen rag already heavy with charcoal, really amounted to nothing but a steady production of dust."

And in 1990, when Sebald urgently undertook to search out the life of the refugee Max Ferber and the history of his lost German Jewish family, he seemed to be duplicating Ferber's own pattern of reluctant consummation, overlaid with haltings, dissatisfactions, fears, and erasures: "Not infrequently I unravelled what I had done, continuously tormented by scruples that were taking tighter hold and steadily paralyzing me. These scruples concerned not only the subject of the narrative, which I felt I could not do justice to, no matter what approach I tried, but also the entire questionable act of writing. I had covered hundreds of pages. . . . By far the greater part had been crossed out, discarded, or obliterated by additions. Even what I ultimately salvaged as a 'final' version seemed to me a thing of shreds and patches, utterly botched."

All this falls out, one imagines, because Sebald is now openly permitting himself to "become" Max Ferber—or, to put it less emblematically, because in these concluding pages he begins to move, still sidling, still hesitating, from the oblique to the head-on; from intimation to declaration. Here, terminally—at the last stop, so to speak—is a full and direct narrative of Jewish exile and destruction, neither hinted at through an account of a loosely parallel flight from Lithuania a generation before, nor obscured by a quarter-Jew who served in Hitler's army, nor hidden under the copper roof of a German synagogue, nor palely limned in Uncle Adelwarth's journey to Jerusalem with a Jewish companion.

Coming on Max Ferber again after a separation of twenty years, Sebald is no longer that uncomprehending nervous junior scholar fresh from a postwar German education—he is middle-aged, an eminent professor in a British university, the author of two novels. Ferber, nearing seventy, is now a celebrated British painter whose work is exhibited at the Tate. The reunion bears unanticipated fruit: Ferber surrenders to Sebald a cache of letters containing what is, in effect, a record of his mother's life, written when the fifteen-year-old Max had already been sent to safety in England. Ferber's father, an art dealer, and his mother, decorated for tending the German wounded in the First World War, remained trapped in Germany, unable to obtain the visas that would assure their escape. In 1941 they were deported from Munich to Riga in Lithuania, where they were murdered. "The fact is," Ferber now tells Sebald, "that that tragedy in my youth struck such deep roots within me that it later shot up again, put forth evil flowers, and spread the poisonous canopy over me which has kept me so much in the shade and dark." Thus the latter-day explication of "I am here to serve under the chimney," uttered decades after the young Sebald loitered, watchful and bewildered, in the exiled painter's ash-heaped studio.

The memoir itself is all liveliness and light. Sebald recreates it lyrically, meticulously—from, as we say, the inside out. It begins with Luisa and Leo Lanzberg, a little brother and sister (reminding us of the brother and sister in *The Mill on the Floss*) in the village of Steinach, near Kissingen, where Jews have lived since the sixteen-hundreds. ("It goes without saying," Sebald interpolates—it is a new note for him—"that there are no Jews in Steinach now, and that those who live there have difficulty remembering those who were once their neighbors and whose homes and property they appropriated, if indeed they remember them at all.") Friday nights in Steinach juxtapose the silver Sabbath candelabrum with the beloved poems of Heine. The day nursery, presided over by nuns, excuses the Jewish children from morning prayers. On Sabbath afternoons in summer, before the men return to the synagogue, there is lemonade and challah with corned beef. Rosh Hashana; Yom Kippur; then the succah hung with apples and pears and chains of rosehips. In winter the Jewish school celebrates both Hanukkah and the Reich. Before Passover "the bustle is dreadful." Father prospers, and the family moves to the middle-class world of Kissingen. (A photo shows the new house: a mansion with two medieval spires. Nevertheless several rooms are rented out.) And so on and so on: the blessing of the ordinary. Luisa grows into a young woman with suitors; her Gentile fiancé dies suddenly, of a stroke; a match-maker finds her a Jewish husband, Max's father. "In the summer of 1921," Ferber's mother writes, "soon after our marriage, we went to the Allgäu ... where the scattered villages were so peaceful it was as if nothing evil had happened anywhere on earth." Sebald, we know, was born in one of those villages.

In 1991—fifty years after the memoirist was deported to Riga—Sebald visits Steinach and Kissingen. (I almost want to say revisits, so identified has he become with Ferber's mother's story.) In the old Jewish cemetery in Kissingen, "a wilderness of graves, neglected for years, crumbling and gradually sinking into the ground amidst tall grass and wild flowers under the shade of trees, which trembled in the slight movements of the air," he stands before the gravestones and reads the names of the pre-Hitler dead, Auerbach, Grunwald, Leuthold, Seeligmann, Goldstaub, Baumblatt, Blumenthal, and thinks how "perhaps there was nothing the Germans begrudged the Jews so much as their beautiful names, so intimately bound up with the country they lived in and with its language." He finds a more recent marker: a relative of Max Ferber's who, in expectation of the outcome, took her own life. (The third suicide in Sebald's quartet.) And then he flees: "I felt increasingly that the mental impoverishment and lack of memory that marked the Germans, and the efficiency with which they had cleaned everything up were beginning to affect my head and my nerves." A sign on the cemetery gates warns that vandals will be prosecuted.

The Emigrants (an ironically misleading title) ends with a mental flash of the Lodz Ghetto—the German occupiers feasting, the cowed Jewish slave laborers, children among them, toiling for their masters. In the conqueror's lens, Sebald sees three young Jewish women at a loom, and recalls "the daughters of night, with spindle, scissors and thread." Here, it strikes me, is the only false image in this ruthlessly moving and profoundly honest work dedicated to the recapture of phantoms. In the time of the German night, it was not the Jews who stood in for the relentless Fates, they who rule over life and death. And no one understands this, from the German side, more mournfully, more painfully, than the author of *The Emigrants*.

The Impossibility of Being Kafka

Franz Kafka is the twentieth century's valedictory ghost. In two incomplete yet incommensurable novels, *The Trial* and *The Castle*, he submits, as lingering spirits will, a ghastly accounting—the sum total of modern totalitarianism. His imaginings outstrip history and memoir, incident and record, film and reportage. He is on the side of realism—the poisoned realism of metaphor. Cumulatively, Kafka's work is an archive of our era: its anomie, depersonalization, afflicted innocence, innovative cruelty, authoritarian demagoguery, technologically adept killing. But none of this is served raw. Kafka has no politics; he is not a political novelist in the way of Orwell or Dickens. He writes from insight, not, as people like to say, from premonition. He is often taken for a metaphysical or even a religious writer, but the supernatural elements in his fables are too entangled in concrete everydayness, and in caricature, to allow for any incandescent certainties. The typical Kafkan figure has the cognitive force of a chess master—which is why the term "Kafkaesque," a synonym for the uncanny, misrepresents at the root. The Kafkan mind rests not on unintelligibility or the surreal, but on adamantine logic—on the sane expectation of rationality. A singing mouse, an enigmatic ape, an impenetrable castle, a deadly contraption, the Great Wall of China, a creature in a burrow, fasting as an art form, and, most famously, a man metamorphosed into a bug—

all these are steeped in reason; and also in reasoning. "Fairy tales for dialecticians," the critic Walter Benjamin remarked. In the two great zones of literary susceptibility—the lyrical and the logical—the Kafkan "K" attaches not to Keats, but to Kant.

The prose that utters these dire analytic fictions has, with time, undergone its own metamorphosis, and only partly through repeated translations into other languages. Something—fame—has intervened to separate Kafka's stories from our latter-day reading of them two or three generations on. The words are unchanged; yet those same passages Kafka once read aloud, laughing at their fearful comedy, to a small circle of friends, are now markedly altered under our eyes—enameled by that labyrinthine process through which a literary work awakens to discover that it has been transformed into a classic. Kafka has taught us how to read the world differently: as a kind of decree. And because we have read Kafka, we know more than we knew before we read him, and are now better equipped to read him acutely. This may be why his graven sentences begin to approach the scriptural; they become as fixed in our heads as any hymn; they seem ordained, fated. They carry the high melancholy tone of resignation unabraded by cynicism. They are stately and plain and full of dread.

And what is it that Kafka himself knew? He was born in 1883; he died, of tuberculosis, in 1924, a month short of his forty-first birthday. He did not live to see human beings degraded to the status and condition of vermin eradicated by an insecticidal gas.*

*His three sisters, Ottla, Valli, and Elli, who survived him, perished at Auschwitz and Lodz between 1941 and 1943. And suppose Kafka had not died of tuberculosis in 1924? Of all the speculations and hypotheses about Kafka, this may be the most significant. In 1940 he would have been fifty-seven. If only he had lived that long —*The Castle* and other works would have been completed, and how many further masterpieces would now be in our possession! Yet what would those extra years have meant for Kafka? By 1940, the Jews of Prague were forbidden to change their addresses or leave the city. By 1941, they could not walk in the woods around Prague, or travel on trolleys, buses, and subways. Telephones were

If he was able to imagine man reduced to insect, it was not because he was prophetic. Writers, even the geniuses among them, are not seers. It was his own status and condition that Kafka knew. His language was German, and that, possibly, is the point. That Kafka breathed and thought and aspired and suffered in German—in Prague, a German-hating city—may be the ultimate exegesis of everything he wrote.

The Austro-Hungarian monarchy, ruled by German-speaking Habsburgs until its dissolution in the First World War, was an amalgam of a dozen national enclaves. Czech-speaking Bohemia was one of these, restive and sometimes rebellious under Habsburg authority. Since the time of Joseph II, who reigned between 1780 and 1790, the imperial parliament—centered in Vienna—had governed in German; all laws were published in German; all outlying bureaucracies and educational systems were conducted in German; German was the language of public offices and law courts; all official books and correspondence were kept in German. Though later rulings ameliorated these conditions somewhat, the struggle for Czech language rights was ongoing, determined, and turbulent. Prague's German-speaking minority, aside from the official linguistic advantage it enjoyed, was prominent both commercially and intellectually. Vienna, Berlin, Munich—these pivotal seats of German culture might be far away, but Prague reflected them all. Here, in Bohemia's major city, Kafka attended a German university, studied German

---

ripped out of Jewish apartments, and public telephones were off-limits to Jews. Jewish businesses were confiscated; firms threw out their Jewish employees; Jewish children were thrown out of school. And so on and so on and so on, until ghettoization, degradation, deportation, and murder. That is how it was for Ottla, Valli, and Elli, and for all of Kafka's tedious and unliterary relatives ("The joys and sorrows of my relatives bore me to my soul," he complained in his diary); and that is how it would have been for Kafka. The work he left behind was at first restricted to Jewish readers only, and then banned as "harmful and undesirable." Schocken, his publisher, escaped to Tel Aviv. It remains doubtful that Kafka would have done the same.

jurisprudence, worked for a German insurance company, and published in German periodicals. German influence was dominant; in literature it was conspicuous.

That the Jews of Prague were German-identified, by language and preference—a minority population within a minority population—was not surprising. There were good reasons for this preference. Beginning with the Edict of Toleration in 1782, and continuing over the next seventy years, the Habsburg emperors had throughout their territories released the Jews from lives of innumerable restrictions in closed ghettos; emancipation meant civil freedoms, including the right to marry at will, to settle in the cities and enter the trades and professions. Among Bohemia's Jews of Kafka's generation, ninety percent were educated in German. Kafka was privately tutored in Czech, but in his academically rigorous German elementary school, thirty of the thirty-nine boys in his class were Jews. For Bohemian patriots, Prague's Jews bore a double stigma: they were Germans, resented as cultural and national intruders, and they were Jews. Though the Germans were as unfriendly to the German-speaking Jews as the Czechs were, militant Czech nationalism targeted both groups.

Nor was modern Czech anti-Semitism without its melancholy history. With the abolition of the ghettos and the granting of civil rights, anti-Jewish demonstrations broke out in 1848, and again in 1859, 1861, and 1866. In neighboring Hungary in 1883, the year of Kafka's birth, a blood-libel charge—a medieval canard accusing Jews of the ritual murder of a Christian child—brought on renewed local hostility. In 1897, the year after Kafka's bar mitzvah observance, when he was fourteen, he was witness to a ferocious resumption of anti-Jewish violence that had begun as an anti-German protest over the government's denial of Czech language rights. Mark Twain, reporting from Vienna on the parliamentary wrangling, described conditions in

Prague: "There were three or four days of furious rioting . . . the Jews and Germans were harried and plundered, and their houses destroyed; in other Bohemian towns there was rioting—in some cases the Germans being the rioters, in others the Czechs—and in all cases the Jew had to roast, no matter which side he was on." In Prague itself, mobs looted Jewish businesses, smashed windows, vandalized synagogues, and assaulted Jews on the street. Because Kafka's father, a burly man, could speak a little Czech and had Czech employees—he called them his "paid enemies," to his son's chagrin—his sundries shop was spared. Less than two years later, just before Easter Sunday in 1899, a teenage Czech girl was found dead, and the blood libel was revived once more; it was the future mayor of Prague who led the country-wide anti-Jewish agitation. Yet hatred was pervasive even when violence was dormant. And in 1920, when Kafka was thirty-seven, with only three years to live and *The Castle* still unwritten, anti-Jewish rioting again erupted in Prague. "I've spent all afternoon out in the streets," Kafka wrote in a letter contemplating fleeing the city, "bathing in Jew-hatred. *Prašivo plemeno*—filthy brood—is what I heard them call the Jews. Isn't it only natural to leave a place where one is so bitterly hated? . . . The heroism involved in staying put in spite of it all is the heroism of the cockroach, which also won't be driven out of the bathroom." On that occasion, Jewish archives were destroyed and the Torah scrolls of Prague's ancient Altneu synagogue were burned. Kafka did not need to be, in the premonitory sense, a seer; as an observer of his own time and place, he *saw*. And what he saw was that, as a Jew in Central Europe, he was not at home; and though innocent of any wrongdoing, he was thought to deserve punishment.

Inexplicably, it has become a commonplace of Kafka criticism to overlook nearly altogether the social roots of the psychological predicaments animating Kafka's fables. To an extent there is justice in this disregard. Kafka's genius will not lend itself to merely local apprehensions; it cannot be reduced to a scarring by a hurtful society. At the other extreme, his stories are frequently addressed as faintly christological allegories about the search for "grace," in the manner of a scarier *Pilgrim's Progress*. It is true that there is not a word about Jews—and little about Prague—in Kafka's formal writing, which may account for the dismissal of any inquisitiveness about Kafka's Jewishness as a "parochialism" to be avoided. Kafka himself is said to have avoided it. But he was less assimilated (itself an ungainly notion) than some of his readers wish or imagine him to have been. Kafka's self-made, coarsely practical father was the son of an impoverished kosher butcher, and began peddling in peasant villages while he was still a child. His middle-class mother was descended from an eminent Talmud scholar. Almost all his friends were Jewish literati. Kafka was seriously attracted to Zionism and Palestine, to Hebrew, to the pathos and inspiration of an East European Yiddish theater troupe that had landed in Prague: these were for him the vehicles of a historic transcendence that cannot be crammed into the term "parochial." Glimmerings of this transcendence seep into the stories, usually by way of their negation. "We are nihilistic thoughts that come into God's head," Kafka told Max Brod, the dedicated friend who preserved the unfinished body of his work. In all of Kafka's fictions the Jewish anxieties of Prague press on, invisibly, subliminally; their fate is metamorphosis.

But Prague was not Kafka's only subterranean torment. His harsh, crushing, uncultivated father, for whom the business drive was everything, hammered at the mind of his obsessively susceptible son, for whom literature was everything. Yet the adult son remained in the parental flat for years, dreading noise, interruption, and mockery, writing through the night. At the family table the son sat in concentration, diligently Fletcherizing his food, chewing each mouthful a hundred times, until it liquified. He experimented with vegetarianism, gymnastics, carpentry, and gardening, and repeatedly went on health retreats, once to a nudist spa. He fell into a stormy, fitfully interrupted but protracted engagement to Felice Bauer, a pragmatic manufacturing executive in Berlin; when he withdrew from it he felt like a felon before a tribunal. His job at the Workers' Accident Insurance Institute (where he was a token Jew) instructed him in the whims of contingency and in the mazy machinery of bureaucracy. When his lungs became infected, he referred to his spasms of cough as "the animal." In his last hours, pleading with his doctor for morphine, he said, "Kill me, or else you are a murderer"—a final conflagration of Kafkan irony.

Below all this travail, some of it self-inflicted, lay the indefatigable clawings of language. In a letter to Max Brod, Kafka described Jews who wrote in German (he could hardly exclude himself) as trapped beasts: "Their hind legs were still stuck in parental Judaism while their forelegs found no purchase on new ground." They lived, he said, with three impossibilities: "the impossibility of not writing, the impossibility of writing German, the impossibility of writing differently. You could add," he concluded, "a fourth impossibility, the impossibility of writing."

The impossibility of writing *German*? Kafka's German—his mother tongue—is spare, somber, comic, lucid, pure; formal without being stilted. It has the almost platonic purity of a language unintruded on by fads or slang or the street, geographically distanced from the tumultuous bruisings of the mean vernacular. The Hebrew poetry written by the Jews of medieval Spain was similarly immaculate; its capital city was not Córdoba or Granada but the Bible. In the same way Kafka's linguistic capital was not German-speaking Prague on the margins of empire, but European literature itself. Language was the engine

and chief motive of his life: hence "the impossibility of not writing." "I've often thought," he ruminated to Felice Bauer, "that
the best way of life for me would be to have writing materials
and a lamp in the innermost room of a spacious locked cellar."
When he spoke of the impossibility of writing German, he never
meant that he was not master of the language; his wish was to be
consecrated to it, like a monk with his beads. His fear was that he
was not entitled to German—not that the language did not
belong to him, but that he did not belong to it. German was
both hospitable and inhospitable. He did not feel innocently—
uncomplicatedly, unself-consciously—German. Put it that Kafka
wrote German with the passion of an ingenious yet stealthy
translator, always aware of the space, however minute, between
his fear, or call it his idea of himself, and the deep ease of at-
homeness that is every language's consolation. *Mutter,* the German word for "mother," was, he said, alien to him: so much for
the taken-for-granted intimacy and trust of *die Muttersprache,*
the mother tongue. This crevice of separation, no thicker than a
hair, may underlie the estrangement and enfeebling distortions
that shock and ultimately disorient every reader of Kafka.

But if there is, in fact, a crevice—or a crisis—of separation
between the psyche and its articulation in Kafka himself, what of
the crevice that opens between Kafka and his translators? If
Kafka deemed it impossible to be Kafka, what chance can a translator have to snare a mind so elusive that it escapes even the
comprehension of its own sensibility? "I really am like rock, like
my own tombstone," Kafka mourned. He believed himself to be
"apathetic, witless, fearful," and also "servile, sly, irrelevant,
unsympathetic, untrue . . . from some ultimate diseased ten-
dency." He vowed that "every day at least one line shall be
directed against myself." "I am constantly trying to communicate something incommunicable, to explain something inexplicable," he wrote. "Basically it is nothing other than . . . fear

spread to everything, fear of the greatest as of the smallest, paralyzing fear of pronouncing a word, although this fear may not
only be fear but also a longing for something that is greater than
any fear." A panic so intuitional suggests—forces on us—still
another Kafkan impossibility: the impossibility of translating
Kafka.

There is also the impossibility of *not* translating Kafka. An
unknown Kafka, inaccessible, mute, secret, locked away, may
now be unthinkable. But it was once thinkable, and by Kafka
himself. At the time of his death the bulk of his writing was still
unpublished. His famous directive (famously unheeded) to Max
Brod to destroy his manuscripts—they were to be "burned
unread"—could not have foreseen their canonization, or the
near-canonization of their translators. For almost seventy years,
the work of Willa and Edwin Muir, a Scottish couple self-taught
in German, has represented Kafka in English; the mystical Kafka
we are long familiar with—and whom the Muirs derived from
Max Brod—reflects their voice and vision. It was they who
gave us *Amerika, The Trial, The Castle,* and nine-tenths of the
stories. And it is because the Muirs toiled to communicate
the incommunicable that Kafka, even in English, stands indisputably among the few truly indelible writers of the twentieth
century—those writers who have no literary progeny, who are
sui generis and cannot be echoed or envied.

Yet any translation, however influential, harbors its own dissolution. Literature endures; translation, itself a branch of literature, decays. This is no enigma. The permanence of a work does
not insure the permanence of its translation—perhaps because
the original remains fixed and unalterable, while the translation
must inevitably vary with the changing cultural outlook and
idiom of each succeeding generation. Then are the Muirs, in
their several redactions, dated? Ought they to be jettisoned? Is
their "sound" not ours? Or, more particularly, is their sound, by

virtue of not being precisely ours, therefore not sufficiently Kafka's? After all, it is Kafka's sound we want to hear, not the nineteen-thirties prose effects of a couple of zealous Britishers.

Notions like these, and also the pressures of renewal and contemporaneity, including a concern for greater accuracy, may account for a pair of fresh English renderings published in 1998: *The Trial*, translated by Breon Mitchell, and *The Castle*, the work of Mark Harman. (Both versions have been brought out by Schocken, an early publisher of Kafka. Formerly a Berlin firm that fled the Nazi regime for Palestine and New York, it is now returned to its origin, so to speak, through its recent purchase by Germany's Bertelsmann.) Harman faults the Muirs for theologizing Kafka's prose beyond what the text can support. Mitchell argues more stringently that "in attempting to create a readable and stylistically refined version" of *The Trial*, the Muirs "consistently overlooked or deliberately varied the repetitions and interconnections that echo so meaningfully in the ear of every attentive reader of the German text." For instance, Mitchell points out, the Muirs shy away from repeating the word "assault" (*"überfallen"*), and choose instead "seize," "grab," "fall upon," "overwhelm," "waylay"—thereby subverting Kafka's brutally intentional refrain. Where Kafka's reiterated blow is powerful and direct, Mitchell claims, theirs is dissipated by variety.

But this is not an argument that can be decided only on the ground of textual faithfulness. The issues that seize, grab, fall upon, waylay, etc., translation are not matters of language in the sense of word-for-word. Nor is translation to be equated with interpretation; the translator has no business sneaking in what amounts to commentary. Ideally, translation is a transparent membrane that will vibrate with the faintest shudder of the original, like a single leaf on an autumnal stem. Translation *is* autumnal; it comes late, it comes afterward. Especially with

Kafka, the role of translation is not to convey "meaning," psychoanalytical or theological, or anything that can be summarized or paraphrased. Against such expectations, Walter Benjamin magisterially notes, Kafka's parables "raise a mighty paw." Translation is transmittal of that which may be made out of language, but is a condition beyond the grasp of language.

The Trial is just such a condition. It is a narration of being and becoming. The title in German, *Der Prozess*, expresses something ongoing, evolving, unfolding, driven on by its own forward movement—a process and a passage. Joseph K., a well-placed bank official, a man of reason, sanity, and logic, is arrested, according to the Muirs, "without having done anything wrong"—or, as Breon Mitchell has it, "without having done anything truly wrong." At first K. feels his innocence with the confidence, and even the arrogance, of self-belief. But through the course of his entanglement with the web of the law, he drifts sporadically from confusion to resignation, from bewilderment in the face of an unnamed accusation to acceptance of an unidentifiable guilt. The legal proceedings that capture K. and draw him into their inescapable vortex are revealed as a series of implacable obstacles presided over by powerless or irrelevant functionaries. With its recondite judges and inscrutable rules, the "trial" is more tribulation than tribunal. Its impartiality is punishing; it tests no evidence; its judgment has no relation to justice. The law ("an unknown system of jurisprudence") is not a law that K. can recognize, and the court's procedures have an Alice-in-Wonderland arbitrariness. A room for flogging miscreants is situated in a closet in K.'s own office; the court holds sessions in the attics of rundown tenements; a painter is an authority on judicial method. Wherever K. turns, advice and indifference come to the same.

"It's not a trial before the normal court," K. informs the out-of-town uncle who sends him to a lawyer. The lawyer is bedrid-

den and virtually useless. He makes a point of displaying an earlier client who is as despairing and obsequious as a beaten dog.
The lawyer's maidservant, seducing K., warns him, "You can't
defend yourself against this court, all you can do is confess."
Titorelli, the painter who lives and works in a tiny bedroom that
proves to be an adjunct of the court, is surrounded by an importuning chorus of phantomlike but aggressive little girls; they too
"belong to the court." The painter lectures K. on the ubiquity
and inaccessibility of the court, the system's accumulation of
files and its avoidance of proof, the impossibility of acquittal. "A
single hangman could replace the entire court," K. protests. "I'm
not guilty," he tells a priest in a darkened and empty cathedral.
"That's how guilty people always talk," the priest replies, and
explains that "the proceedings gradually merge into the judgment." Yet K. still dimly hopes: perhaps the priest will "show
him . . . not how to influence the trial, but how to break out of it,
how to get around it, how to live outside the trial."

Instead the priest recites a parable: Kafka's famed parable of
the doorkeeper. Behind a door standing open is the Law; a man
from the country asks to be admitted. (In Jewish idiom, which
Kafka may be alluding to here, a "man from the country"—*am
ha'aretz*—connotes an unrefined sensibility impervious to spiritual learning.) The doorkeeper denies him immediate entrance,
and the man waits stoically for years for permission to go in.
Finally, dying, still outside the door, he asks why "no one but me
has requested admittance." "No one else could gain admittance
here," the doorkeeper answers, "because this entrance was
meant solely for you. I'm going to go and shut it now." Torrents
of interpretation have washed over this fable, and over every
other riddle embedded in the body of *The Trial*. The priest himself, from within the tale, supplies a commentary on all possible
commentaries: "The commentator tells us: the correct understanding of a matter and misunderstanding the matter are not

mutually exclusive." And adds: "The text is immutable, and the opinions are often only an expression of despair over it." Following which, K. acquiesces in the ineluctable verdict. He is led to a block of stone in a quarry, where he is stabbed, twice, in the heart—after feebly attempting to raise the knife to his own throat.

Kafka's text is by now held to be immutable, despite much posthumous handling. Translations of the work (supposing that all translations are indistinguishable from opinions) are often only expressions of despair; understanding and misunderstanding may occur in the same breath. And *The Trial* is, after all, not a finished book. It was begun in 1914, two weeks after the outbreak of the First World War. Kafka recorded this cataclysm in his diary, in a tone of flat dismissal: "2 August. Germany has declared war on Russia—Swimming in the afternoon," and on August 21 he wrote, "I start 'The Trial' again." He picked it up and left it off repeatedly that year and the next. Substantial fragments—unincorporated scenes—were set aside, and it was Max Brod who, after Kafka's death, determined the order of the chapters and appended the allegorical reflections which so strongly influenced the Muirs. Discussion continues about the looseness of Kafka's punctuation—commas freely and unconventionally scattered. (The Muirs, following Brod, regulate the liberties taken in the original.) Kafka's translators, then, are confronted with textual decisions large and small that were never Kafka's. To these they add their own.

The Muirs aim for a dignified prose, unruffled by any obvious idiosyncrasy; their cadences lean toward a formality tinctured by a certain soulfulness. Breon Mitchell's intent is radically other. To illustrate, let me try a small experiment in contrast and linguistic ambition. In the novel's penultimate paragraph, as K. is brought to the place of his execution, he sees a window in a nearby building fly open, and a pair of arms reach out. The

Muirs translate: "Who was it? A friend? A good man? Someone who sympathized? Someone who wanted to help? Was it one person only? Or was it mankind? Was help at hand?" The same simple phrases in Mitchell's rendering have a different timbre, even when some of the words are identical: "Who was it? A friend? A good person? Someone who cared? Someone who wanted to help? Was it just one person? Was it everyone? Was there still help?" The Muirs' "Was help at hand?" has a Dickensian flavor: a touch of nineteenth-century purple. And "mankind" is not what Kafka wrote (he wrote *"alle,"* everyone), though it may be what he meant; in any case it is what the Muirs, who look to symbolism, distinctly do mean. To our contemporary ears, "Was it one person only?"—with "only" placed after the noun—is vaguely stilted. And surely some would find "a good man" (for *"ein guter Mensch,"* where *"Mensch"* signifies the essential human being) sexist and ideologically wanting. What we hear in the Muirs' language, overall, is something like the voice of Somerset Maugham: British, cultivated, cautiously genteel even in extremis; middlebrow.

Breon Mitchell arrives to sweep all that Muirish dustiness away, and to refresh Kafka's legacy by giving us a handier Kafka in a vocabulary close to our own—an American Kafka, in short. He has the advantage of working with a restored and more scholarly text, which edits out many of Brod's interferences. Yet even in so minuscule a passage as the one under scrutiny, a telltale syllable, therapeutically up-to-date, jumps out: Americans may be sympathetic (*"teilnahm"*), but mainly they *care.* Other current Americanisms intrude: "you'd better believe it" (the Muirs say tamely, "you can believe that"); "without letting myself be thrown by the fact that Anna didn't appear" (the Muirs: "without troubling my head about Anna's absence"); "I'm so tired I'm about to drop"; "you'd have to be a serious criminal to have a commission of inquiry come down on you";

"You're not mad at me, are you?"; "fed up"; and so forth. There is even a talk-show "more importantly." Mitchell's verb contractions ("isn't," "didn't") blanket Kafka's grave exchanges with a mist of Seinfeld dialogue. If the Muirs sometimes write like sticks, Mitchell now and then writes shtick. In both versions, the force of the original claws its way through, despite the foreign gentility of the one and the colloquial unbuttonedness of the other. Unleashed by Kafka's indefinable genius, unreason-thwarting-reason slouches into view under a carapace of ill-fitting English.

Of the hundred theories of translation, some lyrical, some stultifyingly academic, others philologically abstruse, the speculations of three extraordinary literary figures stand out: Nabokov, Ortega y Gasset, and Walter Benjamin. Nabokov, speaking of Pushkin, demands "translations with copious footnotes, footnotes reaching up like skyscrapers. . . . I want such footnotes and the absolutely literal sense." This, of course, is pugnaciously anti-literary—Nabokov's curmudgeonly warning against the "drudge" who substitutes "easy platitudes for the breathtaking intricacies of the text." It is, besides, a statement of denial and disbelief: no translation is ever going to work, so please don't try. Ortega's milder disbelief is finally tempered by aspiration. "Translation is not a duplicate of the original text," he begins; "it is not—it shouldn't try to be—the work itself with a different vocabulary." And he concludes, "The simple fact is that the translation is not the work, but a path toward the work"—which suggests at least the possibility of arrival.

Benjamin withdraws altogether from these views. He will believe in the efficacy of translation as long as it is not of this earth, and only if the actual act of translation—by human hands—cannot be accomplished. A German Jew, a contemporary of Kafka, a Hitler refugee, a suicide, he is eerily close to Kafka in mind and sensibility; on occasion he expresses characteristically

Kafkan ideas. In his remarkable 1923 essay "The Task of the Translator," he imagines a high court of language that has something in common with the invisible hierarchy of judges in *The Trial.* "The translatability of linguistic creations," he affirms, "ought to be considered even if men should prove unable to translate them." Here is Platonism incarnate: the non-existent ideal is perfect; whatever is attempted in the world of reality is an imperfect copy, falls short, and is useless. Translation, according to Benjamin, is debased when it delivers information, or enhances knowledge, or offers itself as a trot, or as a version of Cliffs Notes, or as a help to understanding, or as any other kind of convenience. "Translation must in large measure refrain from wanting to communicate something, from rendering the sense," he maintains. Comprehension, elucidation, the plain import of the work—all that is the goal of the inept: "Meaning is served far better—and literature and language far worse—by the unrestrained license of bad translators."

What is Benjamin talking about? If the object of translation is not meaning, what is it? Kafka's formulation for literature is Benjamin's for translation: the intent to communicate the incommunicable, to explain the inexplicable. "To some degree," Benjamin continues, "all great texts contain their potential translation between the lines; this is true to the highest degree of sacred writings." And yet another time: "In all language and linguistic creations there remains in addition to what can be conveyed something that cannot be communicated . . . that very nucleus of pure language." Then woe to the carpentry work of real translators facing real texts! Benjamin is scrupulous and difficult, and his intimations of ideal translation cannot easily be paraphrased: they are, in brief, a longing for transcendence, a wish equivalent to the wish that the translators of the Psalmist in the King James version, say, might come again, and in our own generation. (But would they be fit for Kafka?)

Benjamin is indifferent to the exigencies of carpentry and craft. What he is insisting on is what Kafka understood by the impossibility of writing German: the unbridgeable fissure between words and the spells they cast. Always for Kafka, behind meaning there shivers an intractable darkness, or (rarely) an impenetrable radiance. And the task of the translator, as Benjamin intuits it, is not within the reach of the conscientious if old-fashioned Muirs, or the highly readable Breon Mitchell, whose *Trial* is a page-turner (and whose glistening contemporaneity may cause his work to fade faster than theirs). Both the superseded Muirs and the eminently useful Mitchell convey information, meaning, complexity, "atmosphere." How can one ask for more, and, given the unparalleled necessity of reading Kafka in English, what, practically, *is* "more"? Our debt to the translators we have is unfathomable. But a look into Kafka's simplest sentences—"*Wer war es? Ein Freund? Ein guter Mensch? . . . Waren es alle?*"—points to Benjamin's nearly liturgical plea for "that very nucleus of pure language" which Kafka called the impossibility of writing German; and which signals also, despairingly, the impossibility of translating Kafka.

The Impious Impatience of Job

The riddles of God are more satisfying
than the solutions of men.
—G. K. Chesterton

1. What the Scholars Say

Twenty-five centuries ago (or perhaps twenty-four or twenty-three), an unnamed Hebrew poet took up an old folk tale and transformed it into a sacred hymn so sublime—and yet so shocking to conventional religion—that it agitates and exalts us even now. Scholars may place the Book of Job in the age of the Babylonian Exile, following the conquest of Jerusalem by Nebuchadnezzar—but to readers of our own time, or of any time, the historicity of this timeless poem hardly matters. It is timeless because its author intended it so; it is timeless the way Lear on the heath is timeless (and Lear may owe much to Job). Job is a man who belongs to no known nation; despite his peerless Hebrew speech, he is plainly not a Hebrew. His religious customs are unfamiliar, yet he is no pagan: he addresses the One God of monotheism. Because he is unidentified by period or place, nothing in his situation is foreign or obsolete; his story cannot blunder into anachronism or archaism. Like almost no other primordial poem the West has inherited, the Book of Job is conceived under the aspect of the universal—if the universal is understood to be a questioning so organic to our nature that no creed or philosophy can elude it.

That is why the striking discoveries of scholars—whether through philological evidences or through the detection of infusions from surrounding ancient cultures—will not deeply unsettle the common reader. We are driven—we common readers—to approach Job's story with tremulous palms held upward and unladen. Not for us the burden of historical linguistics, or the torrent of clerical commentary that sweeps through the centuries, or the dusty overlay of partisan interpretation. Such a refusal of context, historical and theological, is least of all the work of willed ignorance; if we choose to turn from received instruction, it is rather because of an intrinsic knowledge—the terror, in fact, of self-knowledge. Who among us has not been tempted to ask Job's questions? Which of us has not doubted God's justice? What human creature ever lived in the absence of suffering? If we, ordinary clay that we are, are not equal to Job in the wild intelligence of his cries, or in the unintelligible wilderness of his anguish, we are, all the same, privy to his conundrums.

Yet what captivates the scholars may also captivate us. A faithful English translation, for instance, names God as "God," "the Lord," "the Holy One," "the Almighty"—terms reverential, familiar, and nearly interchangeable in their capacity to evoke an ultimate Presence. But the author of Job, while aiming for the same effect of incalculable awe, has another resonance in mind as well: the dim tolling of some indefinable aboriginal chime, a suggestion of immeasurable antiquity. To achieve this, he is altogether sparing in his inclusion of the Tetragrammaton, the unvocalized YHVH (the root of which is "to be," rendered as "I am that I am"), which chiefly delineates God in the Hebrew Bible (and was later approximately transliterated as Yahweh or Jehovah). Instead, he sprinkles his poem, cannily and profusely, with pre-Israelite God-names: El, Eloah, Shaddai—names so lost in the long-ago, so unembedded in usage, that the poem is inevitably swept clean of traditional pieties. Translation veils the

presence—and the intent—of these old names; and the necessary seamlessness of translation will perforce paper over the
multitude of words and passages that are obscure in the original, subject to philological guesswork. Here English allows the
common reader to remain untroubled by scholarly puzzles and
tangles.

But how arresting to learn that Satan appears in the story of
Job not as that demonic figure of later traditions whom we meet
in our translation, but as *ha-Satan*, with the definite article
attached, meaning "the Adversary"—the counter-arguer among
the angels, who is himself one of "the sons of God." Satan's
arrival in the tale helps date its composition. It is under Persian
influence that he turns up—via Zoroastrian duality, which pits,
as equal contenders, a supernatural power for Good against a
supernatural power for Evil. In the Book of Job, the scholars tell
us, Satan enters Scripture for the first time as a distinct personality and as an emblem of destructive forces. But note: when the
tale moves out of the prose of its fablelike frame into the sovereign grandeur of its poetry, Satan evaporates; the poet, an
uncompromising monotheist, recognizes no alternative to the
Creator, and no opposing might. Nor does the poet acknowledge
any concept of afterlife, though Pharisaic thought in the period
of his writing is just beginning to introduce that idea into nor-
mative faith.

There is much more that textual scholarship discloses in its
search for the Job-poet's historical surround: for example, the
abundance of words and phrases in Aramaic, a northwestern
Semitic tongue closely related to Hebrew, which was rapidly
becoming the lingua franca of the post-Exilic Levant. Aramaic is
significantly present in other biblical books as well: in the later
Psalms, in Ecclesiastes, Esther, and Chronicles—and, notably, in
the Dead Sea Scrolls. The Babylonian Talmud is written in

Aramaic; it is the language that Jesus speaks. Possibly the Job-poet's everyday speech is Aramaic—this may account for his many Aramaisms—but clearly, for the literary heightening of poetry, he is drawn to the spare beauty and noble diction of classical Hebrew (much as Milton, say, in constructing his poems of Paradise, invokes the cadences of classical Latin).

And beyond the question of language, the scholars lead us to still another enchanted garden of context and allusion: the flowering, all over the ancient Near East, of a form known as "wisdom literature." A kind of folk-philosophy linking virtue to prudence, and pragmatically geared to the individual's worldly success, its aim is instruction in level-headed judgment and in the achievement of rational contentment. The biblical Proverbs belong to this genre, and, in a more profoundly reflective mode, Ecclesiastes and portions of Job; but wisdom literature can also be found in Egyptian, Babylonian, Ugaritic, and Hellenistic sources. It has no overriding national roots and deals with personal rather than collective conduct, and with a commonsensical morality guided by principles of resourcefulness and discretion. A great part of the Book of Job finds its ancestry in the region's pervasive wisdom literature (and its descendants in today's self-improvement best-sellers). But what genuinely seizes the heart are those revolutionary passages in Job that violently contradict what all the world, yesterday and today, takes for ordinary wisdom.

2. What the Reader Sees

However seductive they are in their insight and learning, all these scholarly excavations need not determine or deter our own reading. We, after all, have in our hands neither the Hebrew original nor a linguistic concordance. What we do have—and it is electrifying enough—is the Book of Job as we readers of English encounter it. And if we are excluded from the sound and texture of an elevated poetry in a tongue not ours, we are also shielded from problems of structure and chronology, and from a confrontation with certain endemic philological riddles. There is riddle enough remaining—a riddle that is, besides, an elemental quest, the appeal for an answer to humankind's primal inquiry.

So there is something to be said for novice readers who come to Job's demands and plaints unaccoutered: we will perceive God's world exactly as Job himself perceives it. Or put it that Job's bewilderment will be ours, and our kinship to his travail fully unveiled, only if we are willing to absent ourselves from the accretion of centuries of metaphysics, exegesis, theological polemics. Of the classical Jewish and Christian theologians (Saadia Gaon, Rashi, ibn Ezra, Maimonides, Gersonides, Gregory, Aquinas, Calvin), each wrote from a viewpoint dictated by his particular religious perspective. But for us to be as (philosophically) naked as Job will mean to be naked of bias, dogma, tradition. It will mean to imagine Job solely as he is set forth by his own words in his own story.

His story, because it is mostly in dialogue, reads as a kind of drama. There is no proscenium; there is no scenery. But there is the dazzling spiral of words—extraordinary words, Shakespearean words; and there are the six players, who alternately cajole, console, contradict, contend, satirize, fulminate, remonstrate, accuse, deny, trumpet, succumb. Sometimes we are reminded of Antigone, sometimes of Oedipus (Greek plays that are contemporaneous with Job), sometimes of Othello. The subject is innocence and power; virtue and injustice; the Creator and His Creation; or what philosophy has long designated as theodicy, the Problem of Evil. And the more we throw off sectarian sophistries—the more we attend humbly to the drama as it plays itself out—the more clearly we will see Job as he emerges from the venerable thicket of theodicy into the heat of our own urgency. Or call it our daily breath.

3. Job's Story

Job's story—his fate, his sentence—begins in heaven, with Satan as prosecuting attorney. Job, Satan presses, must be put to trial. Look at him: a man of high estate, an aristocrat, robust and in his prime, the father of sons and daughters, respected, affluent, conscientious, charitable, virtuous, God-fearing. God-fearing? How effortless to be always praising God when you are living in such ease! Look at him: how he worries about his lucky children and their feasting, days at a time—was there too much wine, did they slide into blasphemy? On their account he brings sacred offerings in propitiation. His possessions are lordly, but he succors the poor and turns no one away; his hand is lavish. Yet look at him—how easy to be righteous when you are carefree and rich! Strip him of his wealth, wipe out his family, afflict him with disease, and *then* see what becomes of his virtue and his piety!

So God is persuaded to test Job. Invasion, fire, tornado, destruction, and the cruelest loss of all: the death of his children. Nothing is left. Odious lesions creep over every patch of Job's skin. Tormented, he sits in the embers of what was once his domain and scratches himself with a bit of shattered bowl. His wife despairs: after all this, he still declines to curse God! She means for him to dismiss God as worthless to his life, and to dismiss his ruined life as worthless. But now a trio of gentlemen from neighboring lands arrives—a condolence call from Eliphaz, Bildad, and Zophar, Job's distinguished old friends. The three weep and are mute—Job's broken figure appalls: pitiable, desolate, dusted with ash, scraped, torn.

All the foregoing is told in the plain prose of a folk tale: a blameless man's undoing through the conniving of a mischievous sprite. A prose epilogue will ultimately restore Job to his good fortune, and, in the arbitrary style of a fable, will even double it; but between the two halves of this simple narrative of loss and restitution the coloration of legend falls away, and a majesty of outcry floods speech after speech. And then Job's rage ascends—a rage against the loathsomeness of "wisdom."

When the horrified visitors regain their voices, it is they who appear to embody reasonableness, logic, and prudence, while Job—introduced in the prologue as a man of steadfast faith who will never affront the Almighty—rails like a blasphemer against an unjust God. The three listen courteously as Job bewails the day he was born, a day that "did not shut the doors of my mother's womb, nor hide trouble from my eyes." In response to which, Eliphaz begins his first attempt at solace: "Can mortal man be righteous before God? Can a man be pure before his Maker? . . . Behold, happy is the man whom God reproves; therefore despise not the chastening of the Almighty." Here is an early and not altogether brutal hint of what awaits Job in the severer discourse of his consolers: the logic of punishment, the dogma of requital. If a man suffers, it must be because of some impiety he has committed. Can Job claim that he is utterly without sin? And is not God a merciful God, "for He wounds, but binds up; He smites, but His hands heal"? In the end, Eliphaz reassures Job, all will be well.

Job is not comforted; he is made furious. He has been accused, however obliquely, of having sinned, and he knows with his whole soul that he has not. His friends show themselves to be as inconstant as a torrential river, icy in winter, vanishing away in the heat. Rather than condole, they defame. They root amelioration in besmirchment. But if Job's friends are no friends, then what of God? The poet, remembering the Psalm—"What is man that thou are mindful of him?"—has Job echo the very words. "What is man," Job charges God, that "thou dost set thy mind upon him, dost visit him every morning, and test him every moment? . . . If I sin, what do I do to thee, thou watcher of men?" And he dreams of escaping God in death: "For now I shall lie in the earth; thou wilt seek me, but I shall not be."

Three rounds of increasingly tumultuous debate follow, with Eliphaz, Bildad, and Zophar each having a turn, and Job replying. Wilder and wilder grow the visitors' accusations; wilder and wilder grow Job's rebuttals, until they are pitched into an abyss of bitterness. Job's would-be comforters have become his harriers; men of standing themselves, they reason from the conventional doctrines of orthodox religion, wherein conduct and consequence are morally linked: goodness rewarded, wickedness punished. No matter how hotly Job denies and protests, what greater proof of Job's impiety can there be than his deadly ordeal? God is just; he metes out just deserts. Is this not the grand principle on which the world rests?

Job's own experience refutes these arguments; and his feverish condemnation of God's injustice refutes religion itself. "I am blameless!" he cries yet again, and grimly concludes: "It is all one: therefore I say, He destroys both the blameless and the wicked. When disaster brings sudden death, He mocks the calamity of the innocent. The earth is given into the hand of the wicked; He covers the face of its judges." Here Job, remarkably, is both believer and atheist. God's presence is incontrovertible; God's moral integrity is nil. And how strange: in the heart of Scripture, a righteous man impugning God! Genesis, to be sure, records what appears to be a precedent. "Wilt thou destroy the righteous with the wicked?" Abraham asks God when Sodom's fate is at stake; but that is more plea than indictment, and anyhow there is no innocence in Sodom. Yet how distant Job is from the Psalmist who sings "The Lord is upright . . . there is no unrighteousness in Him," who pledges that "the righteous shall flourish like the palm tree," and "the workers of iniquity shall be destroyed forever." The Psalmist's is the voice of faith. Job's is the voice of a wounded lover, betrayed.

Like a wounded lover, he envisions, fleetingly, a forgiving afterlife, the way a tree, cut down to a stump, can send forth new shoots and live again—while man, by contrast, "lies down and rises not again." Or he imagines the workings of true justice: on the one hand, he wishes he might bring God Himself to trial; on the other, he ponders man-made law and its courts, and declares that the transcript of his testimony ought to be inscribed permanently in stone, so that some future clansman might one day come as a vindicator, to proclaim the probity of Job's case. (Our translation famously—and not disinterestedly—renders the latter as "I know that my Redeemer lives," a phrase that has, of course, been fully integrated into Christian hermeneutics.) Throughout, there is a thundering of discord and clangor. "Miserable comforters are you all!" Job groans. "Surely there are mockers about me"—while Eliphaz, Bildad, and Zophar press on, from pious apologias to uncontrolled denunciation. You, Job, they accuse, you who stripped the naked of their clothing, gave no water to the weary, withheld bread from the hungry!

And Job sees how the tenets of rectitude, in the mouths of the zealous, are perverted to lies.

But now, abruptly, a new voice is heard: a fifth and so far undisclosed player strides onstage. He is young, intellectually ingenious, confident, a bit brash. Unlike the others, he bears a name with a Hebrew ring to it: Elihu. "I also will declare my opinion," he announces. He arrives as a supplanter, to replace stale wisdom with fresh, and begins by rebuking Job's haranguers for their dogma of mechanical tit-for-tat. As for Job: in his recalcitrance, in his litanies of injured innocence, in his prideful denials, he has been blind to the *uses* of suffering; and doesn't he recognize that God manifests Himself in night visions and dreams? Suffering educates and purifies; it humbles pride, tames the rebel, corrects the scoffer. "What man is like Job, who drinks up scoffing like water?" Elihu points out—but here the reader detects a logical snag. Job has become a scoffer only as a result of gratuitous suffering: then how is such suffering a "correction" of scoffing that never was? Determined though he is to shake Job's obstinacy, Elihu is no wiser than his elders. Job's refusal of meaningless chastisement stands.

So Elihu, too, fails as comforter—but as he leaves off suasion, his speech metamorphoses into a hymn in praise of God's dominion. "Hear this, O Job," Elihu calls, "stop and consider the wondrous work of God"—wind, cloud, sky, snow, lightning, ice! Elihu's sumptuous limning of God's power in nature is a fore-echo of the sublime climax to come.

4. The Voice Out of the Whirlwind

Job, gargantuan figure in the human imagination that he is, is not counted among the prophets. He is not the first to be reluctant to accept God's authority: Jonah rebelled against sailing to Nineveh in order to prophesy; yet he did go, and his going was salvational for a people not his own. But the true prophets are self-starters, spontaneous fulminators against social inequity, and far from reluctant. Job, then, has much in common with Isaiah, Jeremiah, Micah and Amos: he is wrathful that the wicked go unpunished, that the widow and the orphan go unsuccored, that the world is not clothed in righteousness. Like the noblest of the prophets, he assails injustice; and still he is unlike them. They accuse the men and women who do evil; their targets are made of flesh and blood. It is human transgression they hope to mend. Job seeks to rectify God. His is an ambition higher, deeper, vaster, grander than theirs; he is possessed by a righteousness more frenzied than theirs; the scale of his justice-hunger exceeds all that precedes him, all that was ever conceived; he can be said to be the consummate prophet. And at the same time he is the consummate violator. If we are to understand him at all, if we are rightly to enter into his passions at their pinnacle, then we ought to name him prophet; but we may not. Call him, instead, anti-prophet—his teaching, after all, verges on atheism: the rejection of God's power. His thesis is revolution.

Eliphaz, Bildad, and Zophar are silenced. Elihu will not strut these boards again. Job's revolution may be vanity of vanities, but his adversaries have lost confidence and are scattered. Except for Job, the stage is emptied.

Then God enters—not in a dream, as Elihu theorized, not as a vision or incarnation, but as an irresistible Eloquence.

Here I am obliged to remark on the obvious. In recapitulating certain passages, I have reduced an exalted poem to ordinary spoken sentences. But the ideas that buttress Job are not merely "expressed in," as we say, language of high beauty; they are inseparable from an artistry so far beyond the grasp of mind and tongue that one can hardly imagine their origin. We think of the Greek plays; we think of Shakespeare; and still that is not marvel enough. Is it that the poet is permitted to sojourn, for the poem's brief life, in the magisterial Eye of God? Or is it God who allows Himself to peer through the poet's glass, as through a gorgeously crafted kaleidoscope? The words of the poem are preternatural, unearthly. They may belong to a rhapsodic endowment so rare as to appear among mortals only once in three thousand years. Or they may belong to the Voice that hurls itself from the whirlwind.

5. *The Answer*

God has granted Job's demand: "Let the Almighty answer me!" Now here at last is Job's longed-for encounter with that Being he conceives to be his persecutor. What is most extraordinary in this visitation is that it appears to be set apart from everything that has gone before. What is the Book of Job *about*? It is about gratuitous affliction. It is about the wicked who escape whipping. It is about the suffering of the righteous. God addresses none of this. It is as if He has belatedly stepped into the drama without having consulted the script—none of it: not even so much as the prologue. He does not remember Satan's mischief. He does not remember Job's calamities. He does not remember Job's righteousness.

As to the latter: Job will hardly appeal for an accounting from God without first offering one of his own. He has his own credibility to defend, his own probity. "Let me be weighed in a just balance," he insists, "and let God know my integrity!" The case for his integrity takes the form of a bill of particulars that is unsurpassed as a compendium of compassionate human conduct: no conceivable ethical nuance is omitted. It is as if all the world's moral fervor, distilled from all the world's religions, and touching on all the world's pain, is assembled in Job's roster of lovingkindness. Job in his confession of integrity is both a protector and a lover of God's world.

But God seems alarmingly impatient; His mind is elsewhere. Is this the Lord whom Job once defined as a "watcher of men"? God's answer, a fiery challenge, roils out of the whirlwind. "Where were *you*," the Almighty roars, in supernal strophes that blaze through the millennia, "when I laid the foundation of the earth?" And what comes crashing and tumbling out of the gale is an exuberant ode to the grandeur of the elements, to the fecundity of nature: the sea and the stars, the rain and the dew, the constellations in their courses, the lightning, the lion, the raven, the ass, the goat, the ostrich, the horse, the hawk—and more, more, more! The lavishness, the extravagance, the infinitude! An infinitude of power; an infinitude of joy; an infinitude of love, even for the ugly hippopotamus, even for the crocodile with his terrifying teeth, even for creatures made mythical through ancient lore. Even for Leviathan! Nothing in the universe is left unpraised in these glorious stanzas— and one thinks: had the poet access to the electrons, had he an inkling of supernovas, had he parsed the chains of DNA, God's ode to Creation could not be richer. Turn it and turn it —God's ode: everything is in it.

Everything but the answer to the question that eats at Job's soul: why God permits injustice in the fabric of a world so resplendently woven. Job is conventionally judged to be a moral violator because he judges God Himself to be a moral violator. Yet is there any idea in the history of human thought more exquisitely tangled, more furiously daring, more heroically courageous, more rooted in spirit and conscience than Job's question? Why does God not praise the marrow of such a man as Job at least as much as He praises the intricacy of the crocodile's scales? God made the crocodile; He also made Job.

God's answer to Job lies precisely in His not answering; and Job, with lightning insight, comprehends. "I have uttered what I did not understand," he acknowledges, "things too wonderful for me, which I did not know."

His new knowledge is this: that a transcendent God denies us a god of our own devising, a god that we would create out of our own malaise, or complaint, or desire, or hope, or imagining; or would manufacture according to the satisfaction of our own design. We are part of God's design: can the web manufacture the spider? The Voice out of the whirlwind warns against god-manufacture—against the degradation of a golden calf surely, but also against god-manufacture even in the form of the loftiest visions. Whose visions are they? Beware: they are not God's; they are ours. The ways of the true God cannot be penetrated. The false comforters cannot decipher them. Job cannot uncover them. "The secret things belong to the Lord our God," Job's poet learned long ago, reading Deuteronomy. But now: see how Job cannot draw Leviathan out with a hook—how much less can he draw out God's nature, and His purpose!

So the poet, through the whirlwind's answer, stills Job.

But can the poet still the Job who lives in us? God's majesty is eternal, manifest in cell and star. Yet Job's questions toil on, manifest in death camp and hatred, in tyranny and anthrax, in bomb and bloodshed. Why do the wicked thrive? Why do the innocent suffer? In brutal times, the whirlwind's answer tempts, if not atheism, then the sorrowing conviction of God's indifference.

And if we are to take the close of the tale as given, it is not only Job's protests that are stilled; it is also his inmost moral urge. What has become of raging conscience? What has become of lovingkindness? Prosperity is restored; the dead children are replaced by twice the number of boys, and by girls exceedingly comely. But where now is the father's bitter grief over the loss of those earlier sons and daughters, on whose account he once indicted God? Cushioned again by good fortune, does Job remember nothing, feel nothing, see nothing beyond his own renewed honor? Is Job's lesson from the whirlwind finally no more than the learning of indifference?

So much for the naked text. Perhaps this is why—century after century—we common readers go on clinging to the spiritualizing mentors of traditional faith, who clothe in comforting theologies this God-wrestling and comfortless Book.

Yet how astoundingly up-to-date they are, those ancient sages—redactors and compilers—who opened even the sacred gates of Scripture to philosophic doubt!

Who Owns Anne Frank?

If Anne Frank had not perished in the criminal malevolence of Bergen-Belsen early in 1945, she would have marked her seventieth birthday at the brink of the twenty-first century. And even if she had not kept the extraordinary diary through which we know her, it is likely that we would number her among the famous of the twentieth—though perhaps not so dramatically as we do now. She was born to be a writer. At thirteen, she felt her power; at fifteen, she was in command of it. It is easy to imagine—had she been allowed to live—a long row of novels and essays spilling from her fluent and ripening pen. We can be certain (as certain as one can be of anything hypothetical) that her mature prose would today be noted for its wit and acuity, and almost as certain that the trajectory of her work would be closer to that of Nadine Gordimer, say, than that of Françoise Sagan. Put it that as an international literary presence she would be thick rather than thin. "I want to go on living even after my death!" she exclaimed in the spring of 1944.

This was more than an exaggerated adolescent flourish. She had already intuited what greatness in literature might mean, and she clearly sensed the force of what lay under her hand in the pages of her diary: a conscious literary record of frightened lives in daily peril; an explosive document aimed directly at the future. In her last months she was assiduously polishing phrases and editing passages with an eye to postwar publication. *Het Achterhuis,* as she called her manuscript—"the house behind," often translated as "the secret annex"—was hardly intended to be Anne Frank's last word; it was conceived as the forerunner work of a professional woman of letters.

Yet any projection of Anne Frank as a contemporary figure is an unholy speculation: it tampers with history, with reality, with deadly truth. "When I write," she confided, "I can shake off all my cares. My sorrow disappears, my spirits are revived!" But she could not shake off her capture and annihilation, and there are no diary entries to register and memorialize the snuffing of her spirit. Anne Frank was discovered, seized, and deported; she and her mother and sister and millions of others were extinguished in a program calculated to assure the cruelest and most demonically inventive human degradation. The atrocities she endured were ruthlessly and purposefully devised, from indexing by tattoo to systematic starvation to factory-efficient murder. She was designated to be erased from the living, to leave no grave, no sign, no physical trace of any kind. Her fault—her crime—was having been born a Jew, and as such she was classified among those who had no right to exist: not as a subject people, not as an inferior breed, not even as usable slaves. The military and civilian apparatus of an entire society was organized to obliterate her as a contaminant, in the way of a noxious and repellent insect. Zyklon B, the lethal fumigant poured into the gas chambers, was, pointedly, a roach poison.

Anne Frank escaped gassing. One month before liberation, not yet sixteen, she died of typhus fever, an acute infectious disease carried by lice. The precise date of her death has never been determined. She and her sister Margot were among 3,659 women transported by cattle car from Auschwitz to the merciless conditions of Bergen-Belsen, a barren tract of mud. In a cold, wet autumn, they suffered through nights on flooded straw in overcrowded tents, without light, surrounded by latrine ditches, until a violent hailstorm tore away what had passed for shelter. Weakened by brutality, chaos, and hunger, fifty thousand men and women—insufficiently clothed, tormented by lice—succumbed, many to the typhus epidemic.

Anne Frank's final diary entry, written on August 1, 1944, ends introspectively—a meditation on a struggle for moral transcendence set down in a mood of wistful gloom. It speaks of "turning my heart inside out, the bad part on the outside and the good part on the inside," and of "trying to find a way to become what I'd like to be and what I could be if . . . if only there were no other people in the world." Those curiously self-subduing ellipses are the diarist's own; they are more than merely a literary effect—they signify a child's muffled bleat against confinement, the last whimper of a prisoner in a cage. Her circumscribed world had a population of eleven—the three Dutch protectors who came and went, supplying the necessities of life, and the eight in hiding: the van Daans, their son Peter, Albert Dussel, and the four Franks. Five months earlier, on May 26, 1944, she had railed against the stress of living invisibly—a tension never relieved, she asserted, "not once in the two years we've been here. How much longer will this increasingly oppressive, unbearable weight press down on us?" And, several paragraphs on, "What will we do if we're ever . . . no, I mustn't write that down. But the question won't let itself be pushed to the back of my mind today; on the contrary, all the fear I've ever felt is looming before me in all its horror. . . . I've asked myself again and again whether it wouldn't have been better if we hadn't gone into hiding, if we were dead now and didn't have to go through this misery. . . . Let something happen soon. . . . Nothing can be more crushing than this anxiety. Let the end come, however cruel." And on April 11, 1944: "We are Jews in chains."

The diary is not a genial document, despite its author's often

vividly satiric exposure of what she shrewdly saw as "the comical side of life in hiding." Its reputation for uplift is, to say it
plainly, nonsensical. Anne Frank's written narrative, moreover,
is not the story of Anne Frank, and never has been. That the
diary is miraculous, a self-aware work of youthful genius, is not
in question. Variety of pace and tone, insightful humor, insup-
portable suspense, adolescent love-pangs and disappointments,
sexual curiosity, moments of terror, moments of elation, flights
of idealism and prayer and psychological acumen—all these elements of mind and feeling and skill brilliantly enliven its pages.
There is, besides, a startlingly precocious comprehension of the
progress of the war on all fronts. The survival of the little group
in hiding is crucially linked to the timing of the Allied invasion;
overhead the bombers, roaring to their destinations, make the
house quake. Sometimes the bombs fall terrifyingly close. All in
all, the diary is a chronicle of trepidation, turmoil, alarm. Even
its report of quieter periods of reading and study express the
hush of imprisonment. Meals are boiled lettuce and rotted pota-
toes; flushing the single toilet is forbidden for ten hours at a
time. There is shooting at night. Betrayal and arrest always
threaten. Anxiety and immobility rule. It is a story of fear.

But the diary in itself, richly crammed though it is with incident and passion, cannot count as Anne Frank's story. A story
may not be said to be a story if the end is missing. And because
the end is missing, the story of Anne Frank in the fifty years
since *The Diary of a Young Girl* was first published has been
bowdlerized, distorted, transmuted, traduced, reduced; it has
been infantilized, Americanized, homogenized, sentimentalized;
falsified, kitschified, and, in fact, blatantly and arrogantly denied.
Among the falsifiers and bowdlerizers have been dramatists and
directors, translators and litigators, Anne Frank's own father, and
even—or especially—the public, both readers and theatergoers,
all over the world. A deeply truth-telling work has been turned

into an instrument of partial truth, surrogate truth, or anti-truth. The pure has been made impure—sometimes in the name of the reverse. Almost every hand that has approached the diary with the well-meaning intention of publicizing it has contributed to the subversion of history.

The diary is taken to be a Holocaust document; that is overridingly what it is not. Nearly every edition—and there have been innumerable editions—is emblazoned with words like "a song to life," "a poignant delight in the infinite human spirit." Such characterizations rise up in the bitter perfume of mockery. A song to life? The diary is incomplete, truncated, broken off; or, rather, it is completed by Westerbork (the hellish transit camp in Holland from which Dutch Jews were deported), and by Auschwitz, and by the fatal winds of Bergen-Belsen. It is here, and not in the "secret annex," that the crimes we have come to call the Holocaust were enacted. Our entry into those crimes begins with columns of numbers: the meticulous lists of deportations, in handsome bookkeepers' handwriting, starkly set down in German "transport books." From these columns—headed, like goods for export, *"Ausgange-Transporte nach Osten"* (outgoing shipments to the east)—it is possible to learn that Anne Frank and the others were moved to Auschwitz on the night of September 6, 1944, in a collection of 1,019 *Stücke* (or "pieces," another commodities term). That same night, 549 persons were gassed, including one from the Frank group (the father of Peter van Daan), and every child under fifteen. Anne, at fifteen, and seventeen-year-old Margot were spared, apparently for labor. The end of October, from the twentieth to the twenty-eighth, saw the gassing of more than 6,000 human beings within two hours of their arrival, including a thousand boys eighteen and under. In December, 2,093 female prisoners perished, from starvation and exhaustion, in the women's camp; early in January, Edith Frank expired.

But Soviet forces were hurtling toward Auschwitz, and in November the order went out to conceal all evidences of gassing and to blow up the crematoria. Tens of thousands of inmates, debilitated and already near extinction, were driven out in bitter cold on death marches. Many were shot. In an evacuation that occurred either on October 28 or November 2, Anne and Margot were dispatched to Bergen-Belsen. Margot was the first to succumb. A survivor recalled that she fell dead to the ground from the wooden slab on which she lay, eaten by lice, and that Anne, heartbroken and skeletal, naked under a bit of rag, died a day or two later.

To come to the diary without having earlier assimilated Elie Wiesel's *Night* and Primo Levi's *The Drowned and the Saved* (to mention two accounts only), or the columns of figures in the transport books, is to allow oneself to stew in an implausible and ugly innocence. The litany of blurbs—"a lasting testimony to the indestructible nobility of the human spirit," "an everlasting source of courage and inspiration"—is no more substantial than any other display of self-delusion. The success—the triumph—of Bergen-Belsen was precisely that it blotted out the possibility of courage, that it proved to be a lasting testament to the human spirit's easy destructibility. *"Hier ist kein warum,"* a guard at Auschwitz warned Primo Levi: here there is no "why," neither question nor answer, only the dark of unreason. Anne Frank's story, truthfully told, is unredeemed and unredeemable.

These are notions that are hard to swallow—so they have not been swallowed. There are some, bored beyond toleration and callous enough to admit it, who are sick of hearing—yet again!—about depredations fifty years gone. "These old events," one of these fellows may complain, "can rake you over only so much. . . . If I'm going to be lashed, I might as well save my skin for more recent troubles in the world." (I quote from a private letter from a distinguished author.) This may be a popular, if mostly unexpressed, point of view, but it is not socially representative. The more common response respectfully discharges an obligation to pity: it is dutiful. Or it is sometimes less than dutiful. It is sometimes frivolous, or indifferent, or presumptuous. But what even the most exemplary sympathies are likely to evade is the implacable recognition that Auschwitz and Bergen-Belsen, however sacramentally prodded, can never yield light.

And the vehicle that has most powerfully accomplished this almost universal obtuseness is Anne Frank's diary. In celebrating Anne Frank's years in the secret annex, the nature and meaning of her death has been, in effect, forestalled. The diary's keen lens is helplessly opaque to the diarist's explicit doom—and this opacity, replicated in young readers in particular, has led to shamelessness.

It is the shamelessness of appropriation. Who owns Anne Frank? The children of the world, say the sentimentalists. A case in point, then, is the astonishing correspondence, published in 1995 under the title *Love, Otto*, between Cara Wilson, a Californian born in 1944, and Otto Frank, the father of Anne Frank. Wilson, then twelve-year-old Cara Weiss, was invited by Twentieth Century-Fox to audition for the part of Anne in a projected film version of the diary. "I didn't get the part," the middle-aged Wilson writes, "but by now I had found a whole new world. Anne Frank's diary, which I read and reread, spoke to me and my dilemmas, my anxieties, my secret passions. She felt the way I did. . . . I identified so strongly with this eloquent girl of my own age, that I now think I sort of became her in my own mind." And on what similarities does Wilson rest her acute sense of identification with a hunted child in hiding?

> I was miserable being me. . . . I was on the brink of that awful abyss of teenagedom and I, too, needed someone to talk to. . . . (Ironically, Anne, too, expressed a longing for more

attention from her father.) . . . Dad's whole life was a series
of meetings. At home, he was too tired or too frustrated to
unload on. I had something else in common with Anne. We
both had to share with sisters who were prettier and smarter
than we felt we were. . . . Despite the monumental difference
in our situations, to this day I feel that Anne helped me get
through the teens with a sense of inner focus. She spoke for
me. She was strong for me. She had so much hope when I
was ready to call it quits.

A sampling of Wilson's concerns as she matured appears
in the interstices of her exchanges with Otto Frank—which,
remarkably, date from 1959 until his death in 1980. For instance:
"The year was 1968—etched in my mind. I can't ever forget
it. Otis Redding was 'Sittin' on the Dock of the Bay' . . . while we
hummed along to 'Hey Jude' by the Beatles." Or again: "What
a year 1972 was! That was when I saw one of my all-time
favorite movies, *Harold and Maude,* to the tune of Cat Stevens'
incredible sound track. . . . I remember singing along to Don
McLean's 'American Pie' and daydreaming to Roberta Flack's
exquisite 'The First Time Ever I Saw Your Face,' " and so on. "In
1973-74," she reports, "I was wearing headbands, pukka-shell
necklaces, and American Indian anything. Tattoos were a rage"—
but enough. Tattoos were the rage, she neglects to recall, in
Auschwitz; and of the Auschwitz survivor who was her patient
correspondent for more than two decades, Wilson remarks:
"Well, what choice did the poor man have? Whenever an attack
of 'I-can't-take-this-any-longer' would hit me, I'd put it all into
lengthy diatribes to my distant guru, Otto Frank."

That the designated guru replied, year after year, to embarrassing and shabby effusions like these may open a new path-
way into our generally obscure understanding of the character
of Otto Frank. His responses—from Basel, where he had settled
with his second wife—were consistently attentive, formal, kindly.

When Wilson gave birth, he sent her a musical toy, and he faithfully offered a personal word about her excitements as she supplied them: her baby sons, her dance lessons, her husband's work
on commercials, her freelance writing. But his letters were also
political and serious: it is good, he wrote in October 1970, to take
"an active part in trying to abolish injustices and all sorts of
grievances, but we cannot follow your views regarding the Black
Panthers." And in December 1973, "As you can imagine, we
were highly shocked about the unexpected attack of the Arabs
on Israel on Yom Kippur and are now mourning with all those
who lost their families." Presumably he knew something about
losing a family. Wilson, insouciantly sliding past these faraway
matters, was otherwise preoccupied, "finding our little guys sooo
much fun."

The unabashed triflings of Cara Wilson—whose "identification" with Anne Frank can be duplicated by the thousand, though
she may be more audacious than most—point to a conundrum.
Never mind that the intellectual distance between Wilson and
Anne Frank is immeasurable; not every self-conscious young
girl will be a prodigy. Did Otto Frank not comprehend that Cara
Wilson was deaf to everything the loss of his daughter represented? Did he not see, in Wilson's letters alone, how a dena-
tured approach to the diary might serve to promote amnesia of
what was rapidly turning into history? A protected domestic
space, however threatened and endangered, can, from time to
time, mimic ordinary life. The young who are encouraged to
embrace the diary cannot always be expected to feel the difference between the mimicry and the threat. And (like Cara Wilson) most do not. Natalie Portman, then sixteen years old, who
in December 1997 débuted as Anne Frank in the Broadway
revival of the famous play based on the diary—a play that has
itself influenced the way the diary is read—was reported to have

concluded from her own reading that "it's funny, it's hopeful, and she's a happy person."

Otto Frank, it turns out, is complicit in this shallowly upbeat view. Again and again, in every conceivable context, he had it as his aim to emphasize "Anne's idealism," "Anne's spirit," almost never calling attention to how and why that idealism and spirit were smothered, and unfailingly generalizing the sources of hatred. If the child is father of the man—if childhood shapes future sensibility—then Otto Frank, despite his sufferings in Auschwitz, may have had less in common with his own daughter than he was ready to recognize. As the diary gained publication in country after country, its renown accelerating year by year, he spoke not merely about but for its author—and who, after all, would have a greater right? The surviving father stood in for the dead child, believing that his words would honestly represent hers. He was not entitled to such certainty: fatherhood does not confer surrogacy. His own childhood, in Frankfurt, Germany, was wholly unclouded. A banker's son, he lived untrammeled until the rise of the Nazi regime, when he was already forty-four. At nineteen, in order to acquire training in business, he went to New York with Nathan Straus, a fellow student who was heir to the Macy's department-store fortune. During the First World War, Frank was an officer in the German military, and in 1925 he married Edith Holländer, a manufacturer's daughter. Margot was born in 1926 and Anneliese Marie, called Anne, in 1929. His characteristically secular world view belonged to an era of quiet assimilation, or, more accurately, accommodation (which includes a modicum of deference), when German Jews had become, at least in their own minds, well integrated into German society. From birth, Otto Frank had breathed the free air of the affluent bourgeoisie.

Anne's childhood, in contrast, fell into shadows almost

immediately. She was four when the German persecutions of Jews began, and from then until the anguished close of her days she lived as a refugee and a victim. In 1933 the family fled from Germany to Holland, where Frank had commercial connections, and where he founded and directed a spice and pectin business. By 1940 the Germans had occupied the Netherlands. In Amsterdam, Jewish children, Anne among them, were thrown out of the public-school system and made to wear the yellow star. At thirteen, on November 19, 1942, already in hiding, Anne Frank could write:

> In the evenings when it's dark, I often see long lines of good, innocent people accompanied by crying children, walking on and on, ordered about by a handful of men who bully and beat them until they nearly drop. No one is spared. The sick, the elderly, children, babies, pregnant women—all are marched to their death.

And earlier, on October 9, 1942, after hearing the report of an escape from Westerbork:

> Our many Jewish friends and acquaintances are being taken away in droves. The Gestapo is treating them very roughly and transporting them in cattle cars to Westerbork. . . . The people get almost nothing to eat, much less to drink, as water is available only one hour a day, and there's only one toilet and sink for several thousand people. Men and women sleep in the same room, and women and children have their heads shaved. . . . If it's that bad in Holland, what must it be like in those faraway and uncivilized places where the Germans are sending them? We assume that most of them are being murdered. The English radio says they're being gassed.

Perhaps not even a father is justified in thinking he can distill the "ideas" of this alert and sorrowing child, with scenes such as these inscribed in her psyche, and with the desolations of Auschwitz and Bergen-Belsen still ahead. His preference was to accentuate what he called Anne's "optimistical view of life." Yet the diary's most celebrated line (infamously celebrated, one might add)—"I still believe, in spite of everything, that people are truly good at heart"—has been torn out of its bed of thorns. Two sentences later (and three weeks before she was seized and shipped to Westerbork), the diarist sets down a vision of darkness:

> I see the world being transformed into a wilderness, I hear the approaching thunder that, one day, will destroy us too, I feel the suffering of millions. . . . In the meantime, I must hold on to my ideals. Perhaps the day will come when I'll be able to realize them!

Because that day never came, both Miep Gies, the selflessly courageous woman who devoted herself to the sustenance of those in hiding, and Hannah Goslar, Anne's Jewish schoolmate and the last to hear her tremulous cries in Bergen-Belsen, objected to Otto Frank's emphasis on the diary's "truly good at heart" utterance. That single sentence has become, universally, Anne Frank's message, virtually her motto—whether or not such a credo could have survived the camps. But why should this sentence be taken as emblematic, and not, for example, another? "There's a destructive urge in people, the urge to rage, murder, and kill," Anne wrote on May 3, 1944, pondering the spread of guilt. These are words that do not soften, ameliorate, or give the lie to the pervasive horror of her time. Nor do they pull the wool over the eyes of history.

Otto Frank grew up with a social need to please his environment and not to offend it; it was the condition of entering the mainstream, a bargain German Jews negotiated with themselves. It was more dignified, and safer, to praise than to blame.

Far better, then, in facing the larger postwar world the diary had opened to him, to speak of goodness rather than destruction: so much of that larger world had participated in the urge to rage. (The diary notes how Dutch anti-Semitism, "to our great sorrow and dismay," was increasing even as the Jews were being hauled away.) After the liberation of the camps, the heaps of emaciated corpses were accusation enough. Postwar sensibility hastened to migrate elsewhere, away from the cruel and the culpable. It was a tone and a mood that affected the diary's reception; it was a mood and a tone that, with cautious yet crucial excisions, the diary itself could be made to support. And so the diarist's dread came to be described as hope, her terror as courage, her prayers of despair as inspiring. And since the diary was now defined as a Holocaust document, the perception of the cataclysm itself was being subtly accommodated to expressions like "man's inhumanity to man," diluting and befogging specific historical events and their motives. "We must not flog the past," Frank insisted in 1969. His concrete response to the past was the establishment, in 1957, of the Anne Frank Foundation and its offshoot the International Youth Center, situated in the Amsterdam house where the diary was composed, to foster "as many contacts as possible between young people of different nationalities, races and religions"—a civilized and tender-hearted goal that nevertheless washed away into do-gooder abstraction the explicit urge to rage that had devoured his daughter.

But Otto Frank was merely an accessory to the transformation of the diary from one kind of witness to another kind: from the painfully revealing to the partially concealing. If Anne Frank has been made into what we nowadays call an "icon," it is because of the Pulitzer Prize–winning play derived from the diary—a play that rapidly achieved worldwide popularity, and framed the legend even the newest generation has come to believe in. Adapted by Albert Hackett and Frances Goodrich, a

Hollywood husband-and-wife screenwriting team, the theatri-
calized version opened on Broadway in 1955, ten years after the
ovens of Auschwitz had cooled; its portrayal of the "funny,
hopeful, happy" Anne continues to reverberate, not only in how
the diary is construed, but in how the Holocaust itself is understood. The play was a work born in controversy, and was destined to roil on and on in rancor and litigation. Its tangle of
contending lawyers finally came to resemble nothing so much as
the knotted imbroglio of Jarndyce vs. Jarndyce, the unending
court case of *Bleak House*. "This scarecrow of a suit," as Dickens
describes it, "has, in course of time, become so complicated, that
no man alive knows what it means. . . . Innumerable children
have been born into the cause; innumerable young people have
married into it; old people have died out of it." Many of the chief
figures in the protracted conflict over the Hacketts' play have by
now died out of it, but the principal issues, far from fading away,
have, after so many decades, intensified. And whatever the rami-
fications of these issues, whatever perspectives they illumine or
defy, the central question stands fast: who owns Anne Frank?

The hero, or irritant (depending on which side of the controversy one favors), in the genesis of the diary's dramatization was
Meyer Levin, a Chicago-born novelist of the social realist school,
author of such fairly successful works as *The Old Bunch, Com-
pulsion*, and *The Settlers*. Levin began as a man of the left,
though a strong anti-Stalinist: he was drawn to proletarian fiction (*Citizens*, about steel workers), and had gone to Spain in the
thirties to report on the Civil War. In 1945, as a war correspondent attached to the Fourth Armored Division, he was among
the first Americans to enter Buchenwald, Dachau, and Bergen-
Belsen. What he saw there was ungraspable and unendurable.
"As I groped in the first weeks, beginning to apprehend the mon-
strous shape of the story I would have to tell," he wrote, "I knew
already that I would never penetrate its heart of bile, for the

magnitude of the horror seemed beyond human register." The truest telling, he affirmed, would have to rise up out of the mouth of a victim.

His "obsession," as he afterward called it—partly in mockery of the opposition his later views evoked—had its beginning in those repeated scenes of piled-up bodies as he investigated camp after camp. From then on he could be said to carry the mark of Abel. He dedicated himself to helping the survivors get to Mandate Palestine, a goal that Britain had made illegal. In 1946, he reported from Tel Aviv on the uprising against British rule, and during the next two years he wrote and produced a pair of films on the struggles of the survivors to reach Palestine. In 1950 he published *In Search,* an examination of the effects of the European cataclysm on his experience and sensibility as an American Jew; Thomas Mann acclaimed it as "a human document of high order, written by a witness of our fantastic epoch whose gaze remained both clear and steady." Levin's intensifying focus on the Jewish condition in the twentieth century grew more and more heated, and when his wife, the novelist Tereska Torres, handed him the French edition of the diary (it had previously appeared only in Dutch), he felt he had found what he had thirsted after: a voice crying up from the ground, an authentic witness to the German onslaught.

He acted instantly. He sent Otto Frank a copy of *In Search* and offered his services as, in effect, an unofficial agent to secure British and American publication, asserting his distance from any financial gain; his interest, he said, was purely "one of sympathy." He saw in the diary the possibility of "a very touching play or film," and asked Frank's permission to explore the idea. Frank at first avoided reading Levin's book, saturated as it was in passions and commitments so foreign to his own susceptibilities; but he was not unfamiliar with Levin's preoccupations. He had seen and liked one of his films. He encouraged Levin to go ahead—though a dramatization, he observed, would perforce "be rather different from the real contents" of the diary. Hardly so, Levin protested: no compromise would be needed; all the diarist's thoughts could be preserved.

The "real contents" had already been altered by Frank himself, and understandably, given the propriety of his own background and of the times. The diary contained, here and there, intimate adolescent musings—talk of how contraceptives work, and explicit anatomical description: "In the upper part, between the outer labia, there's a fold of skin that, on second thought, looks like a kind of blister. That's the clitoris. Then come the inner labia. . . ." All this Frank edited out. He also omitted passages recording his daughter's angry resistance to her mother's nervous fussiness ("the most rotten person in the world"). Undoubtedly he better understood Edith Frank's protective tremors, and was unwilling to perpetuate a negative portrait. Beyond this, he deleted numerous expressions of religious faith, a direct reference to Yom Kippur, terrified reports of Germans seizing Jews in Amsterdam. It was prudence, prudishness, and perhaps his own diffidently acculturated temperament that had stimulated many of these tamperings. In 1991, eleven years after Frank's death, a "definitive edition" of the diary restored everything he had expurgated. But the image of Anne Frank as merry innocent and steadfast idealist—an image the play vividly promoted—was by then ineradicable.

A subsequent bowdlerization, in 1950, was still more programmatic, and crossed over even more seriously into the area of Levin's concern for uncompromised faithfulness. The German edition's translator, Anneliese Schütz, in order to mask or soft-pedal German culpability, went about methodically blurring every hostile reference to Germans and German. Anne's parodic list of house rules, for instance, includes "*Use of language*: It is necessary to speak softly at all times. Only the language of civilized people may be spoken, thus no German." The German translation reads: *"Alle Kultursprachen . . . aber leise!"*—"all civilized languages . . . but softly!" "Heroism in war or when confronting Germans" is dissolved into "heroism in war and in the struggle against oppression." ("A book intended after all for sale in Germany," Schütz explained, "cannot abuse the Germans.") The diarist's honest cry, in the midst of a vast persecution, that "there is no greater hostility in the world than exists between Germans and Jews," became, in Schütz's version, "there is no greater hostility in the world than between *these* Germans and Jews!" Frank agreed to the latter change because, he said, it was what his daughter had really meant: she "by no means measured all Germans by the same yardstick. For, as she knew so well, even in those days we had many good friends among the Germans." But this guarded accommodationist view is Otto Frank's own; it is nowhere in the diary. Even more striking than Frank's readiness to accede to these misrepresentations is the fact that for forty-one years (until a more accurate translation appeared) no reader of the diary in German had ever known an intact text.

In contemplating a dramatization and pledging no compromise—he would do it, he told Frank, "tenderly and with the utmost fidelity"—Levin was clear about what he meant by fidelity. In his eyes the diary was conscious testimony to Jewish faith and suffering; and it was this, and this nearly alone, that defined for him its psychological, historical, and metaphysical genuineness, and its significance for the world. With these convictions foremost, Levin went in search of a theatrical producer. At the same time he was unflagging in pressing for publication; but the work was meanwhile slowly gaining independent notice. Janet Flanner, in her "Letter from Paris" in *The New*

Yorker of November 11, 1950, noted the French publication of a book by "a precocious, talented little Frankfurt Jewess"— apparently oblivious to the unpleasant echoes, post-Hitler, of "Jewess." Sixteen English-language publishers on both sides of the Atlantic had already rejected the diary when Levin succeeded in placing it with Valentine Mitchell, a London firm. His negotiations with a Boston house were still incomplete when Doubleday came forward to secure publication rights directly from Frank. Relations between Levin and Frank were, as usual, warm; Frank repeatedly thanked Levin for his efforts to further the fortunes of the diary, and Levin continued under the impression that Frank would support him as the playwright of choice.

If a single front-page review in the *New York Times Book Review* can rocket a book to instant sanctity, that is what Meyer Levin, in the spring of 1952, achieved for *Anne Frank: The Diary of a Young Girl*. It was an assignment he had avidly gone after. But Barbara Zimmerman (afterward Barbara Epstein, a founder of *The New York Review of Books*), the diary's young editor at Doubleday, had earlier recognized its potential as "a minor classic," and had enlisted Eleanor Roosevelt to supply an introduction. (According to Levin, it was ghostwritten by Zimmerman.) Levin now joined Zimmerman and Doubleday in the project of choosing a producer. Doubleday was to take over as Frank's official agent, with the stipulation that Levin would have an active hand in the adaptation. "I think I can honestly say," Levin wrote Frank, "that I am as well qualified as any other writer for this particular task." In a cable to Doubleday, Frank appeared to agree: "DESIRE LEVIN AS WRITER OR COLLABORATOR IN ANY TREATMENT TO GUARANTEE IDEA OF BOOK." The catch, it would develop, lurked in a perilous contingency: whose idea? Levin's? Frank's? The producer's? The director's? In any case, Doubleday was already sufficiently doubtful about Levin's ambiguous role: what if an interested producer decided on another playwright?

What happened next—an avalanche of furies and recrimina-
tions lasting years—has become the subject of a pair of arresting
discussions of the Frank-Levin affair. And if "affair" suggests an
event on the scale of the Dreyfus case, that is how Levin saw it:
as an unjust stripping of his rightful position, with implications
far beyond his personal predicament. *An Obsession with Anne
Frank,* by Lawrence Graver, brought out by the University of
California Press in 1995, is the first study to fashion a coherent
narrative out of the welter of claims, counterclaims, letters,
cables, petitions, polemics, and rumbling confusions that accompany any examination of the diary's journey to the stage. *The
Stolen Legacy of Anne Frank,* by Ralph Melnick, published in
1997 by Yale University Press, is denser in detail and in sources
than its predecessor, and more insistent in tone. Both are accomplished works of scholarship that converge on the facts and
diverge in their conclusions. Graver is reticent with his sympathies; Melnick is Levin's undisguised advocate. Graver finds no
villains. Melnick finds Lillian Hellman.

Always delicately respectful of Frank's dignity and rights—
and mindful always of the older man's earlier travail—Levin had
promised that he would step aside if a more prominent playwright, someone "world famous," should appear. Stubbornly
and confidently, he went on toiling over his own version. As a
novelist, he was under suspicion of being unable to write drama.
(In after years, when he had grown deeply bitter, he listed, in
retaliation, "Sartre, Gorky, Galsworthy, Steinbeck, Wilder!")
Though there are many extant drafts of Levin's play, no definitive script is available; both publication and performance were
proscribed by Frank's attorneys. A script staged without autho-
rization by the Israel Soldiers' Theater in 1966 sometimes passes
from hand to hand, and reads well: moving, theatrical, actable,
professional. This later work was not, however, the script sub-

mitted in 1952 to Cheryl Crawford, one of a number of Broadway producers who rushed in with bids in the wake of the diary's acclaim. Crawford, an eminent co-founder of the Actors Studio, was initially encouraging to Levin, offering him first consideration and, if his script was not entirely satisfactory, the aid of a more experienced collaborator. Then—virtually overnight—she rejected his draft outright. Levin was bewildered and infuriated, and from then on became an intractable and indefatigable warrior on behalf of his play—and on behalf, he contended, of the diary's true meaning. In his *Times* review he had summed it up stirringly as the voice of "six million vanished Jewish souls."

Doubleday, meanwhile, sensing complications ahead, had withdrawn as Frank's theatrical agent, finding Levin's presence—injected by Frank—too intrusive, too maverick, too independent and entrepreneurial: fixed, they believed, only on his own interest, which was to stick to his insistence on the superiority of his work over all potential contenders. Frank, too, had begun—kindly, politely, and with tireless assurances of his gratitude to Levin—to move closer to Doubleday's cooler views, especially as urged by Barbara Zimmerman. She was twenty-four years old, the age Anne would have been, very intelligent and attentive. Adoring letters flowed back and forth between them, Frank addressing her as "little Barbara" and "dearest little one." On one occasion he gave her an antique gold pin. About Levin, Zimmerman finally concluded that he was "impossible to deal with in any terms, officially, legally, morally, personally"—a "compulsive neurotic . . . destroying both himself and Anne's play." (There was, of course, no such entity as "Anne's play.")

But what had caused Crawford to change her mind so precipitately? She had sent Levin's script for further consideration to Lillian Hellman, and to the producers Robert Whitehead and

Kermit Bloomgarden. All were theater luminaries; all spurned Levin's work. Frank's confidence in Levin, already much diminished, failed altogether. Advised by Doubleday, he put his trust in the Broadway professionals, while Levin fought on alone. Famous names—Maxwell Anderson, John Van Druten, Carson McCullers—came and went. Crawford herself ultimately pulled out, fearing a lawsuit by Levin. In the end—in a plethora of complications, legal and emotional, and with the vigilant Levin still agitating loudly and publicly for the primacy of his work—Kermit Bloomgarden surfaced as producer and Garson Kanin as director. Hellman had recommended Bloomgarden; she had also recommended Frances Goodrich and Albert Hackett. The Hacketts had a long record of Hollywood hits, from *Father of the Bride* to *It's A Wonderful Life,* and they had successfully scripted a series of lighthearted musicals. Levin was appalled—had his sacred vision been pushed aside not for the awaited world-famous dramatist, but for a pair of frivolous screen drudges, mere "hired hands"?

The hired hands were earnest and reverent. They began at once to read up on European history, Judaism and Jewish practice; they consulted a rabbi. They corresponded eagerly with Frank, looking to satisfy his expectations. They traveled to Amsterdam and visited 263 Prinsengracht, the house on the canal where the Franks, the Van Daans, and Dussel had been hidden. They met Johannes Kleiman, who, together with Harry Kraler and Miep Gies, had taken over the management of Frank's business in order to conceal and protect him and his family in the house behind. Reacting to the Hacketts' lifelong remoteness from Jewish subject matter, Levin took out an ad in the New York *Post* attacking Bloomgarden and asking that his play be given a hearing. "My work," he wrote, "has been with the Jewish story. I tried to dramatize the Diary as Anne would have, in her own words. . . . I feel my work has earned the right to be judged by you, the public." "Ridiculous and laughable," said Bloomgarden. Appealing to the critic Brooks Atkinson, Levin complained—extravagantly, outrageously—that his play was being "killed by the same arbitrary disregard that brought an end to Anne and six million others." Frank stopped answering Levin's letters; many he returned unopened.

The Hacketts, too, in their earliest drafts, were devotedly "with the Jewish story." Grateful to Hellman for getting them the job, and crushed by Bloomgarden's acute dislike of their efforts so far, they flew to Martha's Vineyard weekend after weekend to receive advice from Hellman. "She was amazing," Goodrich crowed, happy to comply. Hellman's suggestions—and those of Bloomgarden and Kanin—were consistently in a direction opposite to Levin's. Wherever the diary touched on Anne's consciousness of Jewish fate or faith, they quietly erased the reference or changed its emphasis. Whatever was specific they made generic. The sexual tenderness between Anne and the young Peter van Daan was moved to the forefront. Comedy overwhelmed darkness. Anne became an all-American girl, an echo of the perky character in *Junior Miss*, a popular play of the previous decade. The Zionist aspirations of Margot, Anne's sister, disappeared. The one liturgical note, a Hanukkah ceremony, was absurdly defined by local contemporary habits ("eight days of presents"); a jolly jingle replaced the traditional "Rock of Ages," with its somber allusions to historic travail. (Kanin had insisted on something "spirited and gay," so as not to give "the wrong feeling entirely." "Hebrew," he added, "would simply alienate the audience.")

Astonishingly, the Nazified notion of "race" leaped out in a line attributed to Hellman and nowhere present in the diary. "We're not the only people that've had to suffer," says the Hacketts' Anne. "There've always been people that've had to . . . sometimes one race . . . sometimes another." This pallid speech,

yawning with vagueness, was conspicuously opposed to the pivotal reflection it was designed to betray:

> In the eyes of the world, we're doomed, but if after all this
> suffering, there are still Jews left, the Jewish people will be
> held up as an example. Who knows, maybe our religion will
> teach the world and all the people in it about goodness, and
> that's the reason, the only reason, we have to suffer. . . . God
> has never deserted our people. Through the ages Jews have
> had to suffer, but through the ages they've gone on living,
> and the centuries of suffering have only made them
> stronger.

For Kanin, this kind of rumination was "an embarrassing
piece of special pleading. . . . The fact that in this play the sym-
bols of persecution and oppression are Jews is incidental, and
Anne, in stating the argument so, reduces her magnificent
stature." And so it went throughout. The particularized plight of
Jews in hiding was vaporized into what Kanin called "the infinite." Reality—the diary's central condition—was "incidental."
The passionately contemplative child, brooding on concrete evil,
was made into an emblem of evasion. Her history had a habitation and a name; the infinite was nameless and nowhere.

For Levin, the source and first cause of these excisions was
Lillian Hellman. Hellman, he believed, had "supervised" the
Hacketts, and Hellman was fundamentally political and inflexi-
bly doctrinaire. Her outlook lay at the root of a conspiracy. She
was an impenitent Stalinist; she followed, he said, the Soviet
line. Like the Soviets, she was anti-Zionist. And just as the Soviets had obliterated Jewish particularity at Babi Yar, the ravine
where thousands of Jews, shot by the Germans, lay unnamed
and effaced in their deaths, so Hellman had directed the Hacketts
to blur the identity of the characters in the play. The sins of the
Soviets and the sins of Hellman and her Broadway deputies

were, in Levin's mind, identical. He set out to punish the man who had allowed all this to come to pass. Otto Frank had allied himself with the pundits of erasure; Otto Frank had stood aside when Levin's play was elbowed out of the way. What recourse remained for a man so affronted and injured? Meyer Levin sued Otto Frank. It was as if, someone observed, a suit were being brought against the father of Joan of Arc.

The bulky snarl of courtroom arguments resulted in small satisfaction for Levin: because the structure of the Hacketts' play was in some ways similar to his, the jury detected plagiarism; yet even this limited triumph foundered on the issue of damages. Levin sent out broadsides, collected signatures, summoned a committee of advocacy, lectured from pulpits, took out ads, rallied rabbis and writers (Norman Mailer among them). He published *The Obsession*, his grandly confessional "J'accuse," rehearsing, in skirmish after skirmish, his fight for the staging of his own adaptation. In return, furious charges flew at him: he was a redbaiter, a McCarthyite. The term "paranoid" began to circulate: why rant against the popularization and dilution that was Broadway's lifeblood? "I certainly have no wish to inflict depression on an audience," Kanin had argued. "I don't consider that a legitimate theatrical end." (So much for *Hamlet* and *King Lear*.)

Grateful for lightness, reviewers agreed. What they came away from was the liveliness of Susan Strasberg as a radiant Anne, and Joseph Schildkraut in the role of a wise and steadying Otto Frank, whom the actor engagingly resembled. "Anne is not going to her death; she is going to leave a dent on life, and let death take what's left," Walter Kerr, on a mystical note, wrote in the *Herald Tribune*. *Variety* seemed relieved that the play avoided "hating the Nazis, hating what they did to millions of innocent people," and instead left a "glowing, moving, frequently humorous" impression, with "just about everything one could wish for. It is not grim." The *Daily News* confirmed what Kanin had striven for: "not in any important sense a Jewish play. . . . Anne Frank is a Little Orphan Annie brought into vibrant life." Audiences laughed and were charmed; but they were also dazed and moved.

And audiences multiplied: the Hacketts' drama went all over the world, including Israel—where numbers of survivors were remaking their lives—and was everywhere successful. The play's reception in Germany was especially noteworthy. In an impressive and thoroughgoing essay entitled "Popularization and Memory," Alvin Rosenfeld, a professor of literature at Indiana University, recounts the development of the Anne Frank phenomenon in the country of her birth. "The theater reviews of the time," Rosenfeld reports, "tell of audiences sitting in stunned silence at the play and leaving the performance unable to speak or look one another in the eye." These were self-conscious and thin-skinned audiences; in the Germany of the fifties, theatergoers still belonged to the generation of the Nazi era. (On Broadway, Kanin had unblinkingly engaged Gusti Huber, of that same generation, to play Anne Frank's mother. As a member of the Nazi Actors Guild until Germany's defeat, Huber had early on disparaged "non-Aryan artists.") But the strange muteness in theaters all over Germany may have derived not so much from guilt or shame as from an all-encompassing compassion; or call it self-pity. "We see in Anne Frank's fate," a German drama critic offered, "our own fate—the tragedy of human existence per se." Hannah Arendt, philosopher and Hitler refugee, scorned such oceanic expressions: "cheap sentimentality at the expense of a great catastrophe," she wrote. And Bruno Bettelheim, a survivor of Dachau and Buchenwald, condemned the play's most touted line: "If all men are good, there was never an Auschwitz." A decade after the fall of Nazism, the spirited and sanitized young girl of the play became a vehicle of German communal identification—with the victim, not the persecutors—and, according to Rosenfeld, a continuing "symbol of moral and intellectual convenience." The Anne Frank whom thousands saw in seven openings in seven cities "spoke affirmatively about life and not accusingly about her torturers." No German in uniform appeared onstage. "In a word," Rosenfeld concludes, "Anne Frank has become a ready-at-hand formula for easy forgiveness."

The mood of consolation lingers on, as Otto Frank meant it to—and not only in Germany, where, even after fifty years, the issue is touchiest. Sanctified and absolving, shorn of darkness, Anne Frank remains in all countries a revered and comforting figure in the contemporary mind. In Japan, because both diary and play mention first menstruation, "Anne Frank" is a code word among teenagers for getting one's period. In Argentina in the seventies, church publications began to link her with Roman Catholic martyrdom. "Commemoration," the French cultural critic Tsvetan Todorov explains, "is always the adaptation of memory to the needs of today."

But there is a note that drills deeper than commemoration: it goes to the idea of identification. To "identify with" is to become what one is not, to become what one is not is to usurp, to usurp is to own—and who, after all, in the half-century since Miep Gies retrieved the scattered pages of the diary, really owns Anne Frank? Who can speak for her? Her father, who, after reading the diary and confessing that he "did not know" her, went on to tell us what he thought she meant? Meyer Levin, who claimed to be her authentic voice—so much so that he dared to equate the dismissal of his work, however ignobly motivated, with Holocaust annihilation? Hellman, Bloomgarden, Kanin, whose interpretations clung to a collective ideology of human interchangeability? (In discounting the significance of the Jewish element, Kanin had asserted that "people have suffered because of being English,

French, German, Italian, Ethiopian, Mohammedan, Negro, and so on"—as if this were not all the more reason to comprehend and particularize each history.) And what of Cara Wilson and "the children of the world," who have reduced the persecution of a people to the trials of adolescence?

All these appropriations, whether cheaply personal or densely ideological, whether seen as exalting or denigrating, have contributed to the conversion of Anne Frank into usable goods. There is no authorized version other than the diary itself, and even this has been brought into question by the Holocaust-denial industry—in part a spinoff of the Anne Frank industry—which labels the diary a forgery. One charge is that Otto Frank wrote it himself, to make money. (Scurrilities like these necessitated the issuance, in 1986, of a Critical Edition by the Netherlands State Institute for War Documentation, including forensic evidence of handwriting and ink—a defensive hence sorrowful volume.)

No play can be judged wholly from what is on the page; a play has evocative powers beyond the words. Still, the Hacketts' work, read today, is very much a conventionally well-made Broadway product of the fifties, alternating comical beats with scenes of alarm, a love story with a theft, wisdom with buffoonery. The writing is skilled and mediocre, not unlike much of contemporary commercial theater. Yet this is the play that electrified audiences everywhere, that became a reverential if robotlike film, that—far more than the diary—invented the world's Anne Frank. Was it the play, or was it the times?

As the Second World War and the Holocaust recede for each new generation into distant fable, no different from tales, say, of Attila the Hun, Holocaust scholarship nevertheless accelerates prodigiously—survivor memoirs, oral histories, wave after wave of fresh documentation and analysis. Under the rubric "recep-

tion studies," Holocaust incidents and figures are being examined for how current cultural perceptions have affected them.
And Stephen Spielberg's *Schindler's List*, about a Nazi industri-
alist as the savior of hunted Jews, has left its transformative
mark. (The security guard who uncovered the Swiss banks' culpability in appropriating survivors' assets is said to have been
inspired by the Spielberg film.) Unsurprisingly, the 1997 revival
of the Hacketts' dramatization entered an environment psycho-
logically altered from that of its 1955 predecessor. The new version's adapter and director were far more scrupulous in keeping
faith with the diary, and went out of their way to avoid stimulat-
ing all the old quarrelsome issues. Yet the later production, with
its cautious and conscientious additions, leaves no trace; it is as if
it never was. What continues in the public consciousness of
Anne Frank is the unstoppable voice of the original play. It was
always a voice of good will; it meant, as we say, well—and, finan-
cially, it certainly did well. But it was Broadway's style of good
will, and that, at least for Meyer Levin, had the scent of ill. For
him, and signally for Bloomgarden and Kanin, the most sensi-
tive point—the focus of trouble—lay in the ancient dispute
between the particular and the universal. All that was a distraction from the heart of the matter: in a drama about hiding, evil
was hidden. History was transcended, ennobled, rarefied. And if
any proof is needed that the puffery of false optimism remains
uneffaced, only recall how the young lead of 1997, forty years
after the furies of the Kanin-Bloomgarden-Levin conflict, saw
her role as Anne: *it's funny, it's hopeful, and she's a happy
person.*

Evisceration, an elegy for the murdered. Evisceration by blurb
and stage, by shrewdness and naïveté, by cowardice and spirituality, by forgiveness and indifference, by success and money, by

vanity and rage, by principle and passion, by surrogacy and affinity. Evisceration by fame, by shame, by blame. By uplift and transcendence. By usurpation.

On Friday, August 4, 1944, the day of the arrest, Miep Gies climbed the stairs to the hiding place and found it ransacked and wrecked. The beleaguered little band had been betrayed by an informer who was paid seven and a half guilders—about a dollar—for each person: sixty guilders for the lot. Miep Gies picked up what she recognized as Anne's papers and put them away, unread, in her desk drawer. There the diary lay untouched, until Otto Frank emerged alive from Auschwitz. "Had I read it," she said afterward, "I would have had to burn the diary because it would have been too dangerous for people about whom Anne had written." It was Miep Gies—the uncommon heroine of this story, a woman profoundly good, a failed savior—who succeeded in rescuing an irreplaceable masterwork. It may be shocking to think this (I am shocked as I think it), but one can imagine a still more salvational outcome: Anne Frank's diary burned, vanished, lost—saved from a world that made of it all things, some of them true, while floating lightly over the heavier truth of named and inhabited evil.

The Rights of History
and the Rights of Imagination

It was not through words that the world first took in the nature and degree of the atrocities wreaked upon Jews by Germans half a century ago. You could not read of the last and worst of these atrocities in the newspaper of record, which suppressed reports of such events even as they were occurring—but certain early depredations you could glimpse, fleetingly, in the newsreels: the crowns of fire and smoke bursting through the roofs of burning synagogues on the night of November 9, 1938, the pyres of burning books in the city squares, the genial faces of young men as they hurled intellect into the flames. Sitting peacefully in an American movie house, you could see all these things with your own eyes, and—through film's illusion of simultaneity—you can see these same scenes today.

The burning synagogues and the burning books are incarnations of a time when, nearly all over Europe, Jews were becoming defenseless human prey. Other images are equally indelible: the photo of the terror-stricken little boy with his cap askew and his hands in the air (impossible not to absorb those desperate eyes, those small elbows, that civilized cap, without belief in the true existence of absolute evil); and, at war's end, the hellish frames of a British bulldozer shoveling a hill of skeletal human corpses into a ditch. In the film the bulldozer blunders forward and shovels, backs up, repositions itself and shovels again. The camera will admit us to this golgotha as often as we dare to revisit it. And we must suppose that some of these images, through repetition, have become so recognizable, so clichéd, that the most liberal hearts can be hardened against them. I continue to recall, inevitably and indefatigably, the comment of a celebrated novelist: "These old events," he wrote, "can rake you over only so much, and then you long for a bit of satire on it all." Satire?

There is another image less well known than the fires and the boy and the bulldozer; it is more overtly brutish by virtue of its being less overtly brutish. And if satire means a parody of normality, then perhaps this scene is travesty enough to gratify the most jaded observer. A city street, modern and clean, lined with leafy bushes and arching trees, on a fine bright autumn day. The road has been cleared of cars to make room for a parade. The marchers are all men, fathers and breadwinners, middle-class burghers wearing the long overcoats and gray fedoras of the thirties; they appear gentlemanly but somber. Along the parade route, behind mild barriers, a cheerful citizenry watches, looking as respectable as the marchers themselves, all nicely dressed, men and women and children, but mostly women and children— these are, let us note, business hours, when fathers and breadwinners are ordinarily in their offices. The weather is lovely, the crowds are pleasant, the women are laughing, the marchers are grave; here and there you will notice a child darting past the barriers, on a dare. The marchers are Jews being taken away in a scheme preparatory for their destruction; they are being escorted by soldiers with guns. Perhaps the watchers do not yet know the destiny of the marchers; but what a diversion it is, what a holiday, to see these dignified gentlemen humiliated, like clowns on show, by the power of the gun!

We may tremble before these images, but we are morally obliged to the German lens that inscribed them. The German lens recorded truthfully; its images are stable and trustworthy: the camera and the act are irrevocably twinned. Though photography can be kin to forgery (consider only the egregious slantedness of so many contemporary "documentaries"), at that time the camera did not lie. It yielded—and preserved—an account of ineffaceable clarity and immutable integrity. And later, when the words disclosing those acts of oppression first began to arrive, we knew them to be as stable and as trustworthy as the camera's images. The scrupulous voice of Elie Wiesel; the scrupulous voice of Primo Levi; the stumbling voices of witnesses who have no fame and have no voice, yet whose eloquence rises up through the scars and stammerings of remembered suffering. The voices of Christian conscience and remorse. All these words were consequential in a way the pictures were not. The pictures belonged to their instant; though they could serve memory, they were not the same as memory. You could not quarrel with the pictures. You could not change what they insistently and irremediably saw. But as the words rushed in in torrents, as they proliferated, becoming more and more various and removed, some broke through the gates of memory into the freer fields of parable, myth, analogy, symbol, story. And where memory was fastidious in honoring history, story turned to the other muses. Where memory was strict, fiction could be lenient, and sometimes lax. Where memory struggled for stringency of historical precision, fiction drifted toward history as a thing to be used, as imagination's stimulus and provocation.

And just here is the crux: the aims of imagination are not the aims of history. Scholars are nowadays calling historiography into radical question; history is seen as the historian's clay; omniscience is suspect, objectivity is suspect, the old-fashioned claims of historical truthfulness are suspect; the causes of the Peloponnesian War are sometimes what I say they are, and sometimes what you say they are. But even under the broken umbrella of contemporary relativism, history has not yet been metamorphosed into fable. Scholars may not agree on what happened, but they do consent to an actual happening. Your Napoleon may not be my Napoleon, but the fact of Napoleon is incontrovertible. To whatever degree, history is that which is owed to reality.

Imagination—fiction—is freer than that; is freed altogether. Fiction has license to do anything it pleases. Fiction is liberty at its purest. It can, if it likes—in the manner of *A Connecticut Yankee in King Arthur's Court*, or Mel Brooks in the French Revolution—place Napoleon in command of the armies of Sparta. It can alter history; it can invent a history that never was, as long as it maintains a hint of verisimilitude. A fictional character represents only itself. You may be acquainted with someone "like" Emma Bovary or "like" Anna Karenina, but if you want the true and only Bovary, you must look to Flaubert, and if you want the true and only Karenina, you must look to Tolstoy. Bovary is not a stand-in for French women; she is Flaubert's invention. Karenina is not a stand-in for Russian women; she is Tolstoy's invention. Imagination owes nothing to what we call reality; it owes nothing to history. The phrase "historical novel" is mainly an oxymoron. History is rooted in document and archive. History is what we make out of memory. Fiction flees libraries and loves lies.

The rights of fiction are not the rights of history.

On what basis, then, can I disdain a story that subverts document and archive? On what basis can I protest a novel that falsifies memory? If fiction annihilates fact, that is the imagination's prerogative. If fiction evades plausibility, that too is the imagination's prerogative. And if memory is passionate in its adherence to history, why should that impinge on the rights of fiction? Why should the make-believe people in novels be obliged to concur with history, or to confirm it? Characters in fiction are not illustrations or representations. They are freely imagined fabrications; they have nothing to do with the living or the dead; they go their own way.

And there the matter ends; or should. Nothing is at issue. But there are, admittedly, certain difficulties. Embedded in the idea of fiction is impersonation: every novelist enters the personae of his or her characters; fiction-writing is make-believe, acting a part, assuming an identity not one's own. Novelists are, after all, professional impostors; they become the people they invent. When the imposture remains within the confines of a book, we call it art. But when impersonation escapes the bounds of fiction and invades life, we call it hoax—or, sometimes, fraud. Three recent exemplars have captured public attention; all have provoked argument and controversy.

In 1995, Alan Dershowitz, known equally for his contribution to the legal defense of O. J. Simpson and for his authorship of books of Jewish self-consciousness, published a review of *The Hand That Signed the Papers*, an Australian novel on a Ukrainian theme. Dershowitz took issue with both plot and substance, and accused the twenty-four-year-old writer, Helen Demidenko, of "the most primitive manifestations of classic Ukrainian anti-Semitism: all Jews are Communists, cheats, smelly animals and otherwise subhuman." According to Dershowitz's summary of the novel, when the Soviet commissars—all Jews—arrive in Ukraine in the nineteen-thirties, they burn down a house with a family inside; understandably, the surviving child becomes the so-called Ivan the Terrible of Treblinka. A Jewish woman from Leningrad, Dershowitz's account continues, "refuses to treat a sick Ukrainian baby, declaring 'I am a physician, not a veterinarian.' " Demidenko's "subtle goal," he concludes, is "to explain the Ukrainian participation in the Holocaust so that the murders go unpunished," and her "greatest anger is directed against the Jewish survivors who sought to bring their Ukrainian tormentors to justice."

Soon after the appearance of Dershowitz's review, the Australian Federation of Ukrainian Organizations threatened to bring a legal action against him under Australia's racial vilification law. Dershowitz responded by welcoming a lawsuit as "an excellent forum for reminding the world of the complicity of so many Ukrainians in the Nazi Holocaust." That the dispute concerned a work of fiction appeared to vanish in the legal and political tumult. Meanwhile, however, the novel rose to fourth on Australia's best-seller list, and received the country's most prestigious literary prize, the Miles Franklin Award. The judges praised Demidenko for illuminating "a hitherto unspeakable portion of the Australian migrant experience." Demidenko herself insisted that her story was based on her own family's travail.

As it turned out, all parties were duped: the protesting reviewer, the infuriated Ukrainians, the publisher, the prize-givers. Helen Demidenko was in reality Helen Darville, a daughter of British immigrants pretending to be Ukrainian in order to augment her credibility. Allen & Unwin, Darville's publisher, confirmed that the novelist "had made some stupid mistakes," but argued that "we still have a book of great power, a book daring to deal with awesome topics." Dershowitz's objections went largely unaddressed. But after the exposure of Demidenko as Darville, the threat of lawsuit was quietly withdrawn.

A more ambiguous instance of novelistic impersonation occurred in Ecuador, when Salomon Isacovici, a Romanian-born survivor of the camps, set out to tell his experiences under the German terror. He enlisted the help—and the Spanish language facility—of Juan Manuel Rodríguez, a Jesuit and former priest; it is not clear whether Rodríguez was amanuensis, ghost, or co-author. In 1990, the manuscript, entitled *Man of Ashes*, was published in Mexico under both names and promoted as "cruel and truthful testimony of the Nazi concentration camps." Mexico's Jewish community praised it as a genuine work of witness and awarded it a prize. Isacovici died early in 1998, but three years before he had announced in a letter that he was "the legitimate author," that *Man of Ashes* was his autobiography, and that Rodríguez was hired only to assist with "the literary and structural parts of the book." Reporting in the *Forward*, Ilan Stavans, a writer and university professor educated in Mexico, quotes Rodríguez as claiming that he "wrote the entire book, its title included, in six months, based upon [Isacovici's] manuscript and mutual conversations."

Rodríguez continues to insist that *Man of Ashes* is not Isacovici's memoir, but is, rather, the product of his own literary imagination. "I transposed many of my philosophical views to Salomon," he told Stavans. "My philosophical formation helped achieve the transplant and succeeded in turning the book from a simple account to a novel of ideas." In the fall of 1999 the University of Nebraska Press issued the book in English as Isacovici's memoir, with Rodríguez named as co-author, and Rodríguez is considering a suit. "Salomon is my novel's protagonist, I am his author," he states. "I invented passages and details, and afterward he believed he had lived through them. For him the book is autobiography; for me it is a charming novel." Quite aside from "charming" as a description of Holocaust suffering, how may we regard what appears to be an act of usurpation? When Rodríguez declares a narrative of survival to be fiction, is the Holocaust being denied? Or is it being affirmed in terms of art?

The same query, steeped in similar murk, can be put to the extraordinary history of *Fragments: A Childhood 1939–1948*, published as the memoir of Binjamin Wilkomirski, a self-declared Latvian Jew. The book, brought out by Germany's

Suhrkamp Verlag in 1995, and a year later by Schocken Books in New York, purports to be the therapy-induced recovered memory of a boy, born in Riga, who was deported at the age of three to Maidanek, a camp in Poland. Lauded as a literary masterpiece, *Fragments* won the Prix Mémoire de la Shoah in France, the Jewish Quarterly Literary Prize in Britain, and a National Jewish Book Award in the United States. It has been endorsed by the Holocaust Memorial Museum in Washington, translated into more than a dozen languages, and eloquently blurbed by established writers. Its success lent credence to the theory that profoundly repressed memory, even of events very early in life, can be retrieved; and it also offered, in a child's pure voice, a narrative of German oppression to set beside the classic accounts of Elie Wiesel and Anne Frank.

All this began to disintegrate when Daniel Ganzfried, a Swiss writer and the son of a Holocaust survivor, undertook to verify Wilkomirski's assertions. He found, instead, inconsistencies of dates and facts, as well as documents identifying Wilkomirski as the child, born in Switzerland in 1941, of an unwed Swiss Protestant woman named Yvonne Grosjean. He also uncovered legal papers proving Wilkomirski's adoption, under the name of Bruno Doesseker, by a middle-class Zürich family. At the same time, Holocaust historians began to note that no child younger than seven would have been spared instant gassing—demurrals that were, however, not voiced during the period of rhapsodic prize-giving. Ganzfried's disclosures ultimately caused grave uneasiness among Wilkomirski's several publishers. Late in 1999, Suhrkamp Verlag withdrew its hardcover edition of *Frag-ments*, a decision followed some weeks afterward by Schocken. Carol Janeway, the book's American translator, affirmed that the "enormous impact that *Fragments* has had upon its readers must not blind us to the truth," and ruminated over the "human bafflement about the psychological processes that went into this." One speculation that arose in Wilkomirski's defense (reminiscent of Rodríguez's charge against Isacovici) is that there was no hoax, and Wilkomirski had committed no fraud, because he believes in his written story, and takes it to be his own. Perhaps he does. In that event we might wish to dub him insane. Even so, his conviction, if conviction it is, has done harm: it led a survivor living in Israel to suppose that he had recovered his lost son, whom he had thought long dead.

There was more. Defending yet another award bestowed on Wilkomirski by the American Orthopsychiatric Association (and eschewing human bafflement), a psychologist who is a member of that organization stated: "We are honoring Mr. Wilkomirksi not as historians or politicians, but as mental-health professionals. What he has written is important clinically." From this it would be fair to conclude that "mental-health professionals" care nothing for historical evidence, and do not recognize when they are, in fact, acting politically. If Wilkomirski is indeed a fabricator, then to laud him is to take a stand— politically—on the side of those who declare the Holocaust to be a fabrication. In any case, how does it advance the public cause of mental health to encourage a possible public liar who is possibly an opportunist and possibly a madman?

The conflict between the freedom to invent and an honest confrontation with the constraints of the historical record remains muddled—and, often enough, muddied. If the subject were, say, the Homeric wars, the muddle might be benign, even frolicsome, a simulacrum of trickster literature. But the subject is the Holocaust, and the issue is probable fraud, hoax, or delusion. What is permissible to the playfully ingenious author of *Robinson Crusoe*—fiction masking as chronicle—is not permitted to those who touch on the destruction of six million souls, and on the extirpation of their millennial civilization in Europe.

Yet the question of the uses of the imagination does not and cannot stop even here. Beyond the acrobatics of impersonation, or the nervy fakery of usurpation, lies a sacred zone consecrated to the power of art: or call it, more modestly, literature's elastic license. I have in mind two novels, *Sophie's Choice*, by William Styron, and *The Reader*, by Bernhard Schlink—one first brought out in 1979, the other published in 1998; one long acclaimed, the work of a contemporary American literary master, the other by a highly praised German writer. Both novels clearly intend to attach their stories to the actuality of the death camps.

Sophie's Choice followed by a dozen years Styron's Pulitzer Prize–winning *Confessions of Nat Turner*, and, like the latter, became a celebrated best-seller. Opening as a richly literary *Bildungsroman*, it recounts the often beguiling fortunes of Stingo, an untried young Southern writer whose attraction to New York lands him in Brooklyn, "the Kingdom of the Jews." In Mrs. Yetta Zimmerman's rooming house, Stingo meets Nathan Landau and his lover, a beautiful Polish woman named Sophie. Nathan is Jewish and mad—a paranoid schizophrenic, erratic when lucid, brutal and suicidal otherwise. Sophie is tormented by a horrific past, which she discloses to Stingo, piecemeal, as the two halves of the novel, Brooklyn and Auschwitz, begin to converge. And it is on account of Sophie's Auschwitz tribulations that *Sophie's Choice* has had an enduring reputation as a "Holocaust novel."

There is some justification for this, at least for the well-researched historical sections dealing with the Final Solution in Poland. Primo Levi, in *The Drowned and the Saved*, affirms that ninety to ninety-five percent of the victims of Auschwitz were Jews, and Styron's factual passages do not depart from this observation. His information concerning Polish Christians in Auschwitz is far thinner; it is, in fact, nearly absent. He gives us Sophie herself, but fails to surround her with the kind of documentation that he supplies for the deportation of Jews—exact dates of arrival in Auschwitz, for instance, as when he recounts the gassing of a contingent of Greek Jews, or when he enumerates figures for the Jewish population of Warsaw before 1939, or when he notes that the "resettlement" from the Warsaw Ghetto took place in July and August of 1942. Wherever the fingerprint of Styron's Holocaust research appears—and it appears frequently and accurately—it points to Jews.

When he turns to Polish Christians, he apprises us of the Nazis' *Lebensborn* project, which sent "Aryan"-looking Polish children to be reared as Germans in Germany; of the Polish resistance movements, many of them zealously anti-Semitic—though the two resistance workers featured in the novel are passionately concerned for Jews; of a boxcar filled with the corpses of Polish children rejected for *Lebensborn;* and of the rescinded plan to tattoo Polish Christian prisoners. Sophie's father and husband are depicted as serious Jew-haters. For the 75,000 Polish Christians murdered in Auschwitz, Styron's novel provides no data, no detail; or, rather, Sophie alone is the detail. But 75,000 Polish Christians *were* murdered in Auschwitz, and that is fact enough. If Styron's Auschwitz research leads voluminously to Jews, it is because the murdered Jews voluminously outnumbered the murdered Polish Christians; yet—incontrovertibly—the factory of inhumanity that was Auschwitz produced complete equality of unsurpassed human suffering. Here there can be no hierarchy, nor may suffering be measured in numbers, or by majorities, or by percentages.

Still, what does it signify—does it signify at all—that the author of *Sophie's Choice* chooses as his protagonist an inmate of Auschwitz who is a Polish Catholic? Here is a fictional decision that by no means contradicts a historical reality. It is the truth—but is it the whole truth, the representative truth? And again, under the rules of fiction, why must a writer's character be representative of a statistical norm? Under the rules of fiction, if Bovary is not typical of most French women, and if Karenina is not typical of most Russian women, why should William Styron's Sophie be representative of the preponderant female population of Auschwitz? What does the autonomy of the imagination owe to a demographic datum? Or ask instead, what does individual suffering owe to the norm? Will the identity of the norm dare to compromise or diminish or denigrate one woman's anguish?

Come now to Bernhard Schlink's *The Reader*, a novel by a practicing judge, a professor of law at the University of Berlin. Its narrator is a law student who is presented as a self-conscious member of the "second generation"—the children of those who were responsible for the Nazi regime. The narrative begins postwar, when an intellectual teenage boy, the future law student, strikes up an unexpected friendship with a streetcar conductor, a woman markedly older than himself. The disparate friends rapidly become lovers, and their affair takes on an unusual routine of added romantic pleasure: in scenes tender and picturesque, as in a Dutch interior, the boy reads aloud to the woman. Only many years later—the occasion is a war crimes trial—is the woman revealed as an illiterate. And as something else besides: she is a former S.S. guard in a camp dedicated to the murder of Jews. An unsuspecting youth in the arms of an unconfessed female Nazi: over this retrospective image falls, unavoidably, the shadow of what some call Nazi porn.

Contemplating the predicament of young Germans after their nation's defeat, the narrator asks, "What should our second generation have done, what should it do with the knowledge of the horrors of the extermination of the Jews? . . . Should we only fall silent in revulsion, shame, and guilt?" "Our parents," he explains, had played a variety of roles in the Third Reich. Several among our fathers had been in the war, two or three of them as officers of the Wehrmacht and one as an officer of the Waffen SS. Some of them had held positions in the judiciary or local government. Our parents also included teachers and doctors and . . . a high official in the Ministry of the Interior.

In short, an educated generation. To the narrator's observations let us add Goebbels, a novelist and playwright, Speer, an accomplished architect, and perhaps also Goering, an art collector—or looter—with a taste for masterpieces. None of this can surprise. Germany before the Second World War was known to have the most educated population in Europe, with the highest standard of literacy. Yet the plot of Schlink's narrative turns not on the literacy that was overwhelmingly typical of Germany, but rather on an anomalous case of illiteracy, which the novel itself recognizes as freakish.

And this freakishness is Schlink's premise and his novel's engine: an unlettered woman who, because she could not read a paper offering her a job in a factory, passed up the chance and was sent instead to serve in a brutal camp. After the war, when she is brought to trial, the narrator acknowledges that she is guilty of despicable crimes—but he also believes that her illiteracy can, to a degree, mitigate her guilt. Had she been able to read, she would have been a factory worker, not an agent of murder. Her crimes are illiteracy's accident. Illiteracy is her exculpation.

Again the fictive imagination presses its question: is the novelist obligated to represent typicality? If virtually universal literacy was the German reality, how can a novel, under the rules of fiction, be faulted for choosing what is atypical? The novelist is neither sociologist, nor journalist, nor demographer, nor reality-imitator; and never mind that the grotesquely atypical turns out to be, in this work by a member of the shamed and remorseful second generation, a means of exculpation. Characters come as they will, in whatever form, one by one; and the rights of imagination are not the rights of history. A work of fiction, by definition, cannot betray history. Nor must a novel be expected to perform like a camera.

If there is any answer at all to this argument (and the argument has force), it must lie in the novelist's intention. Intention is almost always a private, or perhaps a secret, affair, and we may never have access to it. Besides, the writer's motivation does not always reveal itself even to the writer. It would seem, though, that when a novel comes to us with the claim that it is directed consciously toward history, that the divide between history and the imagination is being purposefully bridged, that *the bridging is the very point,* and that the design of the novel is to put human flesh on historical notation, then the argument for fictional autonomy collapses, and the rights of history can begin to urge their own force. The investigation of motive is history's task, and here a suspicion emerges: that Sophie in Styron's novel was not conceived as a free fictional happenstance, but as an inscribed symbolic figure, perhaps intended to displace a more commonly perceived symbolic figure—Anne Frank, let us say; and that the unlettered woman in Schlink's novel is the product, conscious or not, of a desire to divert from the culpability of a normally educated population in a nation famed for *Kultur.*

Everything the camera has guilelessly shown—the burning of Jewish houses of worship, the burning of Jewish books, the humiliation of Jewish fathers, the terrorization of Jewish children, the ditches heaped with Jewish dead—touches on the fate of Jews in twentieth-century Europe. The pictures are fixed. In the less stable realm of words, the ghastly syllables of

"Auschwitz" have resolutely come to denote the intent—and the means—to wipe out every last living Jew, from newborn infants to the moribund elderly in nursing homes. It is sometimes forgotten that the Nuremberg Laws and the Final Solution— the fundamental initiating elements of the Holocaust—were directed at Jews and only at Jews. In a speech in January 1939, Hitler looked forward to "the annihilation [*Vernichtung*] of the Jewish race in Europe"; nothing could be more explicit, and this explicitness succeeded in destroying one-third of the world's total Jewish population.

But the Holocaust is defined by more than the destruction of lives. German national zeal under Nazism exacted an abundance of victims, the Poles painfully and prominently among them. Let us make no mistake about this, and let us not minimize any people's suffering. Eleven million human beings met their deaths during the Nazi period; yet not all eleven million were subject to the Final Solution. The murderous furies of anti-Semitism and the wounds of conquest and war, however lethal, cannot be equated. The invasion and occupation of Poland were deeply cruel; but the Holocaust is not about the invasion and occupation of one nation by another. There is a difference between the brutal seizure of a country (Poland, Czechoslovakia, Holland, etc.) and the achieved extirpation of an entire civilization. In the aftermath of the German occupation, Polish land, language, and Church were still extant. What defines the Holocaust is not the murders alone, but their irreversible corollary: the complete erasure of Jewish academies, libraries, social and religious bodies— the whole vast and ancient organism, spiritual and intellectual, of European Jewish civilization.

Auschwitz is that civilization's graveyard (a graveyard lacking the humanity even of graves); and herein lies the inmost meaning of the ideology of the death camp. Auschwitz represents the end not simply of Jewish society and culture, but of the European Jewish soul. Then how is it possible for a writer to set forth as a purposeful embodiment of Auschwitz anything other than the incised, the historically undisputed, principle and incarnation of the Final Solution? The German occupation of Poland enslaved, abused, murdered; it was a foul evil; it merits its own distinct history and commemoration. But it was not the Final Solution. The attempt to link the two—the annihilation of all traces of Jewish civilization with Poland's fate under Nazi rule—is to dilute and to obscure, and ultimately to expunge, the real nature of the Holocaust.

Sophie, then, is not so much an individual as she is a counter-individual. She is not so much a character in a novel as she is a softly polemical device to distract us from the epitome. The faith and culture of Catholic Poles were not the faith and culture targeted by the explicit dogmas of the German scheme of *Vernichtung*. Styron's Sophie deflects from the total rupture of Jewish cultural presence in a Poland that continues with its religion and institutions intact.

And when a writer describes in his novel the generation complicit in Jewish genocide as rife with members of the judiciary, physicians, lawyers, teachers, government officials, army officers, and so on, what are we to think when he fabricates a tale of German brutality premised on the pitiful absence of the alphabet? Who would not pity the helplessness of an illiterate, even when she belongs to the criminal S.S.? And have we ever before, in or out of fiction, been asked to pity a direct accomplice to Nazi murder? Here again is a softly rhetorical work that deflects from the epitome. It was not the illiterates of Germany who ordered the burning of books.

In the name of the autonomous rights of fiction, in the name of the sublime rights of the imagination, anomaly sweeps away memory; anomaly displaces history. In the beginning was not the word, but the camera—and at that time, in that place, the camera did not mislead. It saw what was there to see. The word came later, and in some instances it came not to illumine but to corrupt.

Public Intellectuals

The term "public intellectual" has been in fashion for some time now, but its embodiment has always been with us. Socrates was what we would call a public intellectual; and Isaiah; and Maimonides; and Voltaire; and Emerson. But observe: presumably not Aristotle, not Montaigne, not George Eliot, not Santayana. George Eliot presided over a salon, of which she was the undisputed center and engine; and still we would not cite her as a public intellectual. Hannah Arendt and Mary McCarthy were certainly public intellectuals; Lionel Trilling was not.

If there are public intellectuals, it must follow that there are also private intellectuals. What is the difference between them? It cannot be a difference of substance or subject matter. William James, despite countless public lectures, was not really a public intellectual; Emerson, who confronted many of the same themes, was. Nor could it have been simply reticence of temperament that separated Lionel Trilling from, say, Irving Howe, an almost prototypical public intellectual. And if we could clearly define the difference, is it important, would it matter?

There recently came into my hands a thin little chapbook, bound in the pallor of an aging blue and entitled "The New Disorder," containing remarks set down in 1941 by E. M. Forster. Now you may instantly object: why bring up Forster, a novelist, an artist, in the context of the public intellectual? The reason is

this. Before we had the dispassionate phrase "public intellectual," there was a simpler name in common use that appeared to
cover everyone who attends to, and rallies around, and pokes at
and palpates ideas. That name was "thinker." No one can deny
that Forster, though distinguished for fiction, was also a thinker.
He surely addressed literary issues, but now and then he
touched on political issues, the hallmark of the public intellectual. *A Passage to India* is inevitably read as a protest against
British colonialism in India; that it is a masterwork able to escape
the fate of a tract is a measure of Forster's both delicate and
robust art. And the indelible epigraph of *Howards End*, "Only
connect," is a slogan as political in its intention as it is private.

Beyond the novels there are the essays—pre-eminently "On
Liberty in England," a talk delivered at an international writers'
conference in Paris in 1935. Here Forster defends freedom of
expression and attacks censorship, particularly of homosexual
writing. And here also he situates himself as any number of
writers and intellectuals situated themselves in the nineteen-
thirties: "As for my politics," he tells his audience, "you will have
guessed that I am not a Fascist—Fascism does evil that evil may
come. And you may have guessed that I am not a Communist,
though perhaps I might be one if I was a younger and braver
man, for in Communism I can see hope. It does many things
which I think evil, but I know that it intends good." Lately, it
goes without saying, these latter words are achingly hollow; and
there were some for whom they were terribly hollow even two-
thirds of a century ago.

But let us return to my little blue pamphlet. It is now 1941;
England has been fighting Hitler for two years; in December
Pearl Harbor will catapult America into the war. Fascism's evil,
recognized as such by Forster six years earlier—the force that
"does evil that evil may come"—is furiously at work. In Germany and elsewhere the Jews have been stripped of citizenship

and are now official prey, ready candidates for a destiny which, while perhaps not yet overtly revealed as murderous, has already plunged whole populations into unspeakable suffering and degradation. Once again the occasion is a writers' conference, this one the seventeenth International PEN Congress. "We had with us," Forster wrote afterward, "representatives from about thirty nations, many of whom had suffered, all of whom had cause for fear. Politics had not ignored them, so how could they ignore politics? . . . They valued literature only if it helped their particular cause or what they regarded as the good of humanity." He granted that his speech was politely dismissed; the Congress "reverted to what it considered important and did not discuss the issue raised."

And the issue Forster raised, in 1941, was this: "Art for Art's sake? I should just think so, and more so than ever at the present time. It is the one orderly product which our muddling race has produced." He offers history as proof: "Ancient Athens made a mess," he says, "but the 'Antigone' stands up. Renaissance Rome made a mess—but the ceiling of the Sistine got painted," and so on. He ends by citing Shelley—the usual quote about poets as the unacknowledged legislators of mankind.

As an adolescent English major in college, I know I would have warmed to this, and taken it as my own life's credo. I did, in fact, do exactly that. But now, when I look at this date—1941!—I can only wonder how, with all of torn-up Europe dangling from German jaws, Forster could dare to take the view from Mount Olympus. Did Forster in 1941 not remember the political impulse out of which he conceived his Indian novel, published in 1924? Yet no one can tell him he is in error: the Sistine Chapel *did* get painted, the "Antigone" *does* stand up (though Forster seems to have forgotten what it stands *for*). But suppose Sophocles had been run through by a tyrant's sword, or suppose Michelangelo had been taken off and shot? Then there would be no play and no painted ceiling. Art may well be the most worthy of all human enterprises; that is why it needs to be defended; and in crisis, in a barbarous time, even the artists must be visible among the defending spear-carriers. Art at its crux—certainly the "Antigone"!—doesn't fastidiously separate itself from the human roil; neither should artists. I like to imagine a conversation between Forster and Isaac Babel—let us say in 1939, the year Babel was arrested and tortured, or early in 1940, when he was sentenced to death at a mock trial. History isn't only what we inherit, safe and sound and after the fact; it is also what we are ourselves obliged to endure.

And just here, you may conclude, is the distinction between the public intellectual and the other kind. Public intellectuals know that history is where we swim, that we are *in* it, that we can't see over or around it, that it is our ineluctable task to grapple with it; and that we may not murmur, with Forster, Look: the past came through, and so will we. Thinkers, after all, do not simply respond to existing conditions; in the buzz, confusion, and chaos of the Zeitgeist they strive to sort out—to formulate—the cognitive and historic patterns that give rise to public issues. That, we may presume, is what Forster thought he was doing when he picked out art-for-art's-sake as the salient issue of 1941. Why this choice was a disappointing one hardly demands analysis. "I realized," he had admitted that same year, living in Cambridge, protected by the British Army, "that as soon as I myself had been hurt or frightened I should forget about books too." Still, he continued, "even when the cause of humanity is lost, the possibility of the aesthetic order will remain and it seems well to assert it at this moment . . . I hope it is not callous to do this, and certainly no callousness is intended."

Intended or not, the callousness was there. Not because Forster was in any way a callous man; the absolute opposite is true. Yet even in 1949, when Forster appended a postscript to that talk—at an hour when the ovens were scarcely cooled and the D.P. camps were filled with wandering ghosts—he did not acknowledge that his 1941 formulation had been inadequate to its own context. Out of the turbulence of a Europe in extremis he had formulated an issue, as thinkers are wont to do, and he had formulated it badly. He put an ideal above immediate reality: the reality that kills. You might protest that Primo Levi did the same when he recited Dante in Auschwitz; but that was because he had the privilege of being a slave laborer rather than a gassed corpse. If you are still barely alive in Auschwitz, it is barely possible that poetry will salve your soul; but if you are comfortably alive well beyond the inferno, the exaltation of art as exclusive of the suffering of your own time does take on the lineaments of callousness.

How do we know when a thinker formulates an issue badly? In just this way: when an ideal, however comely, fails to accord with deep necessity. In 1941, "blood, sweat, and tears" is apropos; in an era of evil joy—Mark Twain's chilling phrase—a dream of the "possibility of aesthetic order" is not. Only a fantasist will not credit the reality of the contagion of evil joy; the world engenders it; it exists. There are those—human beings both like and unlike ourselves—who relish evil joy, and pursue it, and make it their cause; who despise compromise, reason, negotiation; who, in Forster's words, do evil that evil may come—and then the possibility of aesthetic order fails to answer. It stands only as a beautiful thought, and it is not sufficient to have beautiful thoughts while the barbarians rage on. The best ideal then becomes the worst ideal, and the worst ideal, however comely, is that there *are* no barbarians; or that the barbarians will be so impressed by your beautiful thoughts that they too will begin thinking beautiful thoughts; or that in actuality the barbarians are no different from you and me, with our beautiful thoughts;

and that therefore loyalty belongs to the barbarians' cause as much as it belongs to our own.

Some will say, how is it you have the gall to use so unforgivably denigrating a term as "barbarians"? Must you despise your opponents as other, as not of your own flesh? What of the humanity of the other? Are we not all equally flawed, equally capable of mercy? Are we ourselves not in some respects worse? Shall we not be decent to the other?

But—in a jurisprudential democracy especially—a moment may come when it is needful to be decent to our own side, concerning whom we are not to witness falsely or even carelessly in order to prove how worse we are. Without such loyalty—not always a popular notion among the global sentimentalists—you may find you are too weak in self-respect to tell the truth or to commit yourself to the facts. The responsibility of intellectuals ought to include this recognition, or it is no responsibility at all.

The responsibility of intellectuals includes also the recognition that we cannot live above or apart from our own time and what it imposes on us; that willy-nilly we breathe inside the cage of our generation, and must perform within it. Thinkers—whether they count as public intellectuals or the more reticent and less visible sort—are obliged above all to make distinctions, particularly in an age of mindlessly spreading moral equivalence. "I have seen the enemy and he is us" is not always and everywhere true; and self-blame can be the highest form of self-congratulation. People who are privileged to be thinkers are obliged to respect exigency and to admit to crisis. They are obliged to expose and war against those rampant Orwellian coinages that mean their opposite and lead to purposeful deception. And political intellectuals who have the capacity, and the inclination, to reflect on fresh public issues from new perspectives are obliged to reflect on them in so careful a way that their propositions will not seem callous or morally embarrassing or downright despicable decades on.

At the end of the day, a verge can perhaps be measured out: those who favor the guarded life should not risk contemplation in public. Contemplation in public is what political intellectuals commonly do, and what the quieter private thinkers on occasion slip into doing, not always inadvertently. The private thinkers have the advantage of being written off as bunglers when they do speak out, or as cowards when they don't. But for the public thinkers, who are always audible in the forum, the risk is far more perilous, far more destructive to the honor of a generation: they risk being judged mistaken.

The Selfishness of Art

1

Biography, or call it life, attaches to certain writers—but only to certain writers—with the phantom tenacity of a Doppelgänger: history clouding into fable. Who can think of Scott Fitzgerald, say, without the leap into the Plaza fountain, or minus Zelda's madness and Scott's crackup? These emblematic truths are as indelible as the invented parties in the imaginary Gatsby's fictional mansion. And how to contemplate the Brontës in the absence of cramped parsonage, desolate heath, drunken Branwell? Bring George Eliot to mind, and you summon up the drama of her illicit "marriage" to George Henry Lewes. Here sits Jane Austen, eternally in her parlor, hiding her manuscript under her blotter when someone intrudes, as someone eternally does; and over there, in literary fame's more recent precincts, are Virginia and Vanessa and Leonard and Lytton and Clive, and Hemingway and his trophy mammals, including Gertrude Stein, and Alice Toklas, Gertrude's wife and slavey. Incidents, images, archival fragments dissolve into legend. The private life is rival to the work.

Among the great luminaries, Henry James has been relatively free—until lately—of the accretions of personal shock, underground gossip, and the speculations of academic sleuths; he is immaculately sealed, for the most part, within the enameled status of Master. The term Master, of course, is his own (as in

"The Lesson of the Master"), but it is doubtful that he anywhere applied it to himself. It was Leon Edel, in his five-volume biography—a labor of decades—who gave this appellation its contemporary currency, and its lasting aura of literary heroism. Edel's James is heroic in art and heroic in virtue: the virtue of persistent aspiration; the transcendent courage of obsession. Two generations of writers (by now perhaps three) have turned to Edel for the model of an artist committed, through thick and thin, to what James named "our task," "our passion." The celebrated lines continue to reverberate: "We work in the dark—we do what we can—we give what we have. Our doubt is our passion and our passion is our task. The rest is the madness of art."

In his many tales of writers and painters, James was adamant in separating the deliberate and always sacral space of art from the vagaries, contingencies, and frustrations of the artist's life. He did not often speak in his own voice of this demarcation—but once, in the autumn of 1904, during a visit to America (from England, where he had long ago settled), he submitted to a journalist's interview. It was, she reported in the *New York Herald*, the first interview he had ever agreed to—"the marvel is how he has escaped"—and in her description of the "kindly if bewildered welcome from this man who is called intensely shy," we can glimpse him again looking to escape, or at least to elude his interlocutor's more intimate inquiries. "One's craft, one's art, is in his expression," he warned her, "not one's person, as that of some great actress or singer is hers. After you have heard a Patti sing why should you care to hear the small private voice of the woman?"

A credo can be a covert defense of a position not fully admitted to; and in this instance James's credo, despite its vocal flourish, was unmistakably a defense of covertness. He guarded his privacy with a ferocity that could sometimes startle, or even injure. When the invalided Alice James, his gifted and acerbic sister, died in England of breast cancer in 1892, leaving behind an extraordinary diary, Katharine Loring, her companion and caretaker, saw to the printing of four copies: two for herself, one for William—the renowned elder brother—and another for James. James read his copy, grew alarmed at his own role in it, and threw it in the fire; he was peremptory in forbidding publication. (The diary was published only in the following century.) And in 1909, when James was sixty-six, he made what he called a "gigantic bonfire" in the garden behind his house in Sussex and incinerated a lifetime's collection of letters. "I have been easier in my mind ever since," he announced. In an essay on George Sand composed a dozen years before this back-yard conflagration, he wrote with hot sympathy of the subversion of "the cunning of the inquirer" by "the pale forewarned victim, with every track covered, every paper burnt." What could be plainer than that? In 1915, a year before his death, he burned more papers; it took him a week. James intended to disappoint posterity, and to keep his secrets, whatever they were, from exposure.

His secrets, whatever they were, are consequently left to conjecture, whether ideological in the form of a definitive thesis (e.g., queer theory), or psychological in the way of an inspired hunch. Leon Edel fashioned James as a kind of sweeping literary conquistador ("The Conquest of London" is one of his rubrics)—except when Henry was in the presence of William, the brother who was older by two years and a luminary in his own right. Edel's disclosure of the fraternal tension—William superior and high-handedly critical, Henry subordinate and resentful, still struggling to assert against the favored first-born his own power and prestige—is far more the product of Edel's insight than of his research, though there is documentary force behind it. But Edel, in his warmly interpretive narrative of a generous and generously deserving James, did not venture much beyond this. Edel's psychological forays generally follow an outward chronology (his speculations, for example, about the "obscure hurt," James's youthful back injury) and the more modest path of conventional literary criticism; he resists tampering with, or too zealously reconstructing, James's inmost psyche. In the expansive course of those magisterial five volumes, Edel remains a traditional biographer, not an infiltrator. Yet the restrained biographer had second thoughts. In a new preface prepared for an abridged and somewhat revised single-volume edition issued in 1985, he confessed that he was obliged "to keep constantly in mind the changes that have occurred in biographical writing and in social attitudes toward privacy and our sexual lives. These changes are profound. . . . We are able to offer a more forthright record of personal relations, of deeper emotions and sexual fantasies." He added that though he continued to believe in James's lifelong celibacy, he would no longer hesitate to speak of the "homoerotic component." (The societal changes Edel alludes to are acute enough for Lionel Trilling to have acknowledged—looking back in late middle age on his early study of E. M. Forster—that at the time of writing he was entirely ignorant of Forster's homosexuality. It was not, he said, an issue in the culture.)

Eleven years after Edel gave the nod to sex, Sheldon Novick, author of a life of Oliver Wendell Holmes, Jr., brought out his controversial *Henry James: The Young Master*. Taking full advantage of those altered attitudes toward privacy, he challenged the celibacy premise with a spectacular claim. James, he noted, explicitly disapproved of celibacy: after a visit to a Shaker community in 1875, he condemned the Shakers' programmatic asexuality as a "lurking . . . asceticism" characterized by "the capacity for taking a grim satisfaction in dreariness." A comment on a social movement may or may not be personally revelatory;

nevertheless Novick is persuaded of James's sexual activism. "I have taken it for granted," he writes, "that Henry James underwent the ordinary experiences of life," one of which he defines as "realized passion." And: "I have not made any discoveries about James's sexuality; James's sexual orientation, as we now say, has been an open secret for a hundred years." Even so, no biographer before Novick had ever suggested that Henry James and Oliver Wendell Holmes, the future Chief Justice of the United States, went to bed together. Nor is this offered as speculation. "In that epochal spring, in a rooming house in Cambridge and in his own shuttered bedroom in Ashburton Place," Novick states, "Henry performed his first acts of love." James himself, reminiscing in his journal about those Cambridge days decades later, declared that "I knew there, *had* there . . . *l'initiation première* (the divine, the unique) there and in Ashburton Place. . . . Ah, the 'epoch-making' weeks of the spring of 1865!" But whether this cry of remembered delight refers to first-time gay sex, or rather to the rapture of early literary success—James's first published story appeared in the *Atlantic Monthly* in March of that very spring—not even the most intuitive biographer can confirm.

James's bonfire is a blaze of aggressive reticence; it announces—and defends—the borders of the private life. And his admonition to his *New York Herald* interviewer (one imagines her as a type of Henrietta Stackpole, the peppy American journalist in *The Portrait of a Lady*) is a firmly shut gate: do not intrude on the small private life; the large coloratura of the diva's art is sufficient. In "The Private Life," a quasi-ghost story published in 1892, James closets his perpetually dedicated writer-protagonist alone in a room with his pen, while a double—a light-minded social simulacrum—carries out the obligations of the public man. The tale is said to be based on Robert Browning, whose sequestered genius was never evident in his parlor manner; but it also describes James's impatience with "the twaddle of mere graciousness"—his term for the spirit and tone of much of his social correspondence.

T. S. Eliot, who consciously took James as his model in his own conquest of London, elevated Jamesian reticence to intractable dogma. His formulation of the objective correlative, which dominated an era with the unarguability of a papal bull, denied to poetry the presence or influence of any grain of autobiographical matter. Eliot issued a trinity of unassailable declarations: "The progress of an artist is a continual self-sacrifice, a continual extinction of personality"; "Emotion . . . has its life in the poem and not in the history of the poet"; "The more perfect the artist, the more completely separate in him will be the man who suffers and the mind which creates." What all this ideational superstructure actually meant, it turned out, was that Eliot the man had plenty to hide: an anguished personality, desolate emotions, and (especially) years of psychological suffering. The continual extinction of personality was not so much the artist's vaunted self-sacrifice as it was Eliot's attempt to escape from being truly known. A generation passed before his well-made bastion of secrecy was breached; Eliot's lofty strictures, reinforced by an unquestioned authority, held. Like some holy statue, he appeared to his public to have no private life at all; or, at least, nobody dared to inquire after one. It was not until Lyndall Gordon undertook to examine Eliot's experience—going beyond his career as a poet—that various half-concealed poisons (betrayal, misogyny, desertion, racism, anti-Semitism even post-Holocaust) began to spill out of the history of the man who suffered. *Eliot's Early Years* (1977) and *Eliot's New Life* (1988) are now combined, with additions, in Gordon's freshly issued one-volume *T. S. Eliot: An Imperfect Life*. Though she is unfailingly sympathetic to Eliot as an artist, to have read Gordon ten or even twenty years ago was (for those who once worshiped Eliot as lit-

erarily inviolable) akin to seeing the bronze monuments of
Lenin pulled down after the demise of Communism in Russia.
"Hatred is common; perfection rare. In him, the two were inter-
fused" is Gordon's ultimate judgment on Eliot; but on the negative side she suppresses nothing. If others have followed her in
forcing the inscrutable Eliot into the light, she was the first—the
first relentless excavator into his private life.

In *A Private Life of Henry James: Two Women and His Art*,
she is again first. It is possible—it has always been possible—to
fall in love with Edel's tender James, and with the equally
admirable genius in the biographies of R. W. B. Lewis, Frederick
Kaplan, and Sheldon Novick. It is not possible to sink quite so
gratifyingly into the private James (or, rather, the secret one)
whom Gordon scrupulously deduces. "The deeper the silence,
the more intently it speaks," she affirms; but unlike her predecessors, she is not drawn to "the homoerotic component." Her
own project is more discriminating, and more labyrinthine in
the tracing; it lies along the fault line between ambition and feeling. And in moving from Eliot to James, she turns from moral
storm to moral nuance: where the private Eliot can be fiercely
pitiless (after his first wife's permanent incarceration in a mental
asylum, he never once went to see her—one instance among
many), the private James is only selfish. Relying on Edel, and
despite his candid account of James's defeats and depressions, we
are made familiar with sweetness of temperament, courtliness,
affection, humor, the benevolent beaming of a reserved figure
who has learned the ways of an aristocrat. This is James as
Edith Wharton knew him, according to Edel—close and warm as
the drawing room hearth, yet significantly distant; and all the
same beloved. Yet the cause of art inevitably favors—promotes,
urges—selfishness. James himself underlines this idea in tale
after tale, where the artist is either shackled or doomed by

"attachments." In "The Madonna of the Future," the attachment notably overwhelms the art, and the canvas remains blank. Elsewhere artists strain to break free of the claims of the natural. "One has no business to have children," the Master (who has them) declares in "The Lesson of the Master"; "I mean if one wants to do something good." Wife and offspring, he laments, are "an incentive to damnation, artistically speaking." And, as Gordon will take pains to show, so are friends and relations.

2.

A parenthetical reflection, for the moment, on writer's selfishness. From the very beginning James was what even in his own period was called a freelance; he wrote for a living, and when he was not bringing out novels he was voluminously filling the magazines with long essays and stories. Between 1864 and 1910, one hundred and twelve tales—many of them, by our lights, actually novellas or short novels—appeared in the *Atlantic Monthly, Harper's*, the *North American Review*, the *Century*, the *Cornhill*, and numerous other periodicals. The novels themselves ran as serials. He lived in a magazine world, was tied to it, and had deadlines to meet and length requirements to abide by (which he habitually renegotiated and habitually exceeded). He worked, as we say, like a demon; and he was demonically driven by an ambition Balzacian in its appetite for majesty and abundance. One of the marvels of Edel's treatment—and the reason writers especially are magnetized—is its power to excite the reader with the sensation of single-minded literary ambition at its grandest, at the same time defining that sensation as an act of moral radiance. With the exception of James's comedic response to episodes of invasion by Edith Wharton, Edel has little to report about his subject's aversion to interruption. Wharton in her newfangled motor too often descended on James with her "eagle pounce," a terrifying firebird: "the whirr and wind of [her] great pinions is already cold on my foredoomed brow!" he cried. But he complained more gravely of his "inward ache" at the prospect of being swooped up and away from his work table. Edel supplies no further glimpse into that inward ache and what it might imply for an understanding of James's character in general. The fence James erected against intrusion into his private life was itself circumscribed by a second fence—or defense: an instinct to barricade against any distraction from the unrelenting pursuit of his life's appointed task. It made him into a secret monster—a monster on art's behalf; but he encased the monster in so many folds and ribbons and windings that this dissembling webwork of the creature's costume veiled him from easy recognition. As in the terrible metaphor of "The Private Life," the insatiable artist clung frenziedly to his desk, while Wharton and her chauffeur took the friendly gentleman, draped in his elaborate nineteenth-century manners, for a spin in her car. With writer's plentifulness comes writer's selfishness, James's sacred barrier against intrusion and distraction; the pairing of art and defense is ineluctable. For James, the barrier itself partook of the sacral because the exercise of art was acknowledged as holy: in his notebooks he invokes Balzac and Maupassant with what can only be described as petitionary prayers to household gods.

James's age was submerged in a sea of letters. Literature mattered acutely, centrally, and was prized as a fundament of civilization. Even forty years ago we lived in the residue of that notion, and a new novel by a commanding writer galvanized the culture. All that has been eclipsed by film, TV, and dot-com, to say the obvious, and small note is taken nowadays of literary ambition, whether unobtrusively cloaked or savagely naked.

Magazines—those with a reasonable circulation—commonly resist, and probably despise, stories; no more than a handful remain faithful, to a degree, to the old ideal of imaginative prose. Story may still retain its power in print, but only if (as in the name and nature of a long-ago pulp) it is True Story. The tales James published in his forties, saturated in the furiously free force and flow of language, patiently or impatiently sealing brick to telltale brick in the structure of character, above all heedlessly liberated to liberality—how to imagine narratives like these in our own magazines, which no longer welcome such imperiousness? Current editorial inhibition is not so much a question of contemporary taste—the crucial changes of style, attitude, and attention since the pre-modern eighteen-eighties—as it is a revolutionary repudiation of the magazine as an arena for writer's sovereignty. In 1884, at forty-one—the same year he published "The Art of Fiction"—James brought to light, in serial form, two little-known tales, "Georgina's Reasons" and "A New England Winter." The first is an amazing human conundrum (postmodern, in our lingo); the second weaves an ingenious tissue of high comedy. Both display ambition metamorphosed into conscious sovereignty, the writer unimpeded, in full command, a thing inconceivable in popular late-twentieth-century periodicals. (Or, for that matter, in the late-twentieth-century academy, where writer's autonomy has long been undone by politics and deconstruction.) A comparable genius of our own time, if there were one, would not sail so easily with the wind. And since literary fiction is more and more unwanted, and the few writers who embrace it with old-fashioned lust grow more and more irrelevant, the issue of selfishness-for-the-sake-of-art begins to drift, more and more, into the fastness of a superannuated foreign psychology. The past: that alien bourne to which no traveler can return.

3.

Except the canny biographer. It is precisely James's selfishness that Lyndall Gordon meticulously teases out of the archive of extant letters, and out of her own insightful talent for making revelatory connections. As literary detective, she shuns the mischief that is motivated beforehand by what the excavator intends to find; it seems clear that she did not set out to uncover this aspect of James's character, and came upon it as a surprise. (It is certainly a surprise to the Edel-oriented.) Gordon's purpose was to learn more, much more, about two women in James's life—"female partners, posthumous partners," she calls them, "in that unseen space in which life is transformed into art." The two were Mary Temple, known as Minny, James's lively cousin, dead of tuberculosis at twenty-four, and Constance Fenimore Woolson, three years older than James, a successful novelist whose friendship with him was terminated by her suicide in Venice. Both figures have long been staples in all biographies of James. And while Woolson has had the status of a somewhat eccentric walk-on, Minny Temple has been granted the role of a pervasive minor goddess whose luminous influences touched several of James's American heroines. She can be traced most incisively in the dying Milly Theale of *The Wings of the Dove*, and even earlier in the dying Milly Theory of "Georgina's Reasons." Her living spirit animates the independent Daisy Miller, who succumbs to Roman fever, and also the freedom-claiming Isabel Archer of *The Portrait of a Lady*. Such intimations are hardly new; yet Gordon adds richly to what we already know of Minny Temple's variegated and enduring presence in James's imagination. (In the case of Woolson, much of what Gordon has

to tell is altogether fresh disclosure.) But even if we are sufficiently informed of Minny Temple's phantomlike immanence,
we have until now been in the dark about what the real Minny
hoped for—and what she expected of—her cousin Harry.

There were six Temple cousins; four were girls. Minny was
the youngest, James's junior by two years. Their parents had
died of tuberculosis within months of each other, and the
orphaned children were sent to live with the Edmund Tweedys,
relatives of Henry James, Sr., who was their uncle. Minny was
unconventional for her time; she might be unconventional for
ours: once, on an impulse, she cut off all her hair. She had the
recklessness of unfettered individuality; she was spontaneous,
original, thoughtful, witty, passionate—"the amateur priestess
of rash speculation," as James put it. In her teens she cultivated a
fervent bond with Helena de Kay, a fellow school rebel (and
future portraitist). At twenty, with the Civil War just over, she
was surrounded by a body of intellectual young veterans who
were drawn to her exuberance, among them Oliver Wendell
Holmes and John Chipman Gray (a future professor of law
whose correspondence with Minny was put to use by James in
his late memoir). Though James's two younger brothers, Bob
and Wilky, at sixteen and seventeen had been thrown into the
fury of battle—Wilky with the first black regiment, led by
Colonel Robert Shaw—James contrived to sit the war out at
home. On the basis of a bad back (the legendary "obscure hurt,"
dismissed by a specialist as a temporary strain), he managed to
dodge the draft, trying out an unsuccessful term or two at Har-
vard Law School, and devoting himself to turning out stories
which he sent, unsigned, to magazines. William James, too,
avoided army service, but Minny lost a brother to the war, and
Bob and Wilky were permanently broken by it. When Wilky,
severely wounded and hospitalized, pleaded for "a visit of 2 or 3
weeks" from James, he declined; he was preoccupied with the

composition of a tale about murder. And there it was, the beginning of the deliberately blinding discipline of obsession: if a just
war summoned, he would write tales; if a needy brother called
out, he would write tales. It was not that he placed writing above
life—he *used* life—but rather that he placed writing above compassion, and surely above danger. Compassion interrupts, danger
interrupts absolutely.

With Minny, during and after the war, he walked, joked,
talked seriously or playfully, meanwhile pursuing his "long and
secret apprenticeship," as Gordon terms it, hiding his neophyte
efforts from his family. In 1861 the Temple sisters settled with
their guardians in Newport, an outpost of high-minded Boston.
Julia Ward Howe was there, together with artists, historians, and
assorted bluebloods and utopians; some, like the Jameses, came
only for a season. It was here that James took in, for all the
future, the quicksilver shimmer that was Minny—the ease, the
freedom, the candor, the generous stride and the generous
mind. James in old age remembered her, in the "pure Newport
time," the "formative, tentative, imaginative Newport time," as
"absolutely afraid of nothing." She, for her part, confided to
Helena de Kay that her cousin Harry was "as *lovely* as ever, ver-
ily the *goodness* of that boy passeth human comprehension."
Each discovered enchantment in the other, James in a sympathetic recognition of daring unbound by social constraint,
Minny through sensing affectionate approval, as she had failed
to feel it in the other Jameses. Minny reported that William, in
fact, thought her "a *bad* thing." James relied on Minny to see as
he saw, through the imagination; and Minny trusted Harry to be
kind.

He was seventeen, she fifteen, when they began to roam the
Newport landscape together; then he was twenty, she eighteen;
and then he was twenty-six, ready to escape family and country
for a life of autonomy—after which they never again met. He

was on his way to London, with valuable letters of introduction in his pocket. He lunched with Leslie Stephen, and called on George Eliot, William Morris, Dante Gabriel Rossetti, and Charles Darwin; he was inching into the great world of letters. From England he went on to France, Switzerland, and Italy, heading for Rome. Minny, left behind, was compelled to exercise her own large ideas of autonomy within the walls of a society that confined young women to certain clear limits; pushing against commonly accepted restraints, she seemed oddball, a bad thing. She was restrained in still another way: she had contracted tuberculosis. Her sister Kitty, at twenty-five, had married Richard Stockton Emmet, a wealthy man of forty-seven. Minny, thin and ailing, went to live with the Emmets in Pelham, New York, where she was isolated and without real support. The Tweedys, her guardians, had in effect cast her off. As for her James relations, William, Alice, and Mrs. James openly disdained her, while the self-absorbed Henry, Sr., charged her with pride and conceit, and advised her to practice Christian humility. With her lungs hemorrhaging, it was plain to Minny (and to the medical wisdom of the period) that her only chance for improvement lay in a warm climate: "Rome, with its dry winter and cloudless skies, was the common hope of consumptives," Gordon explains. "Another winter in Pelham," Minny wrote to her cousin Harry in Rome, "might go far to finishing me up." In both social and medical terms, she was unable to travel alone, and the Tweedys, who went often to Italy, and who had reared the orphaned girl from the age of nine, never once invited her to go with them. A family proposal that would have taken her to the warmth of California in the company of her sister Elly fell through when Elly's husband, a railroad magnate, decided that remaining in the East was better for business. "The grand plan for Minny's recovery was incidental," Gordon concludes. Minny's recovery, it appeared, was incidental to nearly everyone close to her.

She did not believe it was incidental to cousin Harry. Rome was her coveted goal, and not only for the curative powers of its climate. Rome signified civilization, beauty, the American girl's dream of an idealized Europe; and Harry was there. "I am not very strong nowadays, altho' it is summer," she wrote to James. "I would give anything to have a winter in Italy." "I want to go abroad," she had pressed him earlier, "and I mean to think deeply about it, and try to get there." She went so far as to arrange for a chaperon to accompany and care for her, but soon withdrew from this scheme: she was not well enough. But there was a deeper obstacle. She was slowly growing aware of James's resistance to any tendril of a notion of dependence on him. Even relieved of physical responsibility for his cousin, he did not welcome her presence. He was at this time in a struggle with serious constipation and low spirits; he had fallen into a kind of invalidism. "To think that you should be ill and depressed so far away," she sympathized, "just when I was congratulating myself that you, at all events, were well and happy, even if nobody else was." "Nobody else" was Minny herself, but James was not responsive to this appeal or any other. The true blow came when he left Rome and returned to the dampness of England. She understood then—despite the old consolations of their long-standing intimacy—that she had no part at all in the principle that governed his being; her letters ceased. To William he confided his intention "to write as good a novel one of these days" as *The House of the Seven Gables;* his passions were overridingly directed to literary dominion. He may have cherished what he saw as Minny's "intellectual grace" and "moral spontaneity," but if she threatened, even at a distance, to distract his concentration and his will, he fled. Intellectual grace and moral spontaneity were not to intrude on his siege of the citadel of art—until, after Minny's death, they, and she, became the brightest stuff of his novels and tales.

4.

He had, then, the capacity to disappoint—to disappoint even the tenderest relation of his life. The tenderness, with Minny, was of a purity and a clarity; there might be a skein of romance thrown over their old walks and talks, but there was no question of marriage, no teasing sexuality. And James was still Harry.

Ten years later, at thirty-six, he had become Henry James, acclaimed man of letters, lionized author of the hugely popular *Daisy Miller*. It was at this time that he found himself pursued—at least he felt pursued—by Constance Fenimore Woolson, herself an American expatriate, who had traveled to London to present him with a letter of introduction. The letter wove together certain interesting connections. It had been given to Woolson by Henrietta, another of Minny Temple's sisters, who was now living in Cooperstown, New York—a village named for Woolson's great-uncle, James Fenimore Cooper, the famed novelist of the American frontier. Northern-born, Woolson moved South after the Civil War, visiting battlefields and military cemeteries, interviewing freed slaves, and publishing well-received fiction grounded in these explorations. When her mother died, she began a wandering Continental life, mainly in Italy, in hotels, pensions, or rented flats, industriously bringing out novels and stories. Her reputation grew sufficiently for the *Nation* to charge her, in a swipe at literary women, with "infesting the magazines." She was, in short, a serious professional in an age when women who wrote were ferociously disparaged. "Women aren't literary in any substantial sense of the term,"

James complained, and produced the mocking tale of "Greville Fane" to prove the point. He called female reviewers "the hen-sex," and fumed at being seated at dinner with "a third-rate female novelist." Gordon slyly notes that even the monumental George Eliot did not escape diminishment: if she had seen and known more of life, James said, "she would have done greater things." This from a man who had avoided battle at home, frequented country houses abroad, and charted his characters' secret meditations when they were mostly indoors and sitting still.

Woolson and her letter of introduction missed James in London—he had already left for Paris—and caught him in Florence. It was a friendship that was destined to be unequal. She came to him as an adulator, defining herself—suitably—as the lesser writer; but he made her out to be less than she was. On one occasion he wounded her bitterly when he described her in a letter as "amiable," the kind of blandishment he applied to the generality of ladies whom he was an old hand at charming. She knew she was fiercer than that, and darker, and a hundred times more ambitious. He had met, Gordon tells us, "a writer absorbed in writing even more completely than himself." In their early acquaintance in Florence they made the rounds together of churches and galleries, paintings and sculptures, James leading and discoursing, Woolson rapturously attending. He had begun by thinking of her as a neatly dressed spinster, deaf in one ear, "a good little woman," "a perfect lady," "Miss Woolson." When her intellect and dedication showed themselves indefeasibly, he chose to call her Fenimore: an open recognition of sorts, which led to his talking over with her his current work. "I see her at discreet intervals," he admitted to William Dean Howells, editor of the *Atlantic*, who published both Woolson and James. "She is a very intelligent woman, and understands when she is spoken to." He had advanced, cautiously, to an appreciation of her—but she was always subordinate. She was, in his phrase, a "resource." He sent her his dramatization of *Daisy Miller* (it rankled him that it was never staged); she read and responded during an intense period when she was laboring thirteen hours a day to complete a manuscript of her own. One of her novels, serialized in *Harper's,* was so successful that she felt obligated to apologize to James. "Even if a story of mine should have a large 'popular' sale," she told him, she of course recognized that "the utmost best of my work cannot touch the hem of your first or poorest." And if he exploited her admiration and the usefulness of her literary scrutiny, she did not protest.

Nor did she protest that he hid their friendship; she colluded in his project of secrecy. Ten years of association were suppressed. "None of his London circle knew of her presence in his life," Gordon reveals. He rarely spoke or wrote of Woolson, and then only obliquely, masking the quality of their relationship. In 1886, on a visit to Florence, where she was then residing, he spent three weeks in rooms literally next door to hers, in a house she had rented. It had all the comforts of a private domesticity. A similar arrangement was undertaken the following year; again they divided the house, she on an upper floor, he on a lower. These prolonged occasions, with their meals and talks and inevitable familiarity, were kept carefully screened from James's usual society. And still he could disappear from her ken for eighteen months at a time. She may now and then have been a solace to him, but he dreaded being linked with her—he feared the publicity of an "attachment." As for Woolson, she not only understood when she was spoken to; she understood far more. A character in an 1882 story, "The Street of the Hyacinth," intimates her sense of James: "He was an excellent evader when he chose to exert himself, and he finally got away from the little high-up apartment . . . without any positive promise as to the exact date of his next visit." "My plans are uncertain," the Jamesian persona asserts. "I have a habit of not assuming responsibility, I suppose I have grown selfish."

James evaded Woolson whenever it pleased him. In January of 1894 she evaded him, and horribly: she threw herself from the window of her "little high-up apartment," this one in Venice, recently let. Like James himself (and like William and Alice), she was subject to periods of black depression. When the report of her death arrived, James at first thought it was from influenza, and prepared to go to the funeral. But when he learned she was a suicide, he recoiled, pronounced her "deranged," and insisted that she "was not, she was never, wholly sane." According to Gordon, this "slur of uncontrollable *dementia*" had a self-protective aim. "The coded message is plain: no one," she argues, "not the best of friends, could have prevented this death." The publicity James had always feared did, after all, explode around him. As long as three years after the event, the *New York Herald* was identifying him as "the principal mourner," and offering as "the truth about Mr. James's bachelorhood" his having been "this other author's devoted slave. . . . Miss Woolson was not to be won."

Three months after Woolson's death, James committed himself to an extraordinarily uncharacteristic task. Woolson's sister and niece, Clara and Clare Benedict, were sailing from America to Venice to dismantle the little high-up apartment and all its accumulated treasures. James left London and eagerly joined them in the work of sorting and clearing—sacrificing five full weeks to manual drudgery in Woolson's memory. This seemingly charitable act had a deeply self-serving purpose. The continuing wet weather called for a daily fire, and into it—either trusted or unnoticed by his companions—James tossed every scrap that touched on himself or revealed anything that might cause him uneasiness.

Woolson served James ever afterward. A version of her turns

up as the unnamed woman writer in "The Altar of the Dead"; as May Bartram in "The Beast in the Jungle"; as Miss Gostrey in *The Ambassadors;* and as Miss Staverton in "The Jolly Corner," a title derived from "Cheerful Corner," Woolson's childhood home. It was from a story of Woolson's that James took the phrase, and the metaphor, of "The Figure in the Carpet." Three times he visited her grave in the Protestant Cemetery in Rome. And, most mysteriously, in the autumn of 1894, in Oxford, he sought out the furnished flat she had occupied for the two preceding years and briefly let it; he slept in her bed.

Lyndall Gordon begins her remarkable study—intuitive, scholarly, novel-like, bold—with an amazing image. In 1956, four decades after James's death, a BBC program in his honor recorded, from Florence, the voice of an elderly woman who as a young girl had known James. She was remembering snatches of a scene he had related, all the while oddly laughing, about the death of "some very famous person" in Venice, about having to "do certain things," and about dresses, and a lagoon, and "horrible black balloons." Gordon opens her history with a reconstruction of this fantastic (and perhaps fantasized) memory, drawing also from a passage in "The Aspern Papers." A gentleman in a gondola in the middle of a Venetian lake is in the act of heaving into the water a bundle of lady's garments, all darkcolored and nicely tailored:

> The gondolier's pole would have been useful for pushing them under the still water. But the dresses refused to drown. One by one they rose to the surface, their busts and sleeves swelling like black balloons. Purposefully, the gentleman pushed them under, but silent, reproachful, they rose before his eyes.

It seems unlikely that James, with or without the Benedicts' leave, would have contrived so strange an expedition to dispose of Woolson's clothes. And yet the unlikely, the driven, the weird, were never foreign to his imagination. Gordon's picture of swollen sleeves and torsos resisting drowning, stubbornly bobbing, is as suggestive as she means it to be: a woman returning, a woman refusing to vanish. The two women, Minny Temple and Constance Woolson, whose phantoms took hold of James's vision, fevering and inflaming it, again and again replenish Gordon's thesis. Posthumously, they fed his genius. But when they were alive, his genius beat them off, defending itself with the isolating fortifications that alone sustain literary obsession. Before Harry turned his back on her, Minny believed her cousin's goodness passed comprehension. Woolson, older and worldlier, had a more sardonic view of what to expect. In a story about a literary lion, published a year after the start of her problematic friendship with James, she wrote: "Let us see a man of genius who is 'good' as well." The skeptical quotation marks emphasize her discernment: the ruthless sovereignty of the Master, the defensive selfishness of art.

Cinematic James

There appears to be no record of Henry James's ever having seen a movie. He died in London in 1916, at the age of seventy-three, a dozen years before the introduction of sound. The highbrow term "film" was decades in the future; what people went to was the picture show. And if Charlie Chaplin was deemed an artist by the discerning few, James was assuredly not among them. No one distinguished more stringently between High and Low than this acclaimed literary Master, author of matchless tales and architecturally resplendent novels. And wouldn't he think of movies as Low?

But James was enraptured by drama, and all his life tried to succeed in the theater, the only medium available to his era. "The dramatic form," he wrote in 1882, "seems to me the most beautiful thing possible." And another time: "An acted play is a novel intensified." He was single-mindedly obsessed by the notion of the scene. As a novelist, he explained, he worked on "absolutely scenic lines," and developed dialogue as it might be employed in a script, "with the loose end as gross an imperti-nence on its surface, and as grave a dishonor, as the dangle of a snippet of silk or wool on the right side of a tapestry."

The evidence, then, is that James would have welcomed film, with its quicksilver dissolves, its ghostly special effects (he was in love with the ghost story), its lavish costumes and intensified color, its precision of landscape and weather and sky, and particularly its capacity for living portraiture through the technique of the closeup, rivaling in facial revelation anything he might have seen in the great galleries of Europe. He was, besides, sympathetically open to technical advance. When writer's cramp forced him to abandon his pen, he turned at once to the newfangled typewriter (the "typewriter" being, for James, the typist). Though still mainly in the period of the horse-drawn, he now and then enjoyed tooling up and down the countryside in Edith Wharton's chauffeur-driven motorcar. The progress of sophisticated film technology, had he lived to see it, would not have daunted or inhibited him.

Yet there was a Hollywood side, in the negative sense, to James's script-writing experience. Theater managers—who at that time were both producers and directors—got in the way of his purist ideas of dramatic art. Like many television and movie potentates nowadays, they were apt to fix solely and wholly on mass taste and mass profits, hoping to woo the trendiest and most sentimental audiences. After several unsatisfactory theatrical ventures, and especially after the humiliating failure of his 1905 play, *Guy Domville,* when he was subjected to jeers and howls from the pit, James gave up trying to please a larger public. In shame and fury he railed against showbiz, its "vulgarities and disgusts, all the dishonor and chronic insult," and said he intended "to chuck the whole intolerable experiment and return to more elevated and independent courses. I have come," he burst out, "to *hate* the whole theatrical subject."

And in *The Tragic Muse,* his 1888 theater novel, he has a character cry: "What crudity compared to what the novelist does!"

There is a temptation to say the same about any film adaptation of a complex and nuanced work of fiction. A novel is, first of all, made out of language; it is language that determines whether a novel's storytelling trajectory will land it in the kingdom of art or in the rundown neighborhood of the hackneyed. *The Portrait of a Lady*, James's earliest full-scale masterpiece, is at its core an effective melodrama, chillingly equipped with an unsuspecting victim and sinister schemes and disclosures. What lifts it beyond melodrama is exactly what movies have no use for: acute, minute examination of motives; the most gossamer vibrations of the interior life; densely conceived villains and comic figures who cast unexpected shadows of self-understanding; a rich population of minor characters, each of whom has a history. And more: something atmospheric, something akin to what we might call a philosophy of the soul—a thing different from up-to-date sensibility.

A movie, by contrast, despite its all-encompassing arsenal of skills, probing angles, mood-inducing music, and miraculous technologies, is still a picture show. It shows us pictures above all, and Jane Campion's backgrounds and views in her film version of *The Portrait of a Lady* are immaculately beautiful—reminiscent of nineteenth-century canvases, and of the era of Beaux Arts. And if they breathe out a kind of museum insularity, that is what confirms their power: we know we are in another time, another and older England and Europe. Fabled sites become fresh pageants. An English country house, Rome and Florence, ancient churches and crypts and palaces and plazas, the Colosseum itself, all pass before us with the picturesque glow of authentic old lantern slides. But they are not sentimental; they convince.

At least three in Campion's cast* are unerringly persuasive in the same way. John Malkovich plays the callous, languorous

---

* A film in a canister (and who today would dispute that movies are an art form?) is nevertheless not the same as a book in a library. The names of James's characters endure; nothing is more ephemeral than the names of the actors who portray them. The difference between characters in literature and actors in performance is the difference, say, between a waterfall and a drink of water. No matter how pretty the cup, the drink is short-lived.

dilettante, Gilbert Osmond, precisely as James imagined him: an aesthete devoted to objets d'art, for whom human beings too are objects to be turned in the hand at will. Martin Donovan, as Ralph Touchett, the heroine's consumptive cousin, sees omnisciently with eyes marvelously lit by both irony and longing. As Madame Merle, Barbara Hershey fully incarnates James's idea of the schemer, as vulnerable as she is dangerous, who lures Isabel Archer into a pitiless marriage with Osmond, Madame Merle's former lover and the father of her unacknowledged child.

But Nicole Kidman as Isabel Archer, Madame Merle's dupe, is far more Campion's creation than James's—even though, given the confinements of her medium, Campion keeps reasonably close to James's plot. Fatherless and motherless, a spirited young beauty, Isabel is plucked out of provincial Albany, New York, by her aunt, Mrs. Touchett (Shelley Winters, banally miscast), and brought into the wider opportunities of aristocratic England.

There she enters the life of the grand country estates, and declines the offer of a brilliantly advantageous marriage to Lord Warburton, a member of Parliament (Richard E. Grant). Alone and dependent, she has seemingly given up her chance of access to a glittering society, and old Mr. Touchett, her wealthy banker uncle (John Gielgud), is bemused by such perversity. She has earlier refused a persistent American suitor, Caspar Goodwood (Viggo Mortensen)—she is ambitious beyond the velvet enclosures of marriage.

Just here is the conceptual spine of James's novel, its electrifying and chancy theory. Isabel Archer dreams of living hugely, of using her vivid capacities to take in the great and various world of boundless experience. Ralph Touchett, her admiring invalid cousin, sympathizes, understands, and makes it all possible. He persuades his dying father to leave Isabel a magnificent fortune. The Albany orphan is now an heiress, freed to infinite choice.

This is the point Campion unluckily loses sight of. She misses it both in detail and in scope. Isabel's first and buoyant choice is to voyage around the world, the bold outward sign of her valued new freedom—a freedom that Campion burlesques in a series of scenes (Isabel riding a camel, visiting the Pyramids) rendered playfully but reductively in silent-film style. Yet James recounts Isabel's worldly education as a serious enrichment: "She had ranged . . . through space and surveyed much of mankind, and was therefore now, in her own eyes, a very different person from the frivolous young woman from Albany who had begun to take the measure of Europe."

And while Nicole Kidman is lovely, slender, and effectively winning, Campion has omitted the buoyancy and the ambition. Kidman's Isabel takes the measure mainly of herself, in erotic and autoerotic fantasies: Isabel caressing her own lips and cheek, Isabel prone in a vortex of three suitors who surround her like a whirligig, Isabel walking moodily through a landscape with a hand at her breast.

The film's opening moments startle with the faces and voices of a group of contemporary young women who comment on the act of kissing—and though such a prologue may seem extraneous to what follows, it is plainly offered as a key to the director's sensibility. Self-oriented eroticism (or call it, more generally, a circumscribed interest in one's body), a current theme of a certain order of feminism, here replaces James's searching idea of a large and susceptible imagination roiling with world-hunger. James describes Isabel, fresh from America, as "at all times a keenly-glancing, quickly-moving, completely animated young woman" who emits a "radiance, even a slight exaltation." No flicker of this expressive vitality can be glimpsed in Kidman's passive, morose, tearfully suffering Isabel.

This is partly because a film based on a novel is, perforce, essentially an excerpt, and Campion mostly gives us the climax and sorrowful denouement of Isabel's story, and little of its eagerly yearning premise. Of motives there is nothing. Isabel, who had earlier eschewed marriage as too narrow for her possibilities, marries after all, and discovers herself to be Gilbert Osmond's unsatisfactory, even inferior, bibelot. The palatial interiors darken, husband and wife turn bitter. The two old lovers, Madame Merle and Osmond, working together, have seized on Isabel only for her money, to assure their daughter's future. And the daughter, Pansy, a pitifully obedient child warehoused in a convent, is still another victim of this pair of polished plotters. (But Valentina Cervi, a robust young Italian actor, is irritatingly unsuited for the timorously fragile Pansy.)

Here, in these final concentrated scenes—trust tainted by malignancy—Campion is wholly faithful to the outer progress of James's narrative. Beyond this, her art supplies what no novel can: the direct sensation of voluptuous gazing—so many doors opening into spaciousness, objects, liveried servants, a boiling, dizzying ballroom.

Yet the aim of Campion's film is surely not a literal faithfulness to the crowded, chesslike movements of the original. A film strives to be, so to speak, a condensed *second* original, which means that it will fail if it strays from or perverts the discriminations of its source. Campion sets out to alter and coarsen those discriminations. Ralph Touchett on his deathbed is hurled, in Campion's hands, from deeply held cousinly love ("Oh my brother!" James has Isabel cry in her grief) to driven lover's love, in wholesale repudiation of James. It is as if he is not to be trusted to tell the truth about men and women, and about the justice of willed reticence. And if James's Isabel is generously and earnestly outward-turning, Campion's Isabel is just the opposite—fastened, as that mischievously anachronistic prologue warns, on the inner chamber of the sensual kiss.

James's Isabel, in the hope of freedom, looks to the broadening world. Campion's Isabel, all too programmatically, looks to the limits of self. That is why the novel is a tragedy—it enacts the defeat of freedom. And that is why the movie, through its governing credo, adds up to little more than a beautifully embroidered anecdote of a bad marriage.

What crudity compared to what the novelist saw!

A Prophet of Modernism

What is the difference between a literary icon and an ordinary writer? The writer is sometimes read, the icon almost never; a symbol is independent of readers. The writer transfigured into symbol leaves behind such earthbound circumstances as reputation, controversy, acclaim, fame—including the highest degree of fame. All these are swallowed up in the Representation of an Era. Consider those nineteen-sixties luminaries (they are all male) who have come to personify—indelibly and incontrovertibly—one liberating scenario after another: the mystical vagabond, the Whitman-like bard, the macho rebel, the generational clown, the soused ex-prodigy. They are like medieval "humors," confined to the narrowest temper of their noisiest time. They have transcended their own labors: they denote, they delineate, they typify. They stand for an age. Of their celebrated passions, only a handful of stray phrases and shockworthy gestures survive. They have ascended—or fallen—into legend. Though alive, they are no longer urgent. They are animate statues.

Literary women are less likely to suffer such wholesale deportations into the straits of American personification. Emily Dickinson, Willa Cather, Edith Wharton, and Susan Sontag go on being newly and hotly read: they speak in the language of life, not of monument. Not that we are altogether without female monuments. The poet Emma Lazarus is mostly indistinguishable from her inscription on the Statue of Liberty. Julia Ward Howe, of "The Battle Hymn of the Republic," is thumpingly memorialized by those ungodly grapes of wrath (unless John Steinbeck has stolen them away). "So you're the little woman who started this big war," President Lincoln is said to have declared to Harriet Beecher Stowe, as if she were Helen of Troy. Yet not even the emblematic author of *Uncle Tom's Cabin* could fully embody the bleeding psychological wilderness of the Civil War. And neither she nor Howe nor Lazarus ever became the goddess of an age.

One woman did, and she did it by abandoning America and settling in Paris. She became the goddess of her age; she became the incarnation of that age; she became its legend; she became its symbol. "I have been the creative literary mind of the century," she announced. And another time: "Think of the Bible and Homer, think of Shakespeare and think of me." But we do not remember Gertrude Stein for saying any of these outrageous things. As a writer she is defined for us by four quotations only—egoless catchphrases, her logo and trademark: "Pigeons on the grass alas." "Rose is a rose is a rose is a rose." (Four roses: heavier brew than the three commonly cited.) To Ernest Hemingway, after the First World War: "You are all a lost generation." On her deathbed: "What is the question?"

She intended to seize and personify modernism itself, and she succeeded. Consequently we cannot imagine Gertrude Stein without Picasso. Like him, she wanted to invent Cubism—not in oils but in words, where refraction produces not abstraction but subtraction. She worked to subtract plain meaning from English prose. Whether she was a charlatan or a philosopher, it is even now hard to say. William James, with whom she studied psychology at Radcliffe, sent her on to Johns Hopkins to do research on automatic writing. (She earned an M.D. while she was at it.)

Certainly there appears to be more than a little of the subconscious in many of her sentences, but mainly they are mindful, calculated, striven after, arranged. "Think well of the difference between thinking with what they are thinking"—is this nonsense, or is it an idea too gossamer to capture? She was deliberately, extravagantly, ferociously extreme, and as concentrated and imperial as Picasso himself, who painted Stein just the way her companion Alice Toklas described her: a woman with the head of a Roman emperor.

No one now reads Gertrude Stein, though a few of her titles have a life of their own: *Four Saints in Three Acts,* which Virgil Thomson made into an opera; *The Autobiography of Alice B. Toklas,* written by Gertrude Stein about Gertrude Stein. Those who valiantly read her in her heyday often gave up. Clifton Fadiman's view was that her prose "puts you at once in the condition resembling the early stages of grippe—the eyes and legs heavy, the top of the skull wandering around in an uncertain and independent manner, the heart ponderously, tiredly beating." "A cold, black suet-pudding," Wyndham Lewis concluded. "All fat, without nerve."

And still the modernist pantheon came to sit at her feet. The visitors who passed through the bohemian dazzle of her Paris apartment—Picasso and Matisse on the walls—were nearly all illustrious; she knew what she was after, and so did they. Hemingway said that he and Stein were "just like brothers." Juan Gris, Sherwood Anderson, Clive Bell, Wyndham Lewis, Carl Van Vechten, Ezra Pound, Ford Madox Ford, André Gide, John Reed, Paul Robeson, Jo Davidson, and the geniuses on her walls, Picasso and Matisse—all these paraded by her witty tongue, while squat Alice Toklas looked loyally on. During the German occupation of Paris, when Jews were being hunted by the thousands in every neighborhood, these two Jewish women of Montparnasse were somehow left unmolested. And when Gertrude

Stein died in 1946, at seventy-two, her name was a household word (or quip), her mannish head an avant-garde image; and she had become one with the movement she touted.

At the close of its century of brilliance and triumph, modernism begins now to look a little old-fashioned, even a bit stale or exhausted, and certainly conventional—but what is fresher, and sassier, and more enchantingly silly, than "Rose is a rose is a rose . . ."? This endearing, enduring, durable and derisible chant of a copycat Cubist is almost all that is left of Gertrude Stein. It signifies what was once a mammoth revolution in literature and art. Gertrude Stein was modernism's outermost manifestation and prophet; and so she remains.

Imaginary People

Readers often ask—and writers ask themselves—where a work of fiction "comes from." A captivating question: it implies that stories don't always originate in the writer's mind, but in some outside source or force, like the sting of a passing insect. Henry James, in fact, concocted a germ theory to account for the sudden recognition that a tale is already *there*, at least in embryo. The "germ," in James's view, was the smallest fructifying hint, no bigger than a seed, out of which a story might grow. He collected these useful germs at dinner parties, listening to anecdotes and gossip—but he turned away, on principle, as the teller moved on to the story's real-life outcome.

What gripped James was not what had actually happened, but what *might* happen, what lay implicit in any overheard circumstance—the intimation, the possibility, the initiating spore. His notebooks swarm with such germs. "Mrs. F.F. mentioned to me," he would write, "a little local fact that strikes me as a good small 'short-story' ... The man had engaged himself to a young woman, but afterward had thought better of it," etc. James's elaborations would soon massively depart from the original "little local fact"—but this, the germ of the narrative, was indispensable to his imagination.

Writers' inspiration tends to divide itself between memory and observation—or call it between the self and ideas about the world. For writers on the memory side, it is autobiography that engenders story—or if not autobiography literally, then the matrix where psychology and personality and social surroundings meet. Memory-writers begin with character and situation, as James does. For writers magnetized by ideas—think of Hawthorne or Kafka—it is idea that precedes character. But of course no writer is purely on one side or the other; every novel is a complex partnership of both memory and idea, with one finally outweighing the other, as on a seesaw.

The act of reading, too, has a stake in this divide. Readers ride the seesaw along with the writer, but may weigh in against the writer's proclivity. E. M. Forster's early novel, *The Longest Journey* (a novel I reread obsessively in my twenties and thirties), is mainly—possibly exclusively—a memory work, rooted in autobiography, and far more dedicated to the exposition of character than to idea in the "philosophical" sense. But what I have taken away from it, over decades, is an idea about the nature of the moral life. (Readers discover their own "germs.") The idea—an insight into vice—resides in a single sentence in Chapter Eight. Agnes and Rickie have just announced that they will marry. Ansell, Rickie's blunt friend, asks when the marriage will take place. "Not for years, as far as we can see," Agnes replies.

Whereupon Ansell, who knows Rickie's heart, condemns Agnes as a liar—because, he explains, "she said 'we see' instead of 'I see.' "

A moment like this in a novel is equal to a dozen chapters of Kant. In one small shrewd scene, Forster penetrates into the peril of "I" speaking for "we"—untruth; arrogance; demagoguery.

Unlike James, Forster left no written record of how he came upon the germ for this youthful fiction. And the writer's germ, that crucial instant of revelation, may not be the reader's. For me, the germ of this novel—what is most germane to a reading life in its youth—is the tiny horror (it will later become an enormity) of hearing Agnes say "we."

Now it may be objected that Rickie and Agnes do not exist— that, as people go, they are only imaginary. All the same, imaginary people can, often enough, claim a reality greater than, for instance, our relatives. I may find Mrs. Dalloway a bit cloudy, but I believe absolutely in Mrs. Ramsay. Bellow's Einhorn, Forster's Aziz, Flaubert's Emma, A. B. Yehoshua's Abulafia, Jane Austen's Elizabeth, George Eliot's Dorothea, Chaim Grade's Hersh Rasseyner, Philip Roth's Swede, and on and on and on: these lives are more lasting than our own. We, whatever our current station on the span of three-score-and-ten, are ephemeral. Only make-believe people can endure for long; and some, like Hamlet, are permanent—at least until the sun burns out.

It is the curious identity of books in general that history and philosophy, invaluable though they are, cannot, by their very nature, contain novels; yet novels can contain history and philosophy. We need not quarrel about which genre is superior; all are essential to human striving. But somehow it is enchanting to think that the magic sack of make-believe, if one wills it so, can always be fuller and fatter than anything the historians and philosophers can supply. Make-believe, with its uselessness and triviality, with all its falseness, is nevertheless frequently praised for telling the truth via lies. Such an observation seems plainly not to the point. History seeks truth; philosophy seeks truth. They may get at it far better than novels can. Novels are made for another purpose. They are made to allow us to live, for a little time, another life; a life different from the one we were ineluctably born into. Truth, if we can lay our hands on it, may or may not confer freedom. Make-believe always does.

The Ladle

I came late to the ladle. For years it lay in a kitchen drawer, its wooden handle split—from age, not use. A practical friend's practical gift, for which I felt no gratitude. The truth is I have no affinity for pans and colanders and other culinary devices; my friendliest utensils have always been a trustworthy can opener screwed to the wall and a certain ancient red-handled wrench designed to twist the covers off recalcitrant grocery jars. The ladle, I believed, was a serious instrument for serious cooks, an accessory to the fact of real soups and real stews. I saw no need for it.

Yet the first time I dipped the ladle into a stew-laden pot (a real stew, finally, but by then my hair had turned white), I knew its value. The ladle, though made of commonplace stainless steel, was pure gold. I had all along been feebly spooning things out; but in the depth of a true stew a spoon is an inept, lazy, shallow fellow, poor kin to a ladle. Your spoon will bring up a pair of peas in a mild flat puddle—a spoon is nearly as feckless as a sieve. But your ladle is a powerful radar-equipped submarine churning into the wild deeps of an undertow, capable of trawling the sea-floor, a driving authentic vessel that will raise a rich authentic freight.

A spoon is an effete and timid little mouth, good enough for teacups and sweet puddings. A ladle is a great guzzling inebriate, given to gargantuan draughts; a swiller of oceanic wassail; a diver into densest abysses.

It is no surprise, then, to look up to the sea of stars—the well of infinity that is the sky at night—and find there two ladles, one Big, one Little. The Big Dipper's seven stars are hitched to the nearby constellations of Draco and Leo; the hollow of its ladle has been transformed into a kind of Cinderella-coach driven not by mice but by a dragon and a lion. The Little Dipper, in contrast, is the perfected form of the purified, unmetaphoricized ladle; it is the very incarnation of a Platonic notion of a ladle. (That the ancients should have seen it as Ursa Minor, a small bear, is no credit to them. But of course eyeglasses, never mind the telescope, hadn't yet been invented, so let it pass.)

As a reward for such precision of celestial engineering, a divine Hand long ago placed a diamond at the tip of the Little Dipper's handle. The diamond is called Polaris: the North Star, which connects the sky's seas with the earth's seas. For thousands of years before there were compasses, sailors fixed on Polaris to map the way from here to there, and back again. Without the ladle there would have been no navigation, no trade, no cross-culturalization. Without the ladle, how would Greece have learned geometry from Egypt? How would the alphabet have voyaged from the land of the Semites across the Mediterranean to Europe? How would Marco Polo have met the silkworm in China?

The ladle is, after all, the ultimate cosmic receptacle. It dips into knowledge and brings up wisdom, in the shape of a hundred images. The ladle *is* image: it is configuration in all its variety. It is the world's well. "Very deep is the well of the past. Should we not call it bottomless?" Thomas Mann asks in *Joseph and His Brothers*. Leave off the handle on occasion, or attach it afterward if you like, and you have scooped up a universe of stories. For Joseph, the ladle had no handle; it was a pit, out of which he rose to sit at the right hand of Pharaoh. For Joseph's father, Jacob, the ladle kept its handle, and went down into the bucket that Rachel drew up from the well in Haran to water Jacob's sheep and win his strenuous love. Isaac, Jacob's father, dug three wells—their names were Esek, Sitnah, and Rehoboth—in remembrance of the wells his father Abraham had dug a generation before.

With its handle attached, the ladle is always activist: it will delve, scoop, dip, gouge, shovel, excavate. It will fetch up a mess of vegetables from the maw of a stewpot. Or an archaeological plinth; or a shard of what was itself once a Middle Bronze dipper.

Without its handle, the ladle can be laid-back, hammocklike, a cradle (the rhyme is, at least in the etymology of the psyche, plainly no accident): it can be the cavity of a crescent moon for Wynken, Blynken, and Nod to lie in. It can be civilized or primitive, enameled or rough, utilitarian or luxuriant. It can be tank, vat, barrel, keg, cask, or stoup; it can be urn or calabash shell, bowl or basin, silver salver or Shaker firkin, Roman simpulum or Greek kyathos. It can be Ali Baba's jars to catch forty thieves in. It can be Tom Sawyer's scary cave. It can be the tunnel of love.

Hook the handle on again, and it can become the long haft of a fountain pen terminating in a well of black ink.

And just here we come (though for most of us the fountain pen has been superseded by the compact cavern of the computer, with its interior cybernetic cosmos)—we come to the ladle's deepest work: deeper than the ocean floor, deeper than the reach of the heavenly Dippers, deeper, in a way, than history itself. This is the ladle as it dips down, down, down into memory and imagination, into the bottomlessness of the word. It is the enchanted ladle that storytellers and writers grasp, or hope to grasp. Its handle (or hilt) is as long as the record of human habitation on our planet—or, some might wish to say, as long as thought and insight, as long as music and mathematics and science and art. And at the end of this longest handle of all is the dipper, the scoop, the vessel that raises up from the poet's or the philosopher's well something deeper, and higher, than we knew we knew.

Once upon a time there really used to be an inkwell and a dipper; I recollect it myself. In my childhood every elementary-school desk had, in its upper right corner, a round hole into which would fit a round glass cup. The ink monitor—generally a self-important factotum—filled the cup weekly, from a large glass bottle. Invariably the ink would spill and stain the wooden desk. We pupils dipped our pens (metal nibs in wooden slots) and were drilled in "penmanship," and dipped our pens again. Every few words necessitated a fresh dip. The inkwell was not deep— yet every year, as the grades ascended, it deepened. It deepened with *Travels with a Donkey*; it deepened with "Ode to the West Wind"; it deepened with Ichabod Crane.

And the well of sensibility goes on deepening, the ladle goes on dipping. A month or so ago I heard a man my own age, a brilliant editor—of books, and also of a famous magazine—scoop up out of his mind a lifetime's worth of ecstatic reading, novel after novel. His brain was mobbed with literature; the remembering dipper fetched and fetched. What a pity, he said at last, that all this joyful mental stock is impermanent; ephemeral; it will go to waste; it will vanish when I vanish.

That same week I saw a newborn infant, and marveled at how perfectly it was formed, a complete human simulacrum; but it had no mental stock at all. It was a freshly made ladle: a replenishing ladle ready soon enough to dip into pictures and melodies and rhymes. The well of stories and ideas is eternal. But the ladle must be renewed. So decrees the Hand that put the diamond on the Little Dipper.

What Is Poetry About?

To ask the question "What is poetry about?" is different from asking what *poems* are about. "Poems," in the plural, will mean an aggregate of individual poems—and despite the bundling together, we think of singularity: one poem, and then another poem, and then another. Each poem is the unique vessel of its own intent, focus, tone, theme, language, discovery, astonishment. A poem is "a" or "the" poem: it resists category, except perhaps the category of form. A poem may consent to being called a haiku, or a sonnet, or a villanelle; it may be content to being called "free," and once upon a time—a time that now begins to take on a kind of autumnal browning—it was delighted to stand under the eaves of the term "modern." And still it is possible, or nearly possible, to say what any single poem is "about"—although a poem may be less about what it is about, and more about its intimations, its penumbra, its scent, its own hiddenness or elusiveness. A poem is "edgelit," to borrow a word from Adrienne Rich.

So if we can say, even if only more or less, what a single poem is about, can we say what "poetry" is about? Is "poetry" a collective? Is it a plural? Is it a universe? Is it an emanation, and if so, an emanation of what? From what does it derive? Is it endemic in our biological being, like the human hand with its opposable thumb? Does it belong to song, or is it the child, or perhaps the parent, of philosophy?

Turn for a moment from poetry to pots. The archaeologist's pots: vessels to store grain in, or mead, or wine; vessels to cook with, over an open fire. Pots have been the intimate companions of humankind since humankind evolved; pots *define* humankind. They are present, omnipresent, in every human culture. Utility ordained that the prehistoric clay pot would indeed be a pot: a concave object. Utility also prescribed a base suitable for standing or storage or shipping, and often enough, when it was to the purpose, a spout, a lid, a handle or a pair of handles. But utility did not contemplate imaginative departures and additions of form, it did not envision the fanciful shapes of animals or birds; and utility did not demand decorative design, coarser in one culture, more brilliantly complex in another. The drive to mark the most ordinary articles with the impress of art was and is humanly universal and appears to be humanly innate. Always and everywhere, art attaches itself to the utilitarian.

And not only to the utilitarian. Even, and especially, to the imagery of the divine: so that, from Osiris and Ishtar to Athena and Zeus, from Vishnu and Shiva to Buddha and Jesus, there has been figuration. Art may have gravitated to utensils, mere utensils, to express a human drive; but it *inhabited* religion—or put it that religion inhabited art. The thousands of talismans unearthed in the excavations of extinct settlements; the monumental sculptures of ancient Egypt; the towering statue of Athena in the Parthenon; the torrent of Christian carvings and paintings, both Western and Eastern, and the talismanic cross and crucifix; the manifold Hindu representations of deities; the serene Buddha-busts, both mammoth and domestic—all these testify to religion's habitation in art. Through the ministrations of art, concept became concrete, idea turned into thing, mystery metamorphosed into matter. Some may regard this nearly universal flood of representation as a tribute to the human imagination, and so it is. But Judaism, Islam, and iconoclastic elements of the Protestant Reformation, all under the influence of the Second Commandment, refused representations of the divine. The Second Commandment is usually thought to be the instrument of the suppression of art—yet what ultimately flowered from this denial of divine representation was, paradoxically, the freer flowering of art itself.

The Second Commandment, alone in the ancient world in its opposition to graven images, sought to liberate religion from art, and the Creator from anthropomorphism—so that, in the second century before the Common Era, when the Greek Syrians conquered Jerusalem and invaded the First Temple and found there no statue of a god, they instantly supposed the Jews to be an atheist people. But in freeing the metaphysical from the limits of literalism, the Second Commandment also freed art to impulse, permitting it to wander limitlessly, to become purely itself, manumitted from clerical servitude. It is the Second Commandment that is the author of Picasso.

For poetry—for Word—there can be no Second Commandment. Creation and the Creator cannot be separated from Word. We will look in vain for a scriptural admonition that omits or prohibits or silences poetry. *"Va-y'hi or,"* says the God of Genesis: Let there be light: and light, and, after light, life, are spoken into existence. "In the beginning was the Word," says the Gospel in Greek, summing up the Hebrew of Genesis. Something there is in poetry that clings and clings to what we lamely and tamely call the metaphysical—the questions that are beyond our capacity to formulate, the portraits that are beyond our capacity to trace. Poetry is not often prophecy, and surely poets are not often prophets, but it is inescapable that all true prophets are poets.

Poetry itself, because it is written, because it is spoken, because it creates a world in the mind, tends to the scriptural. "The heterocosm," Harold Bloom calls it in an essay on Yeats, "or the poem as an alternative world to that of nature." But poetry also aspirates the given and actual cosmos, and rounds the mundane earth—mundane yet not profane. Here is Charles Wright, fashioning a scripture of plum blossoms:

> Belief in transcendence,
> > belief in something beyond belief,
> Is what the blossoms solidify
> In their fall through the two worlds—
> The imaging of the invisible, the slow dream of metaphor,
> Sanction our going up and our going down, our days
> And the lives we infold inside them,
> > our *yes* and *yes*.

There is no Second Commandment to inhibit the imagery of the invisible in words. The visual arts cannot make scripture—they can only falsify it. God's promise was that God's Face would never be shown; who can copy what isn't revealed? But poetry is an echo of revelation itself: in Adrienne Rich's lines,

> . . . poetry means refusing
> the choice to kill or die,

and this succinct refusal is not unlike Abraham's hot refusal of God's judgment of the Cities of the Plain. Milton wrote a scripture parallel with the sacral scripture of the ages; Blake did the same.

Yet no one would claim that every poet is a metaphysical poet, or that every poem is written in the breeze made by the turning-away of God's unknowable Face, or the turning of the earth on its axis, or the spiraling of the galaxies. Nor does every poem aspire to be a heterocosm, or intend to hold a mirror up to nature, or existence, or eternity. "I measure time by how a body sways," says Theodore Roethke, declining eternity. And Anne Sexton looks at an earthworm cut in half and asks, ontologically, teleologically: "Have you no beginning and end?" To be saturated with eternality means to feel the ache of the ephemeral; to take precise note of the immediate means to sink into contemplation of the eternal.

A poem can be about anything at all: a mouse, a bat, a plum, a jar, a wind, a sigh, a thigh: whatever is thought or sought or caught or wrought. But *poetry* is about what is eternal, and *therefore* about the fracture in time that is a single moment. Or say it the other way around: poetry is about impingements on the senses, including the sense of innerness, and is *therefore* about what the senses, including the sense of innerness, cannot grasp in the outer oceans of Being.

Whatever any single poem may be about, poetry is about the trail, the trace, the veil of gossamer motes, that fall from the outskirts of Genesis. Poetry is the Word that can send its dipper into the formless void—*tohu va-vohu,* as Genesis has it—and draw up light.

"I, too, dislike it," said the poet who wore a tricornered hat: she who took note of how every corner of her surround was stocked. This is a sentiment, however ironic, that a poet has a right to, since poetry is generally more skeptical than romantic. But poetry has its party of opposition, its passionate dispraisers, who go even further into negation: call them our contemporary cultural anthropologists. "Irrelevant," they say—a term that has been abused for three decades, having been put to use chiefly for purposes of contempt. Yet irrelevant to what? To the three Screens that, like the three Fates, absorb and shape our span: movie, TV, computer? Unlike those Screens, poetry is not a universal toy of our society.

And so it is true—no one can successfully deny it—that a poem, even when it concerns the everyday, is disjunctive with the everyday, collides with it, or veers away from it. Poetry belongs to the *strange*—and in saying that, there are two meanings, or inferences, that I would instantly reject. The first is "strange" wearing its aura of "the uncanny," a formula that comes to us from the fashionable academic theorists via Freud. And the second is "strange" in the sense of "spiritual," a term that, in my view, resists poetry at its root. The uncanny is beyond words, beyond human expression—the work of succubi, of ghosts. The idea of the spiritual is equally ghostly, with an added faith in the penetrating power of external magicking. Neither derives from the human labor of the human imagination; both leave the work of discovery and revelation, and even the work of instinct, to mysterious forces outside human capacity. The so-called uncanny and the so-called spiritual thrive in the dilution or absence of language; both skirt intelligibility.

But when we say that poetry is strange, we mean not that it is less than intelligible, but exactly the opposite: poetry is intelligibility heightened, strengthened, distilled to the point of astounding us; and also made manifold. Metaphor is intelligibility's great imperative, its engine of radical amazement.

What is strange about poetry is what is most manifest: not so much the unpredictable surge of its music as the words of which it is made. Everyone uses words; from minute to minute, from a million million larynxes, a deluge of words falls on the air. And every word, spoken or written, has its own history, and is a magnet for cultural accretion. A poet has the same access to the language-pool as a tailor, an archaeologist, or a felon. How strange that, scooping up words from the selfsame pool that everyone else draws from, a poet will reconfigure, startle, and restart those words! How strange that what we call the norms of life—the findings of sociology, of anthropology, the common sense of common observations of nature: call it whatever you like—how strange that all these habits and pursuits poetry is said to be irrelevant to are precisely what poetry has the magisterial will and the intimate attentiveness to decode!

Let us come back to pots. I read, the other day, an essay on translation of the *Analects* of Confucius. One of these is recorded as follows: "A gentleman is not a pot." Other renderings are: "A gentleman is not a utensil," "A gentleman is not an implement." This is taken to be a declaration on behalf of a generalized cultivation of insight as opposed to the specialist's performance of a narrow concrete task. To those who insist that poetry is irrelevant to our common preoccupations, or that it contributes nothing "real" to society, one can only reply: Poetry is not a pot.

And poetry, because it is timeless, takes time. Let W. H. Auden have the last word on the things both infinite and infinitesimal that poetry is about:

> Were all stars to disappear or die,
> I should learn to look at an empty sky
> And feel its total dark sublime,
> Though this might take me a little time.

A Swedish Novel

A confession of omission: *The Christmas Oratorio,* by Sweden's celebrated Göran Tunström, is only the second Swedish novel I have ever read—the first was Pär Lagerkvist's *The Sibyl*—and this alone is an anomaly, or possibly an indictment. Where, on my American bookshelves, are the Swedish novels? On the other hand, is it at all proper (I mean proper in a purely literary sense) to think of any novel as a work of national expression? A novel, after all, is one of the two blessèd forms (poetry is the other) that stand in opposition to generalization or co-optation. In a novel we encounter *this* woman, *this* child, *this* man. We are also led to *this place:* but place, though it may shape a human being, is almost always—for a novel—less than a human being. If I am enthralled by Moscow and Dublin, it is because that is where I have met Anna Karenina and Molly Bloom.

And so the question is inescapable: is there really such a thing as a "Swedish" novel, a "Russian" novel, an "American" novel? Is Göran Tunström a sort of summary or repository of the Swedish sensibility? Does national temperament inevitably inform a writer, or is every writer sui generis, an unduplicatable fingerprint, a unique force never to be replicated? In short: when I read *The Christmas Oratorio,* am I reading representative Swedish fiction, or—the difference counts—am I simply reading Göran Tunström?

The Christmas Oratorio (translated by Paul Hoover) is a lyrical novel; it instantly put me in mind of D. H. Lawrence's *Sons and Lovers,* another work of unashamedly high romantic song.

> It was very still. The tree was tall and straggling. It had thrown its briers over a hawthorne-bush, and its long streamers trailed thick, right down to the grass, splashing the darkness everywhere with great spilt stars, pure white. In bosses of ivory and in large splashed stars the roses gleamed on the darkness of foliage and stems and grass. Paul and Miriam stood there together, silent, and watched. Point after point the steady roses shone out to them, seeming to kindle something in their souls.

That is Lawrence. Now here is a passage from Tunström.

> He wanders over the field of oats, through the pasture land. Ends up standing, looking at something which, after a while, reveals itself as a stone, a cowpile, a dried branch. Slowly, if it happens at all, the properties glide out of the object, take form, put themselves in proper order, become one with their name. Often there is a white moment just before, which can last minutes, when the stone refuses to be a stone, when the hand refuses to be a hand, when one cannot die since one is not alive.

The difference between these scenes (read in or out of context) is self-evident. The first describes nature's beauty made still more beautiful by the sensations of the two young lovers observing it. The second presents the natural world, lovely and innocently steadfast in itself, made strange and unreliable by the grief of a husband whose young wife has died in an accident.

But there is a difference far more crucial than any superficial disparity of narrative circumstance: what do we mean when we speak of a "poetic novel"? Lawrence's poetry is a novelist's poetry—it may be ripe, it may be voluptuous, but it is never phantasmagorical, it never flies off into an independent reverie, it is grounded at every moment in the reality and need of the scene in hand. (Seamus Heaney: "A grounded strength as well as a perfect tact.") Tunström's poetry, in contrast, almost instantly departs from the narrative center to sail upward to the meta-metaphorical: a "white moment" perforates reality, and through that hole in the curtain of our five senses "the properties glide out of the object."

In *The Christmas Oratorio* Platonism rules, and the properties glide out of their objects again and again. The narrative is strong, the visionary flights have their gauzy beauty; but it is a beauty stripped of strength, furred by mist. A free-floating lyricism fogs over the palpable bodies and burning minds of the human actors in the tale, so that we can see them only dimly, as through a blemished window, and are shut off from their mental cues. Now and then the poetry settles, like crystal deposits, and the fog clears; and then we know what is there.

And what is there is a series of country tragedies that spread to the other side of the planet, entangling three idiosyncratic generations. Sidner, an inward and precocious farm boy, gives his mother's bicycle a push as she heads downhill to the church to rehearse Bach; the bicycle crashes into a cow and Solveig is killed. Aron, Sidner's father, is inconsolable, and moves his orphaned family into town to take a job in a hotel. The town seethes with strangeness: a child named Splendid, a genial type of Huck Finn; the hotel's Sauce Queen; and even an imaginary and forlorn Selma Lagerlöf, riding a raft. Sidner, who loves books and music, is seduced in his teens by an eccentric older woman; she gives birth to his son. And meanwhile Aron, in a hallucinatory overseas correspondence, comes to believe that Solveig has been returned to him in the form of an odd young woman in far-off New Zealand. On the ship carrying him there,

Aron throws himself overboard and drowns. Sidner, yearning to know his little son and kept away, falls into temporary madness; ultimately he follows his father's track across the sea. The novel ends in the voice of Sidner's grown son. Ordinary life is extraordinary, and hard.

All this is the spine, so to speak, of *The Christmas Oratorio*— and by "spine" nothing remotely like plot is intended. There is no plot, but there is something eerier: call it destiny. Or call it teleology: a sense of universal purpose to which mortals are blind. Events fall out as naturally and arbitrarily, and yet as astonishingly, as leaves from a tree in autumn. Göran Tunström is a master of earthly truths.

But he is a writer powerfully tempted by the unearthly: "And unseen I went by, inside a huge scream. . . . Someone had lost a mirror in the moss by the shore. My eye was caught by it, deep down I saw how my tears fell upward toward me." And: "What flickering flames we are. How easily darkness washes over us, extinguishing our lives. It is a wonder that we exist at all." And: "As soon as I turn my dwarfish eyes to God, trying to define him, he disappears, becoming manifest everywhere he is not. His absence is the prerequisite for his existence." And, to cap the rest: "You wanted to know what it's like to write a book. It's exhausting! It's like forcing yourself over a desert. . . . But then you come to an oasis: words pour out, every leaf opens, everything wants to become poetry."

And just here is the difficulty: in a novel *not* everything wants to become poetry. Nor does a novel's everything want to be coated with the silvery blur of the unearthly, the magical, the legendary, the wistful, the dreamlike. A novel—*any* novel, Swedish, English, French, Russian, Italian, American, Japanese— cries out for structure: the structure, one might venture, of society itself. The novel, after all, was born out of societal experience. Modernism turned it subjective, introspective. But introspection let loose into the purely visionary is in danger of losing so much perspective that it will become indistinguishable from sentimentality. What I miss in *The Christmas Oratorio* is social bite, something more stringent than the merely bizarre; irony, one of the deep gifts of the Western mind; and finally the sense that, often enough, a stone is really a stone and a hand no more than a hand. Too much metaphor overloads us with softness. And Göran Tunström, in all the wisdom of his hard lives, knows profoundly that the human condition is anything but soft.

She: Portrait of the Essay as a Warm Body

An essay is a thing of the imagination. If there is information in an essay, it is by-the-by, and if there is an opinion in it, you need not trust it for the long run. A genuine essay has no educational, polemical, or sociopolitical use; it is the movement of a free mind at play. Though it is written in prose, it is closer in kind to poetry than to any other form. Like a poem, a genuine essay is made out of language and character and mood and temperament and pluck and chance.

And if I speak of a genuine essay, it is because fakes abound. Here the old-fashioned term poetaster may apply, if only obliquely. As the poetaster is to the poet—a lesser aspirant—so the article is to the essay: a look-alike knockoff guaranteed not to wear well. An article is gossip. An essay is reflection and insight. An article has the temporary advantage of social heat—what's hot out there right now. An essay's heat is interior. An article is timely, topical, engaged in the issues and personalities of the moment; it is likely to be stale within the month. In five years it will have acquired the quaint aura of a rotary phone. An article is Siamese-twinned to its date of birth. An essay defies its date of birth, and ours too. (A necessary caveat: some genuine essays are popularly called "articles"—but this is no more than an idle, though persistent, habit of speech. What's in a name? The ephemeral is the ephemeral. The enduring is the enduring.)

A small historical experiment. Who are the classical essayists that come at once to mind? Montaigne, obviously. Among the nineteenth-century English masters, the long row of Hazlitt, Lamb, De Quincey, Stevenson, Carlyle, Ruskin, Newman, Arnold, Harriet Martineau. Of the Americans, Emerson. It may be argued that nowadays these are read only by specialists and literature majors, and by the latter only when they are compelled to. However accurate the claim, it is irrelevant to the experiment, which has to do with beginnings and their disclosures. Here, then, are some introductory passages:

> One of the pleasantest things in the world is going a journey; but I like to go by myself. I can enjoy society in a room; but out of doors, nature is company enough for me. I am then never less alone than when alone.
>
> —William Hazlitt, "On Going a Journey"

> To go into solitude, a man needs to retire as much from his chamber as from society. I am not solitary whilst I read and write, though nobody is with me. But if a man would be alone, let him look at the stars.
>
> —Ralph Waldo Emerson, "Nature"

> I have often been asked how I first came to be a regular opium eater; and have suffered, very unjustly, in the opinion of my acquaintance, from being reputed to have brought upon myself all the sufferings which I shall have to record, by a long course of indulgence in this practice purely for the sake of creating an artificial state of pleasurable excitement. This, however, is a misrepresentation of my case.
>
> —Thomas De Quincey, "Confessions of an
> English Opium Eater"

The human species, according to the best theory I can form of it, is composed of two distinct races, the men who borrow, and the men who lend.

—Charles Lamb, "The Two Races of Men"

I saw two hareems in the East; and it would be wrong to pass them over in an account of my travels; though the subject is as little agreeable as any I can have to treat. I cannot now think of the two mornings thus employed without a heaviness of heart greater than I have ever brought away from Deaf and Dumb Schools, Lunatic Asylums, or even Prisons.

—Harriet Martineau, "From Eastern Life"

The future of poetry is immense, because in poetry, where it is worthy of its high destinies, our race, as time goes on, will find an ever and surer stay. There is not a creed which is not shaken, not an accredited dogma which is not shown to be questionable, not a received tradition which does not threaten to dissolve. . . . But for poetry the idea is everything; the rest is a world of illusion, of divine illusion.

—Matthew Arnold, "The Study of Poetry"

The changes wrought by death are in themselves so sharp and final, and so terrible and melancholy in their consequences, that the thing stands alone in man's experience, and has no parallel upon earth. It outdoes all other accidents because it is the last of them. Sometimes it leaps suddenly upon its victims, like a Thug; sometimes it lays a regular siege and creeps upon their citadel during a score of years. And when the business is done, there is a sore havoc made in other people's lives, and a pin knocked out by which many subsidiary friendships hung together.

—Robert Louis Stevenson, "Aes Triplex"

It is recorded of some people, as of Alexander the Great, that their sweat, in consequence of some rare and extraordinary constitution, emitted a sweet odor, the cause of which

Plutarch and others investigated. But the nature of most bodies is the opposite, and at their best they are free from smell. Even the purest breath has nothing more excellent than to be without offensive odor, like that of very healthy children.

—Michel de Montaigne, "Of Smells"

What might such a little anthology of beginnings reveal? First, that language differs from one era to the next: there are touches of archaism here, if only in punctuation and cadence. Second, that splendid minds may contradict each other (outdoors, Hazlitt never feels alone; Emerson urges the opposite). Third, that the theme of an essay can be anything under the sun, however trivial (the smell of sweat) or crushing (the thought that we must die). Fourth, that the essay is a consistently recognizable and venerable—or call it ancient—form. In English: Addison and Steele in the eighteenth century, Bacon and Browne in the seventeenth, Lyly in the sixteenth, Bede in the eighth. And what of the biblical Koheleth—Ecclesiastes— who may be the oldest essayist reflecting on one of the oldest subjects: world-weariness?

So the essay is ancient and various: but this is a commonplace. There is something else, and it is more striking yet—the essay's power. By "power" I mean precisely the capacity to do what force always does: coerce assent. Never mind that the shape and inclination of any essay is against coercion or suasion, or that the essay neither proposes nor purposes to get you to think like its author—at least not overtly. If an essay has a "motive," it is linked more to happenstance and opportunity than to the driven will. A genuine essay is not a doctrinaire tract or a propaganda effort or a broadside. Thomas Paine's "Common Sense" and Emile Zola's "J'accuse" are heroic landmark writings; but to call them essays, though they may resemble the form, is to misunderstand. The essay is not meant for the barricades; it is a stroll through someone's mazy mind. Yet this is not to say that there has never been an essayist morally intent on making an argument, however obliquely—George Orwell is a case in point. At the end of the day, the essay turns out to be a force for agreement. It co-opts agreement; it courts agreement; it seduces agreement. For the brief hour we give to it, we are sure to fall into surrender and conviction. And this will occur even if we are intrinsically roused to resistance.

To illustrate: I may not be persuaded by Emersonianism as an ideology, but Emerson—his voice, his language, his music—persuades me. When we look for superlatives, not for nothing do we speak of "commanding" or "compelling" prose. If I am a skeptical rationalist or an advanced biochemist, I may regard (or discard) the idea of the soul as no better than a puff of warm vapor. But here is Emerson on the soul: "when it breathes through [man's] intellect, it is genius; when it breathes through his will, it is virtue; when it flows through his affection, it is love." And then—well, I am in thrall, I am possessed; I believe.

The novel has its own claims on surrender. It suspends our participation in the society we ordinarily live in, so that—for the time we are reading—we forget it utterly. But the essay does not allow us to forget our usual sensations and opinions; it does something even more potent: it makes us deny them. The authority of a masterly essayist—the authority of sublime language and intimate observation—is absolute. When I am with Hazlitt, I know no greater companion than nature. When I am with Emerson, I know no greater solitude than nature.

And what is most odd about the essay's power to lure us into its lair is how it goes about this work. We feel it when a political journalist comes after us with a point of view—we feel it the way the cat is wary of the dog. A polemic is a herald, complete with feathered hat and trumpet. A tract can be a trap. Certain magazine articles have the scent of so-much-per-word. What is indisputable is that all of these are more or less in the position of a lepidopterist with his net: they mean to catch and skewer. They are focused on prey—i.e., us. The genuine essay, in contrast, never thinks of us; the genuine essay may be the most self-centered (the politer word would be subjective) arena for human thought ever devised.

Or else, though still not having you and me in mind (unless as an exemplum of common folly), it is not self-centered at all. When I was a child, I discovered in the public library a book that enchanted me then, and the idea of which has enchanted me for life. I have no recollection either of the title or of the writer—and anyhow very young readers rarely take note of authors; stories are simply and magically *there*. The characters included, as I remember them, three or four children and a delightful relation who is a storyteller, and the scheme was this: each child calls out a story-element—most often an object—and the storyteller gathers up whatever is supplied (blue boots, a river, a fairy, a pencil box) and makes out of these random, unlikely, and disparate offerings a tale both logical and surprising. An essay, it seems to me, may be similarly constructed—if so deliberate a term applies. The essayist, let us say, unexpectedly stumbles over a pair of old blue boots in a corner of the garage, and this reminds her of when she last wore them—twenty years ago, on a trip to Paris, where on the banks of the Seine she stopped to watch an old fellow sketching, with a box of colored pencils at his side. The pencil wiggling over his sheet is a grayish pink, which reflects the threads of sunset pulling westward in the sky, like the reins of a fairy cart . . . and so on. The mind meanders, slipping from one impression to another, from reality to memory to dreamscape and back again.

In the same way Montaigne, in our sample, when contemplating the unpleasantness of sweat, ends with the pure breath of children. Or Stevenson, starting out with mortality, speaks first of ambush, then of war, and finally of a displaced pin. No one is freer than the essayist—free to leap out in any direction, to hop from thought to thought, to begin with the finish and finish with the middle, or to eschew beginning and end and keep only a middle. The marvel of it is that out of this apparent causelessness, out of this scattering of idiosyncratic seeing and telling, a coherent world is made. It is coherent because, after all, an essayist must be an artist, and every artist, whatever the means, arrives at a sound and singular imaginative frame—or call it, on a minor scale, a cosmogony.

And it is into this frame, this work of art, that we tumble like tar babies, and are held fast. What holds us there? The authority of a voice, yes; the pleasure—sometimes the anxiety—of a new idea, an untried angle, a snatch of reminiscence, bliss displayed or shock conveyed. An essay can be the product of intellect or memory, lightheartedness or gloom, well-being or disgruntlement. But always there is a certain quietude, on occasion a kind of detachment. Rage and revenge, I think, belong to fiction. The essay is cooler than that. Because it so often engages in acts of memory, and despite its gladder or more antic incarnations, the essay is by and large a serene or melancholic form. It mimics that low electric hum, sometimes rising to resemble actual speech, that all human beings carry inside their heads—a vibration, garrulous if somewhat indistinct, that never leaves us while we wake. It is the hum of perpetual noticing: the configuration of someone's eyelid or tooth, the veins on a hand, a wisp of string caught on a twig, some words your fourth-grade teacher said, so long ago, about the rain, the look of an awning, a sidewalk, a bit of cheese left on a plate. All day long this inescapable hum drums on, recalling one thing and another, and pointing out this and this and this. Legend has it that Titus, emperor of Rome, went mad because of the buzzing of a gnat that made her home in his ear; and presumably the gnat, flying out into the great world and then returning to her nest, whispered what she had seen and felt and learned there. But an essayist is more resourceful than an emperor, and can be relieved of this interior noise, if only for the time it takes to record its murmurings. To seize the hum and set it down for others to hear is the essayist's genius.

It is a genius bound to leisure, and even to luxury, if luxury is measured in hours. The essay's limits can be found in its own reflective nature. Poems have been wrested from the inferno of catastrophe or war, and battlefield letters too: these are the spontaneous bursts and burnings that danger excites. But the meditative temperateness of an essay requires a desk and a chair, a musing and a mooning, a connection to a civilized surround; even when the subject itself is a wilderness of lions and tigers, mulling is the way of it. An essay is a fireside thing, not a conflagration or a safari.

This may be why, when we ask who the essayists are, it turns out—though novelists may now and then write essays—that true essayists rarely write novels. Essayists are a species of metaphysician: they are inquisitive—also analytic—about the least grain of being. Novelists go about the strenuous business of marrying and burying their people, or else they send them to sea, or to Africa, or (at the least) out of town. Essayists in their stillness ponder love and death. It is probably an illusion that men are essayists more often than women (especially since women's essays have in the past frequently assumed the form of unpublished correspondence). And here I should, I suppose, add a note about maleness and femaleness as a literary issue—what is popularly termed "gender," as if men and women were French or German tables and sofas. I *should* add such a note; it is the fashion, or, rather, the current expectation or obligation—but there is nothing to say about any of it. Essays are written by men. Essays are written by women. That is the long and the short of it. John Updike, in a genially confident discourse on maleness ("The Disposable Rocket"), takes the view—though he admits to admixture—that the "male sense of space must differ from that of the female, who has such an interesting, active, and significant inner space. The space that interests men is outer." Except, let it be observed, when men write essays: since it is only inner space—interesting, active, significant—that can conceive and nourish the contemplative essay. The "ideal female body," Updike adds, "curves around the centers of repose," and no phrase could better describe the shape of the ideal essay—yet women are no fitter as essayists than men. In promoting the felt salience of sex, Updike nevertheless drives home an essayist's point. Essays, unlike novels, emerge from the sensations of the self. Fiction creeps into foreign bodies; the novelist can inhabit not only a sex not his own, but also beetles and noses and hunger artists and nomads and beasts; while the essay is, as we say, personal.

And here is an irony. Though I have been intent on distinguishing the marrow of the essay from the marrow of fiction, I confess I have been trying all along, in a subliminal way, to speak of the essay as if it—or she—were a character in a novel or a play: moody, fickle, given on a whim to changing her clothes, or the subject; sometimes obstinate, with a mind of her own; or hazy and light; never predictable. I mean for her to be dressed—and addressed—as we would Becky Sharp, or Ophelia, or Elizabeth Bennet, or Mrs. Ramsay, or Mrs. Wilcox, or even Hester Prynne. Put it that it is pointless to say (as I have done repeatedly, disliking it every moment) "the essay," "an essay." The essay—an essay—is not an abstraction; she may have recognizable contours, but she is highly colored and individuated; she is not a type. She is too fluid, too elusive, to be a category. She may be bold, she may be diffident, she may rely on beauty, or on cleverness, on eros or exotica. Whatever her story, she is the protagonist, the secret self's personification. When we knock on her door, she opens to us, she is a presence in the doorway, she leads us from room to room; then why should we not call her "she"? She may be privately indifferent to us, but she is anything but unwelcoming. Above all, she is not a hidden principle or a thesis or a construct: she is *there,* a living voice. She takes us in.

A Drug Store Eden

In 1929 my parents sold their drug store in Yorkville—a neighborhood comprising Manhattan's East Eighties—and bought a pharmacy in Pelham Bay, in the northeast corner of the Bronx. It was a move from dense city to almost country. Pelham Bay was at the very end of a relatively new stretch of elevated train track that extended from the subway of the true city all the way out to the small-town feel of little houses and a single row of local shops: shoemaker's, greens store, grocery, drug store, bait store. There was even a miniature five-and-ten where you could buy pots, housedresses, and thick lisle stockings for winter. Three stops down the line was the more populous Westchester Square, with its bank and post office, which old-timers still called "the village"—Pelham Bay had once lain outside the city limits, in Westchester County.

This lost little finger of the borough was named for the broad but mild body of water that rippled across Long Island Sound to a blurry opposite shore. All the paths of Pelham Bay Park led down to a narrow beach of rough pebbles, and all the surrounding streets led, sooner or later, to the park, wild and generally deserted. Along many of these streets there were empty lots that resembled meadows, overgrown with Queen Anne's lace and waist-high weeds glistening with what the children termed "snake spit"; poison ivy crowded between the toes of clumps of sky-tall oaks. The snake spit was a sort of bubbly botanical excretion, but there were real snakes in those lots, with luminescent skins, brownish-greenish, crisscrossed with white lines. There were real meadows, too: acres of downhill grasses, in the middle of which you might suddenly come on a set of rusty old swings—wooden slats on chains—or a broken red-brick wall left over from some ruined and forgotten Westchester estate.

The Park View Pharmacy—the drug store my parents bought—stood on the corner of Colonial Avenue, between Continental and Burr: Burr for Aaron Burr, the Vice President who killed Alexander Hamilton in a duel. The neighborhood had a somewhat bloodthirsty Revolutionary flavor. Not far away you could still visit Spy Oak, the venerable tree on which captured Redcoats had once been hanged; and now and then Revolutionary bullets were churned up a foot or so beneath the front lawn of the old O'Keefe house, directly across the street from the Park View Pharmacy. George Washington had watered his horses, it was believed, in the ancient sheds beyond Ye Olde Homestead, a local tavern that, well after Prohibition, was still referred to as the "speak-easy." All the same, there were no Daughters of the American Revolution here: instead, Pelham Bay was populated by the children of German, Irish, Swedish, Scottish, and Italian immigrants, and by a handful of the original immigrants themselves. The greenhorn Italians, from Naples and Sicily, kept goats and pigs in their back yards, and pigeons on their roofs. Pelham Bay's single Communist—you could tell from the election results that there was such a rare bird—was the Scotsman who lived around the corner, though only my parents knew this. They were privy to the neighborhood's opinions, ailments, and family secrets.

In those years a drug store seemed one of the world's permanent institutions. Who could have imagined that it would one day vanish into an aisle in the supermarket, or re-emerge as a kind of supermarket itself? What passes for a pharmacy nowadays is all open shelves and ceiling racks of brilliant white neon suggesting perpetual indoor sunshine. The Park View, by contrast, was a dark cavern lined with polished wood cabinets rubbed nearly black and equipped with sliding glass doors and mirrored backs. The counters were heaped with towering ziggurats of lotions, potions, and packets, and under them ran glassed-in showcases of the same sober wood. There was a post office (designated a "substation") that sold penny postcards and stamps and money orders. The prescription area was in the rear, closed off from view: here were scores of labeled drawers of all sizes, and rows of oddly shaped brown bottles. In one of those drawers traditional rock candy was stored, in two flavors, plain and maple, dangling on long strings. And finally there was the prescription desk itself, a sloping lecternlike affair on which the current prescription ledger always lay, like some sacred text.

There was also a soda fountain. A pull at a long black handle spurted out carbonated water; a push at a tiny silver spout drew out curly drifts of whipped cream. The air in this part of the drug store was steamy with a deep coffee fragrance, and on wintry Friday afternoons the librarians from the Traveling Library, a green truck that arrived once a week, would linger, sipping and gossiping on the high-backed fountain chairs, or else at the little glass-topped tables nearby, with their small three-cornered seats. Everything was fashioned of the same burnished chocolate-colored wood; but the fountain counters were heavy marble. Above the prescription area, sovereign over all, rose a symbolic pair of pharmacy globes, one filled with red fluid, the other with blue. My father's diploma, class of 1917, was mounted on a wall; next to it hung a picture of the graduates. There was my very young father, with his round pale eyes and widow's peak—a fleck in a mass of black gowns.

Some time around 1937, my mother said to my father, "Willie, if we don't do it now, we'll never do it."

It was the trough of the Great Depression. In the comics, Pete the Tramp was swiping freshly baked pies set out to cool on windowsills; and in real life, tramps (as the homeless were then called) were turning up in the Park View nearly every day. Sometimes they were city drunks—"Bowery bums"—who had fallen asleep on the subway downtown and had ended up in Pelham Bay. Sometimes they were exhausted Midwesterners who had been riding the rails, and had rolled off into the obscuring cattails of the Baychester marsh. But always my father sat them down at the fountain and fed them a sandwich and soup. They smelled bad, these penniless tramps, and their eyes were red and rheumy; often they were very polite. They never left without a meal and a nickel for carfare.

No one was worse off than the tramps, or more desolate than the family who lived in an old freight car on the way to Westchester Square; but no one escaped the Depression. It stalked the country, it stalked Pelham Bay, it stalked the Park View. Drugstore hours were famously long—monstrously long: seven days a week the Park View opened at nine a.m. and closed at two the next morning. My mother scurried from counter to counter, tended the fountain, unpacked cartons, climbed ladders; her varicose veins oozed through their strappings. My father patiently ground powders, and folded the white dust into translucent paper squares with elegantly efficient motions. The drug store was, besides, a public resource: my father bandaged cuts, took specks out of strangers' eyes, and once removed a fishhook from a man's cheek—though he sent him off to the hospital, on the other side of the Bronx, immediately afterward. My quiet father had cronies and clients, grim women and voluble men who flooded his understanding ears with the stories of their

sufferings, of flesh or psyche. My father murmured and comforted, and later my parents would whisper sadly about who had
"the big C," or, with an ominous gleam, they would smile over a
geezer certain to have a heart attack: the geezer would be newly
married to a sweet young thing. (And usually they were right
about the heart attack.)

Yet no matter how hard they toiled, they were always in peril.
There were notes to pay off; they had bought the Park View
from a pharmacist named Robbins, and every month, relent-
lessly, a note came due. They never fell behind, and never missed
a payment (and, in fact, were eventually awarded a certificate
attesting to this feat); but the effort—the unremitting pressure,
the endless anxiety—ground them down. "The note, the note," I
would hear, a refrain that shadowed my childhood, though I had
no notion of what it meant.

What it meant was that the Depression, which had already
crushed so many, was about to crush my mother and father:
suddenly their troubles intensified. The Park View was housed
in a building owned by a catlike woman my parents habitually
referred to, whether out of familiarity or resentment, only as
Tessie. The pharmacy's lease was soon to expire, and at this
moment, in the cruelest hour of the Depression, Tessie chose to
raise the rent. Her tiger's eyes narrowed to slits: no appeal could
soften her.

It was because of those adamant tiger's eyes that my mother
said, "Willie, if we don't do it now, we'll never do it."

My mother was aflame with ambition, emotion, struggle. My
father was reticent, and far more resigned to the world as given.
Once, when the days of the Traveling Library were over, and a
real library had been constructed at Westchester Square—you
reached it by trolley—I came home elated, carrying a pair of
books I had found side by side. One was called *My Mother Is a*

Violent Woman; the other was *My Father Is a Timid Man.* These seemed a comic revelation of my parents' temperaments. My mother was all heat and enthusiasm. My father was all logic and reserve. My mother, unrestrained, could have run an empire of drug stores. My father was satisfied with one.

Together they decided to do something revolutionary; something virtually impossible in those raw and merciless times. One street over—past McCardle's sun-baked gas station, where there was always a Model-T Ford with its hood open for repair, and past the gloomy bait store, ruled over by Mr. Isaacs, a dour and reclusive veteran of the Spanish-American War who sat reading military histories all day under a mastless sailboat suspended from the ceiling—lay an empty lot in the shape of an elongated lozenge. My parents' daring plan—for young people without means it was beyond daring—was to buy that lot and build on it, from scratch, a brand-new Park View Pharmacy.

They might as well have been dreaming of taking off in Buck Rogers' twenty-fifth-century rocket ship. The cost of the lot was a stratospheric $13,500, unchanged from the Boom of 1928, just before the national wretchedness descended; and that figure was only for the land. After that would come the digging of a foundation and the construction of a building. What was needed was a miracle.

One sad winter afternoon my mother was standing on a ladder, concentrating on setting out some newly arrived drug items on a high shelf. (Although a typical drug store stocked several thousand articles, the Park View's unit-by-unit inventory was never ample. At the end of every week I would hear my father's melodious, impecunious chant on the telephone, ordering goods from the jobber: "A sixth of a dozen, a twelfth of a dozen . . .") A stranger wearing a brown fedora and a long overcoat entered, looked around, and appeared not at all interested in making a purchase; instead he went wandering from case to case, picking things up and putting them down again, trying to be inconspicuous, asking an occasional question or two, all the while scrupulously observing my diligent and tireless parents. The stranger turned out to be a mortgage officer from the American Bible Society, and what he saw, he explained afterward, was a conscientious application of the work ethic; so it was the American Bible Society that supplied the financial foundation of my parents' Eden, the new Park View. They had entertained an angel unawares.

The actual foundation, the one to be dug out of the ground, ran into instant trouble. An unemployed civil engineer named Levinson presided over the excavation; he was unemployed partly because the Depression had dried up much of the job market, but mostly because engineering firms in those years were notorious for their unwillingness to hire Jews. Poor Levinson! The vast hole in the earth that was to become the Park View's cellar filled up overnight with water; the bay was near, and the water table was higher than the hapless Levinson had expected. The work halted. Along came Finnegan and rescued Levinson: Finnegan the plumber, who for a painful fee of fifty dollars (somehow squeezed out of Levinson's mainly empty pockets) pumped out the flood.

After the Park View's exultant move in 1939, the shell of Tessie's old place on Colonial Avenue remained vacant for years. No one took it over; the plate-glass windows grew murkier and murkier. Dead moths were heaped in decaying mounds on the inner sills. Tessie had lost more than the heartless increase she had demanded, and more than the monthly rent the renewed lease would have brought: there was something ignominious and luckless—tramplike—about that fly-specked empty space, now dimmer than ever. But within its freshly risen walls, the Park View Redux gleamed. Overhead, fluorescent tubes—an indoor innovation—shed a steady white glow, and a big square skylight poured down shifting shafts of brilliance. Familiar objects appeared clarified in the new light: the chocolate-colored fixtures, arranged in unaccustomed configurations, were all at once thrillingly revivified. Nothing from the original Park View had been left behind—everything was just the same, yet zanily out of order: the two crystal urns with their magical red and blue fluids suggestive of alchemy; the entire stock of syrups, pills, tablets, powders, pastes, capsules; tubes and bottles by the hundreds; all the contents of all the drawers and cases; the fountain with its marble top; the prescription desk and its sacrosanct ledger; the stacks of invaluable cigar boxes stuffed with masses of expired prescriptions; the locked and well-guarded narcotics cabinet; the post office, and the safe in which the post office receipts were kept. Even the great, weighty, monosyllabically blunt hanging sign—"DRUGS"—had been brought over and rehung, and it too looked different now. In the summer heat it dropped its black rectangular shadow over Mr. Isaacs' already shadowy headquarters, where vials of live worms were crowded side by side with vials of nails and screws.

At around this time my mother's youngest brother, my uncle Rubin, had come to stay with us—no one knew for how long—in our little house on Saint Paul Avenue, a short walk from the Park View. Five of us lived in that house: my parents, my grandmother, my brother and I. Rubin, who was called Ruby, was now the sixth. He was a bachelor and something of a family enigma. He was both bitter and cheerful; effervescence would give way to lassitude. He taught me how to draw babies and bunnies, and could draw anything himself; he wrote ingenious comic jingles, which he illustrated as adroitly, it struck me, as Edward Lear; he cooked up mouth-watering corn fritters, and designed fruit salads in the shape of ravishing unearthly blossoms. When now and then it fell to him to put me to bed, he always sang the same heartbreaking lullaby: "Sometimes I fee-eel like a motherless child, a long, long way-ay from ho-ome," in a deep and sweet quaver. In those days he was mostly jobless; on occasion he would crank up his Tin Lizzie and drive out to upper Westchester to prune trees. Once he was stopped at a police roadblock, under suspicion of being the Lindbergh baby kidnapper—the back seat of his messy old Ford was strewn with ropes, hooks, and my discarded baby bottles.

Ruby had been disappointed in love, and was somehow a disappointment to everyone around him. When he was melancholy or resentful, the melancholy was irritable and the resentment acrid. As a very young man he had been single-minded in a way none of his immigrant relations, or the snobbish mother of the girlfriend who had been coerced into jilting him, could understand or sympathize with. In Czarist Russia's restricted Pale of Settlement, a pharmacist was the highest vocation a Jew could attain to. In a family of pharmacists, Ruby wanted to be a farmer. Against opposition, he had gone off to the National Farm School in New Jersey—one of several Jewish agricultural projects sponsored by the German philanthropist Baron Maurice de Hirsch. Ruby was always dreaming up one sort of horticultural improvement or another, and sometimes took me with him to visit a certain Dr. McClain, at the Bronx Botanical Gardens, whom he was trying to interest in one of his inventions. He was kindly received, but nothing came of it. Despite his energy and originality, all of Ruby's hopes and strivings collapsed in futility.

All the same, he left an enduring mark on the Park View. It was a certain circle of stones—a mark more distinctive than his deserted bachelor's headstone in an overgrown cemetery on Staten Island.

Ruby assisted in the move from Tessie's place to the new location. His presence was fortuitous—but his ingenuity, it would soon develop, was benison from the goddess Flora. The Park View occupied all the width but not the entire depth of the lot on which it was built. It had, of course, a welcoming front door, through which customers passed; but there was also a back door, past a little aisle adjoining the prescription room in the rear of the store, and well out of sight. When you walked out this back door, you were confronted by an untamed patch of weeds and stones, some of them as thick as boulders. At the very end of it lay a large flat rock, in the center of which someone had scratched a mysterious X. The X, it turned out, was a surveyor's mark; it had been there long before my parents bought the lot. It meant that the property extended to that X and no farther.

I was no stranger either to the lot or its big rock. It was where the neighborhood children played—a sparse group in that sparsely populated place. Sometimes the rock was a pirate ship; sometimes it was a pretty room in a pretty house; in January it held a snow fort. But early one summer evening, when the red ball of the sun was very low, a little girl named Theresa, whose hair was as red as the sun's red ball, discovered the surveyor's X and warned me against stamping on it. If you stamp on a cross, she said, the devil's helpers climb right out from inside the earth and grab you and take you away to be tortured. "I don't believe that," I said, and stamped on the X as hard as I could. Instantly Theresa sent out a terrified shriek; chased by the red-gold zigzag of her hair, she fled. I stood there abandoned—suppose it was true? In the silence all around, the wavering green weeds seemed taller than ever before.

Looking out from the back door at those same high weeds stretching from the new red brick of the Park View's rear wall all the way to the flat rock and its X, my mother, like Theresa, saw hallucinatory shapes rising out of the ground. But it was not the devil's minions she imagined streaming upward; it was their very opposite—a vision of celestial growths and fragrances, brilliant botanical hues, golden pears and yellow sunflower-faces, fruitful vines and dreaming gourds. She imagined an enchanted garden. She imagined a secret Eden.

Ruby was angry at my mother; he was angry at everyone but me: I was too young to be held responsible for his lost loves and aspirations. But he could not be separated from his love of fecund dirt. Dirt—the brown dirt of the earth—inspired him; the feel and smell of dirt uplifted him; he took an artist's pleasure in the soil and all its generative properties. And though he claimed to scorn my mother, he became the subaltern of her passion. Like some wizard commander of the stones—they were scattered everywhere in a wild jumble—he swept them into orderliness. A pack of stones was marshaled into a low wall. Five stones were transformed into a perfect set of stairs. Seven stones surrounded what was to become a flower bed. Stones were borders, stones were pathways, stones—placed just so—were natural sculptures.

And finally Ruby commanded the stones to settle in a circle in the very center of the lot. Inside the circle there was to be a green serenity of grass, invaded only by the blunders of violets and wandering buttercups. Outside the circle the earth would be a fructifying engine. It was a dreamer's circle, like the moon or the sun; or a fairy ring; or a mystical small Stonehenge, miniaturized by a spell.

The back yard was cleared, but it was not yet a garden. Like a merman combing a mermaid's weedy hair, my uncle Ruby had unraveled primeval tangles and brambles. He had set up two tall metal poles to accommodate a rough canvas hammock, with a wire strung from the top of one pole to the other. Over this wire a rain-faded old shop-awning had been flung, so that the hammock became a tent or cave or darkened den. A backyard hammock! I had encountered such things only in storybooks.

And then my uncle was gone. German tanks were biting into Europe. Weeping, my grandmother pounded her breast with her fist: the British White Paper of 1939 had declared that ships packed with Jewish refugees would be barred from the beaches of Haifa and Tel Aviv and returned to a Nazi doom. In P.S. 71, our neighborhood school, the boys were drawing cannons and warplanes; the girls were drawing figure skaters in tutus; both boys and girls were drawing the Trylon and the Perisphere. The Trylon was a three-sided obelisk. The Perisphere was a shining globe. They were already as sublimely legendary as the Taj Mahal. The official colors of the 1939 World's Fair were orange and blue—everyone knew this; everyone had ridden in noise-lessly moving armchairs into the Fair's World of Tomorrow, where the cloverleaf highways of the impossibly futuristic nineteen-sixties materialized among inconceivable suburbs. In the magical lanes of Flushing you could watch yourself grin on a television screen as round and small as the mouth of a teacup. My grandmother, in that frail year of her dying, was taken to see the Palestine Pavilion, with its flickering films of Jewish pioneers.

Ruby was drafted before the garden could be dug. He sent a photograph of himself in Army uniform, and a muffled record-ing of his voice, all songs and jolly jingles, from a honky-tonk arcade in an unnamed Caribbean town.

So it was left to my mother to dig the garden. I have no inkling of when or how. I lived inside the hammock all that time, under the awning, enclosed; I read and read. Sometimes, for a treat, I would be given two nickels for carfare and a pair of quar-ters, and then I would climb the double staircase to the train and go all the way to Fifty-ninth Street: you could enter Blooming-dale's directly from the subway, without ever glimpsing day-light. I would run up the steps to the book department on the mezzanine, moon over the Nancy Drew series in an agony of choosing (*The Mystery of Larkspur Lane, The Mystery of the Whispering Statue,* each for fifty cents), and run down to the subway again, with my lucky treasure. An hour and a half later, I would be back in the hammock, under the awning, while the afternoon sun broiled on. But such a trip was rare. Mostly the books came from the Traveling Library; inside my hammock-cave the melting glue of new bindings sent out a blissful redolence. And now my mother would emerge from the back door of the Park View, carrying—because it was so hot under the awning—half a cantaloupe, with a hillock of vanilla ice cream in its scooped-out center. (Have I ever been so safe, so happy, since? Has consciousness ever felt so steady, so unimperiled, so immortal?)

Across the ocean, synagogues were being torched, refugees were in flight. On American movie screens Ginger Rogers and Fred Astaire whirled in and out of the March of Time's grim newsreels—Chamberlain with his defeatist umbrella, the Sudetenland devoured, Poland invaded. Meanwhile my mother's garden grew. The wild raw field Ruby had regimented was ripening now into a luxuriant and powerful fertility: all around my uncle's talismanic ring of stones the ground swelled with thick savory smells. Corn tassels hung down over the shut greenleaf lids of pearly young cobs. Fat tomatoes reddened on sticks. The bumpy scalps of cucumbers poked up. And flowers! First, as tall as the hammock poles, a flock of hunchbacked sunflowers, their heads too weighty for their shoulders—huge heavy heads of seeds, and a ruff of yellow petals. At their feet, rows of zinnias and marigolds, with tiny violets and the weedy pink buds of clover sidling between.

Now and then a praying mantis—a stiffly marching fake leaf—would rub its skinny forelegs together and stare at you with two stern black dots. And butterflies! These were mostly white and mothlike; but sometimes a great black-veined monarch would alight on a stone, in perfect stillness. Year by year the shade of a trio of pear trees widened and deepened.

Did it rain? It must have rained—it must have thundered—in those successive summers of my mother's garden; but I remember a perpetual sunlight, hot and honeyed, and the airless boil under the awning, and the heart-piercing scalliony odor of library glue (so explicit that I can this minute re-create it in my very tear ducts, as a kind of mourning); and the fear of bees.

Though I was mostly alone there, I was never lonely in the garden. But on the other side of the door, inside the Park View, an unfamiliar churning had begun—a raucous teeming, the world turning on its hinge. In the aftermath of Pearl Harbor, there were all at once jobs for nearly everyone, and money to spend in any cranny of wartime leisure. The Depression was receding. On weekends the subway spilled out mobs of city picnickers into the green fields of Pelham Bay Park, bringing a tentative prosperity to the neighborhood—especially on Sundays. I dreaded and hated this new Sunday frenzy, when the Park View seemed less a pharmacy than a carnival stand, and my own isolation grew bleak. Open shelves sprouted in the aisles, laden with anomalous racks of sunglasses, ice coolers, tubes of mosquito repellent and suntan lotion, paper cups, colorful towers of hats—sailors' and fishermen's caps, celluloid visors, straw topis and sombreros, headgear of every conceivable shape. Thirsty picnickers stood three deep at the fountain, clamoring for ice-cream cones or sodas. The low, serious drug-store voices that accompanied the Park View's weekday decorum were swept away by revolving laughing crowds—carnival crowds. And at the close of these frenetic summer Sundays, my parents would anxiously count up the cash register in the worn night of their exhaustion, and I would hear their joyful disbelief: unimaginable riches, almost seventy-five dollars in a single day!

Then, when the safe was locked up, and the long cords of the fluorescent lights pulled, they would drift in the dimness into the garden, to breathe the cool fragrance. At this starry hour the katydids were screaming in chorus, and fireflies bleeped like errant semaphores. In the enigmatic dark, my mother and father, with their heads together in silhouette, looked just then as I pictured them looking on the Albany night boat, on June 19, 1921, their wedding day. There was a serial photo from that long-ago time I often gazed at—a strip taken in an automatic-photo booth in fabled, faraway Albany. It showed them leaning close, my young father quizzical, my young mother trying to smile, or else trying not to; the corners of her lips wandered toward one loveliness or the other. They had brought back a honeymoon souvenir: three sandstone monkeys joined at the elbows: see no evil, hear no evil, speak no evil. And now, in their struggling forties, standing in Ruby's circle of stones, they breathed in the night smells of the garden, onion grass and honeysuckle, and felt their private triumph. Seventy-five dollars in eighteen hours!

No one knew the garden was there. It was utterly hidden. You could not see it, or suspect it, inside the Park View, and because it was nested in a wilderness of empty lots all around, it was altogether invisible from any surrounding street. It was a small secluded paradise.

And what vegetable chargings, what ferocities of growth, the turbulent earth pushed out! Buzzings and dapplings. Birds dipping their beaks in an orgy of seed-lust. It was as if the ground itself were crying peace, peace; and the war began. In Europe the German death factories were pumping out smoke and human ash from a poisoned orchard of chimneys. In Pelham Bay, among bees and white-wing flutterings, the sweet brown dirt pumped ears of corn.

Nearly all the drug stores—of the old kind—are gone, in Pelham Bay and elsewhere. The Park View Pharmacy lives only in a secret Eden behind my eyes. Gone are Bernardini, Pressman, Weiss, the rival druggists on the way to Westchester Square. They all, like my father, rolled suppositories on glass slabs and ground powders with brass pestles. My mother's garden has returned to its beginning: a wild patch, though enclosed now by brick house after brick house. The houses have high stoops; they are city houses. The meadows are striped with highways. Spy Oak gave up its many ghosts long ago.

But under a matting of decayed pear pits and thriving ragweed back of what used to be the Park View, Ruby's circle of stones stands frozen. The earth, I suppose, has covered them over, as—far off in Staten Island—it covers my dreaming mother, my father, my grandmother, my resourceful and embittered farmer uncle.

Lovesickness

1

Once, when I had already been married for a time, I went to a friend's wedding and fell in love with the bridegroom. It happened out of the blue, in an instant, as unexpectedly as a sneeze. I was not responsible for it; it came upon me; it was an incursion, an invasion—a possession, like that of a dybbuk. Or it was what diplomats call an "intervention," an intact sovereign tract subjected without warning to military fire. Or it was a kind of spell, the way the unearthly music of a fairy-tale pipe casts a helpless enchantment, so that, willy-nilly, you are compelled to dance and dance without surcease.

The bride had a small head and a Cheshire-cat smile. I had known her since childhood. Together, under the heavy-hanging trees, we had gathered acorns and pretended to dine on them. But we were not confidantes; we were not close. We had differing temperaments. She was humorous: her jokiness cut with an icy ironic blade. I was naïve and grave and obtuse. She was diligent at the violin and played it well. I hid when the piano teacher rang the doorbell. She was acutely and cleverly mathematical. I was an arithmetical imbecile. She was tall and I was short: we were seriously divided by our arms' reach. Often I felt between us a jealous tremor. I was jealous because she was almost two years younger, and even in girlhood I lamented the passing of my prime. At eleven, I scribbled a story and appended a lie: "By the Young Author," I wrote, "Age Nine."

The bride was standing under the wedding canopy in a white dress, her acorn head ringed by a wreath, when lovesickness struck. The venerable image of arrow or dart is crucially exact. Though I had met the bridegroom once before, in the long green darkening tangle of a meadow at dusk—it was a game of Frisbee—I had been unmoved. His thighs were taut, his calf-sinews thick; he had the inky curly hair of a runner on a Greek amphora. The white plastic disk arced into a blackening sky, along the trajectory of an invisible yet perfect night-rainbow. He sprinted after it; his catch was deft, like the pluck of a lyre. He was an Englishman. He was a mathematician. He was nothing to me.

But when I saw him under the wedding canopy next to my childhood friend, I was seized and shaken by a dazing infatuation so stormy, so sibylline, so like a divination, that I went away afterward hollowed-out. Infatuation was not an added condition: it was loss—the strangeness of having lost what had never been mine.

The newly married pair departed for England, by sea, in a sluggishly churning vessel. A shipboard postcard arrived: on the one side a view of the ship itself, all serene white flanks pocked by portholes, and on the other an unfamiliar script. It was the new husband's. I studied his handwriting—examined its loops and troughs, the blue turns of ink where they thickened and narrowed, the height of the l's and d's, the width of the crossbars, the hillocks of the m's and n's, the connecting tails and the interrupting gaps. The sentences themselves were sturdy and friendly, funny and offhand—entirely by-the-by. Clearly, composing this note was a lunch-table diversion. "You do it," I imagined the new wife telling the new husband. In a minute and a half it was done.

For weeks I kept the card under my eye; it was as if the letters of each word were burning, as if the air above and below the letters were shuddering in an invisible fire. The words, the sentences, were of no moment; I hardly saw them; but the letters crazed me. They were the new husband's nerves, they were the vibrations of his pulse, his fingers' pressure, his most intimate mark. They were more powerful than the imprint of his face and shoulders, which had anyhow begun to fade. What I remembered was the hand leaping up into the dark to snatch the Frisbee out of the sky. That same hand had shaped these intoxicating yet regimented letters. A mathematician's letters: as upright and precise as numbers.

Infatuation has its own precision. It focuses on its object as directly and sharply as sunlight through a magnifying glass: it enlarges and clarifies, but it also scorches. What we call love-sickness, or desire, is deliberate in that way—the way of exactitude and scrupulous discrimination—and at the same time it is wildly undeliberate, zigzag, unpremeditated, driven, even loony.

What I finally did with—or *to*—that postcard was both meticulously focused and rapaciously mad.

It was the hand that my desire had fixed on—or, rather, the force and the brain that flowed from that hand. I wanted to get *into* that hand—to become it, to grow myself into its blood vessels, to steal its fire. I had already felt the boil of that fire under my own hand: the phosphorescent threads of the letters, as blue as veins, bled hotly into the paper's grain.

And I knew what I would do. I took my pencil and slowly, slowly traced over the letters of the first word. Slowly, slowly. The sensation was that of a novice dancer mimicking the movements of a ballet master; or of a mute mouth speaking through a ventriloquist; or of a shadow following a light; or of a mountain climber ascending the upward slope of a *t*, stopping to rest on the horizontal shelf of the crossbar, again toiling upward, turning, again resting on a ledge, and then sliding downward along a sheerly vertical wall.

Letter by letter, day by day, I pressed the point of my pencil into the fleshly lines of the sea-borne bridegroom's pen; I jumped my pencil over his jumps and skips, those minute blank sites of his pen's apnea.

In a week or so it was finished. I had coupled with him. Every word was laboriously Siamese-twinned. Each of the letters bore on its back the graphite coat I had slowly, slowly laid over it. Breath by breath, muscle by muscle, nerve by nerve, with the concentration of a monkish scribe, with the dedication of a Torah scribe, I had trod in his tracks and made his marks. Like a hunter, I had pursued his marks; I had trapped and caged them. I was his fanatical, indelible Doppelgänger. And a forger besides.

2.

All this was done in secret: lovesickness is most often silent, private, concealed. But sometimes it is wily and reckless, thrusting itself into the world like a novelist on the loose. To wit: I once observed an illustrious young professor of philosophy swinging a small boy between his knees. The child was rapturous; the man went on teasing and swinging. He had a merry, thin, mobile face—not at all professorial. And yet his reputation was dauntingly fierce: he was an original; his famous Mind crackled around him like an electric current, or like a charged whip fending off mortals less dazzlingly endowed. It was said that his intellectual innovations and uncommon insights had so isolated him from ordinary human pursuits, and his wants were so sparse, that he slept on a couch in his mother's apartment in an outer borough. And here he was, laughing and swinging— himself a boy at play.

The blow of lovesickness came hammering down. I had no connection of any kind with this wizard of thought. It was unlikely that I could ever aspire to one.

But I had just then been reading Peter Quennell's biography of Lord Byron, and was captivated by its portrait of Lady Caroline Lamb, a married flirt who had seduced and conquered Byron (or vice-versa—both were mercurial and inclined toward escapades). Quennell described Lady Caroline as a volatile woman in search of "some violent, self-justificatory explosion, some crisis in which she could gather up the spasmodic and ill-directed energies that drove her. . . . The fever of Romanticism was in her blood." She delighted in spats and subterfuges and secret letters delivered to her lover by a page, who turned out to be Lady Caroline in disguise. It was she who invented Byron's most celebrated epithet—*mad, bad, and dangerous to know.* This would do admirably for Lady Caroline.

Certainly Byron found her dangerous to know. When, exasperated, he tired of her, he discovered she was impossible to get rid of. He called her "a little volcano," and complained that her fascination was "unfortunately coupled with a total want of common conduct." In the end she became a pest, an affliction, a plague. In vindictive verses he pronounced her a fiend. She was a creature of ruse and caprice and jealousy; she would not let him go. She chased after him indefatigably, she badgered him, she burned him in effigy, she stabbed herself. And she wrote him letters.

The fever of Romanticism was in my blood; I had been maddened by a hero of imagination, a man who could unravel the skeins of logic that braid human cognition. Byron had his clubfoot; my philosopher was still spending his nights on his mother's couch. Byron spoke of his pursuer as a volcano; I could at least leak quantities of epistolary lava. And so, magnetized and wanting to mystify, I put on a disguise and began my chase: I wrote letters. They were love letters; they were letters of enthrallment, of lovesickness. I addressed them to the philosopher's university and signed them all, in passionately counterfeit handwriting, "Lady Caroline Lamb."

3.

But what of lovesickness in reverse? The arrow not suffered but inadvertently shot? The wound not taken but blindly caused?

The Second World War was just over; the college cafeteria swarmed with professed Communists, grim veterans on the G.I. Bill, girls flaunting Edwardian skirts down to their ankles in the New Look style, and a squat square mustached fellow who, when anyone inquired after his politics, insisted he was a monarchist working for the restoration of his dynasty. There was, in addition, an aristocratic and very young Turkish boy, a prodigy, whose father was attached to the United Nations and whose mother wore the veil. The Turkish boy and I studied Latin together, and sometimes spoke of *amor intellectualis*—but intellectual love rooted in a common admiration of Catullus's ode to kissing was too heated, or not heated enough. In the cafeteria I was often ambushed by spasms of bewitchment—over a green-eyed sophomore, for instance, with a radio-announcer voice, who was himself in love with a harpist called Angel. I waited for him at the foot of a certain staircase, hoping he might come down it. I cultivated one of his classmates in the expectation that I might learn something intimate about my distant love, and I did: his nickname, I was told, was Beanhead. "Beanhead, Beanhead," I would murmur at the bottom of the stairs. All my loves at that time were dreamlike, remote, inconclusive, evanescent.

But one afternoon in winter, a foreign-seeming young man (I had noticed him in the cafeteria, curled over a notebook) followed me home. What made him appear foreign was his intensity, his strict stride, his unembarrassed persistence; and also the earnest luster of his dangling black bangs, which shielded his eyes like a latticed gate, and freed him to gaze without moderation. Following me home was no easy journey—it was a long, long subway ride to the end of the line. Despite that curtained look, I saw in his face an urgency I knew in myself. Unaccountably, I had become his Beanhead, his Byron, his bridegroom. I pleaded with him not to undertake the trek to the northeast Bronx—what, I privately despaired, would I *do* with him?

He filled an underground hour by explaining himself: he was a Persian in command of the history and poetry of his beautiful country, and with my permission, because at this moment he was unluckily without a nosegay (he was prone to words like nosegay, garland, attar), he would offer me instead a beautiful poem in Arabic. He drew out his notebook and a pen: from its nib flowed a magical calligraphy.

"This is my poem, my original own," he said, "for you," and folded the sheet and slipped it into my copy of Emily Dickinson, exactly at the page where I had underlined "There's a certain Slant of light / On winter afternoons."

"You don't really want to ride all this distance," I said, hoping to shake him off. "Suppose you just get out at the East 86th Street express stop and go right back, all right?"

"Ah," he said, "will the moon abandon the sun?"

But the third time he demanded to come home with me, it was the sun who abandoned the moon. I had had enough of lovelorn importuning. He accepted his dismissal with Persian melancholy, pressing on me yet another poem, his original own, that he had set down in those melodious, undulating Scheherazadean characters. At the entrance to the subway, forbidden to go farther, he declaimed his translation: "There is a garden, a wall, a brook. You are the lily, I am the brook. O wall, permit me to refresh the lily!"

No one is crueler than the conscious object of infatuation: I blew back the black veil of hair, looked into a pair of moonstruck black eyes, and laughed. Meanly, heartlessly.

4.

And once I made a suitor cry. He was, I feared, a genuine suitor. By now the war had long been over, and nearly all the former G.I.s had gladly returned to civilian life. My suitor, though, was still in uniform; he was stationed at an army base on an island in the harbor. He had a tidy blond head on which his little soldier's cap rested; he had little blunt fingers; everything about him was miniature, like a toy soldier. He was elfin, but without elfishness: he was sober, contained, and as neutral as khaki. He put me in mind of a drawing in a children's coloring book: those round clear pale eyes anticipating blueness, that firm outline beyond which no crayon would ever stray. He had a kind of blankness waiting to be filled in. On weekends, when he was free, he came to call with a phonograph record under his arm. We sat side by side, sternly taking in the music. We were two sets of blank outlines. The music was coloring us in.

One Sunday he brought Richard Strauss's *Death and Transfiguration*. The jacket supplied the title in German, *Tod und Verklärung*, and a description—tone poem. But it was "transfiguration" that held me. Transfiguration! Would the toy soldier be transformed into live human flesh and begin to move and think on his own?

When he returned to his island, I put *Death and Transfiguration* on the record player and, alone, listened to it over and over again. It colored the empty air, but I saw there would be no transfiguration. Stasis was the toy soldier's lot.

The next Sunday, I piled all the records that had been his gifts into his arms. "At least keep this one. You liked it," he said dolefully: it was *Tod und Verklärung*. But I dropped it on top of the farewell pile and watched him weep, my marble heart immune to any arrow.

5.

Not long afterward, a young man whose eyes were not green, who inspired nothing eccentric or adventurous, who never gave a thought to brooks and lilies or death and transfiguration, who never sought to untangle the knots in the history of human thought, began, with awful consistency, to bring presents of marzipan. So much marzipan was making me sick—though not lovesick.

Ultimately the philosopher learned the true identity of the writer of those love letters; it was reported that he laughed. He is, I believe, still sleeping on his mother's couch.

I never saw the bridegroom again. He never sent another postcard. I suppose he is an unattractive old man by now. Or anyhow I hope so.

The marzipan provider? Reader, I married him.

How I Got Fired from
My Summer Job

The summer after graduate school, when I was twenty-two years old, I wanted to get a job. I had just come back from Ohio State University in Columbus, Ohio, at that time a hotbed of the New Criticism, where I had completed a fat M.A. thesis on the later novels of Henry James. In those distant days, an M.A. was like a mini-Ph.D.; I had even had to endure a grilling by a committee of three professors. It was important not to go after a Ph.D., though, because it meant you were not in earnest about becoming a writer; it was, in fact, an embarrassment, a cowardly expedient that could shame you. The models for the young of my generation, after all, Hemingway and Faulkner and Willa Cather, had rushed straight into life. Yet when the chairman of the English Department summoned me into his office, I was certain that he was going to urge me to continue. To forestall him, I instantly offered my confession: I was not planning to stick around for a higher degree. I expected him to say, "But you did so nicely with Henry James, so you *must* stay." Instead he said, "Well, right, you should go home and get married." I was hurt; I didn't want to marry anyone; what I really wanted was to write a metaphysical novel.

But first I wanted a summer job.

Even though I was not serious about a Ph.D., I was very serious about the New Criticism. Its chief tenet was that you could pry meaning out of any sort of mysterious parlance, especially if Ezra Pound had written it. Ezra Pound and T. S. Eliot were the New Criticism's archbishops (and faith and mystery were what kept it going), but *A Theory of Literature,* by René Wellek and Austin Warren—"Wellek-and-Warren" for short—was its Bible. Piously, I carried Wellek-and-Warren with me everywhere, and it was on my desk the very first day of my summer job. I had answered an ad by Margate, Haroulian, a firm of accountants. What had attracted me was its location: a short walk from Bryant Park, the green rectangle behind the Forty-second Street Library. I plotted lunch hours on a bench under a hot and dreamy city sun, eating a sandwich out of a paper bag and inhaling the philosophical fragrance of Wellek-and-Warren.

The man who interviewed me was neither Mr. Margate nor Mr. Haroulian. He introduced himself as George Berkeley, Mr. Haroulian's second-in-command. Disciplined blond wisps were threaded across his reddish scalp, and his mouth made a humorless line. He was dry and precise and acutely courteous. Though I had no previous office experience, he seemed pleased with my credentials.

"So you've got a Master's," he said. "What in?"

"English," I said.

"That's fine. That's all right," he said, and asked if I could type. I said I could, and he explained what the work would require. I was to copy lists of numbers onto different printed forms, with three sets of carbons. He showed me my desk and the forms, each with its vertical rows of small oblong boxes. He opened a drawer filled with carbon paper and staples. "That's all you'll need," he said.

"But your *name,*" I marveled. "It's so thrilling to have a name like that!"

"I don't see anything special about my name."

"George Berkeley—Bishop Berkeley, the eighteenth-century idealist! He said no existence is conceivable that isn't conscious spirit. He believed in Universal Mind. He's the one that infuriated Samuel Johnson so much that Dr. Johnson kicked a stone and said 'I refute it *thus*.' "

"I don't think we're related," George Berkeley said, and disappeared into an inner office. It was Mr. Haroulian's office. I never saw Mr. Margate, who seemed to have no office.

I put my sandwich into the drawer with the carbons and arranged my desk. First I placed Wellek-and-Warren next to the typewriter, so as to remind me of the nature of my soul. Then I plucked up three sheets of carbon paper and three sheets of blank paper, and stacked them behind one of the forms, and got ready to begin. I had a page of numbers to copy from—clusters of numbers: some had six digits, some four, some ten, and each set of digits had to be typed into an oblong box. It was hard to keep track, and I discovered in alarm that I had typed the same group of digits twice. I found a typewriter eraser (a stiff round thing, with a miniature whiskbroom at one end) and tried to erase the mistake on the form, but the eraser scraped the paper and almost tore it through; it made an unsightly translucent lozenge. Worse, I had forgotten about the carbons underneath. When I inspected them, they were hopelessly smudged. There was nothing to do but toss the whole mess into the trash and start over.

I started over many times.

"How're you doing?" George Berkeley asked, passing by.

"I'm afraid I've wasted some forms."

"Not to worry, you'll get the hang of it," he said. "The girl you're replacing didn't have a Master's, believe me."

At lunchtime I walked to Bryant Park with my sandwich, and rapturously mooned through the densities of Wellek-and-Warren. Summer in the city! Pigeons preened in the grass;

young women in white sandals and light skirts sauntered by; the shoulders of the great Library baked serenely in the heat; an ice-cream wagon floated out its jolly carillon.

But by the end of that first day—it was Monday—I still had not managed to type the right numbers into the right boxes on a single form.

"Now I don't want you to get discouraged," George Berkeley said. "All this is routine stuff, and I know you've been dealing with things a whole lot more complicated than a bunch of fig-ures. I notice you're doing some studying on the side, and that's what I call desirable. I've been waiting a long while to get hold of someone like you, a smart girl who thinks about more than the color of her nail polish. It struck me right away that you don't *wear* any nail polish, and that's why I hired you—that and the fact that you lug that book around and keep up with your study-ing. I expect you to get somewhere with this firm. I give myself credit for being a pretty fair judge of people. I can spot someone who's going to go far with us. Potential," he said, "that's what I'm interested in."

He dragged a chair over from a nearby desk, and settled him-self just opposite me; he was all earnestness. We were sitting almost knee to knee, with his big milky face so close to mine that I could see the pores, large and clean, in the wings of his nostrils. Healed pockmarks ran up the sides of his cheeks. He looked scrubbed and tidy, and it came to me that he might be the kind of man who went to bed under a framed slogan, like those I had seen in landladies' rooming houses in Columbus: BLESS THIS HOME, or GOD LOVES ME, or the pure-hearted TRUTH MAY BE BLAMED, BUT CANNOT BE SHAMED. The truth was that just then, in the middle of a peroration intended for my improvement, I was feeling considerably shamed. I had been taken into Margate, Haroulian under false colors; I had commit-ted a lie of omission. George Berkeley, himself in a position of

permanent allegiance to Margate, Haroulian, assumed I was
what he termed "entry-level," a young person in pursuit of
advancement in business. I did not disabuse him.

"Now let me tell you something about all these lists of figures," he went on. "They may not seem very glamorous, but
they are our lifeline. They are the lifeline of our country. A
really intelligent person can see right through to what these lists
of figures actually stand for, and just as soon as you get the gist
of all that, I have every confidence you'll be as impressed as I am
with how figures like ours keep this country safe and strong.
Some people may think that keeping the books the way we do it
around here is the exact opposite of the sort of charge a person
like you gets out of . . . well, let's say poetry, a poem like 'The
Midnight Ride of Paul Revere,' let's say. Well, I get the same
charge out of business that you get out of . . . that's Henry
Wordsworth Longfellow, isn't it?"

There was no way out. "Henry *Wads*worth Longfellow," I
said weakly. "Wordsworth is a different poet."

"That's fine," he said, "that's very good. I like it that you're
enthusiastic that way, and by this time tomorrow, watch and see,
you'll be just as expert with our figures. Now here's my suggestion. Suppose instead of going out to lunch tomorrow, you join
me in Mr. Margate's office. I'll order in some sandwiches and we
can have a talk about books—I'm a book lover myself. I'll bring
in a couple to show you that've been helpful to me in my career
here. You might find them just as useful as I have."

I said, "I didn't know Mr. Margate had an office."

"Mr. Margate passed away eight years ago. It's my office now,
but we still call it Mr. Margate's office. Mr. Margate was the
founder of this firm, and even though he got to be very old, he
was remarkable to the end. He could carry columns and columns
of figures in his head. One look at a column of figures and Mr.
Margate *had* them. Mr. Haroulian is certainly a brilliant man,

but Mr. Margate was a genius. He was married to an authoress—
she passed on right after he did. It was Mr. Margate who gave me
these books I'm going to lend you, and believe me they had an
effect on my whole attitude and behavior in the office. One of
them was written by Mrs. Margate herself."

I was reluctant to give up my Bryant Park lunch hour to sit in
Mr. Margate's office with George Berkeley. Besides, I was discov-
ering that my lie had a living pulse in it, and was likely to go on
ticking: it appeared to be leading me to a future in accounting.
That future was visible in George Berkeley, but it was still more
visible in Mr. Haroulian, even though Mr. Haroulian was a kind
of apparition. His door was always shut; whatever he did behind
it was secret, significant, worldly. But several times a day a small
bony man with copper-penny eyes and a domelike head would
glide by, expressionlessly, monarchically, caressing his mustache
and speaking to no one. Once or twice he halted in front of my
wastebasket and stared down into the crumpled heap of my dis-
cards and sad mistakes.

On Tuesday at twelve-thirty, a delivery boy carried in a card-
board tray with two lettuce-and-tomato sandwiches on it, and
two paper cups filled with a urine-yellow liquid, which proved to
be apple juice. George Berkeley, it developed, was a vegetarian
and a health theorist.

He asked where I had eaten lunch the day before.

"On a bench in the park," I said.

"Not in the sun?" he said. "You should keep out of the sun. It
affects the nerves. And I hope you didn't have meat or cheese.
My rule is, if it comes from anything that has a head on it, don't
eat it."

He reached into Mr. Margate's desk drawer and brought out
two well-worn books. It was plain that they had been zealously
read and reread. One was *How to Win Friends and Influence*

People, by Dale Carnegie. The full title of the other, by Bertha N. Margate, was *Changing Losses into Bosses: A Handbook for Talented and Ambitious Young People Who Feel They Have Come to a Dead End Yet Wish to Succeed in the Business World.*

"Mrs. Margate knew whereof she wrote. According to what she says here, when she met Mr. Margate he was making fifteen dollars a week, but with her on board to inspire him he ended up on top. Look at this! Solid mahogany!" He slapped the ruddy flanks of Mr. Margate's glossy desk. "You just take these couple of books and look them through, and you'll feel the difference they make. But whatever you do, don't skip Mrs. Margate's Chapter Six, the one called 'Inspiration Increaseth Potential.' You'll notice she uses Biblical language all through. Now tell me," he finished, "how did it go this morning? How're you doing?"

"A little better," I fibbed, and opened to Mrs. Margate's Table of Contents.

"That's fine, that's just fine," George Berkeley said in his flat way. I wondered whether he was putting to instant use Mrs. Margate's Chapter Twelve: "A Cheerful Word Encourageth Subordinates." He wrapped his sandwich crumbs in a paper napkin, made a little wad of it, and threw the wad into Mr. Margate's otherwise pristine wastebasket with a force that startled me. Under all that restraint and hollow optimism, something boiled; behind those nondescript syllables what unknown yet colorful life lay in passionate ambush? Perhaps the god of figures did not suffice. I wanted to romanticize George Berkeley, but all at once he romanticized himself: he turned inquisitive, peering over the bow of Margate, Haroulian into the uncharted sea beyond. "I'm interested in that kick," he said. "What's that name again, the fellow who kicked the stone?"

"Dr. Johnson? Who refuted Bishop Berkeley?"

"That's the one. Well, I don't see it. How did that *settle* any-thing?"

"Berkeley insisted that matter wasn't real, only mind was real. So Dr. Johnson kicked the stone to prove the reality of mat-ter. Or you could say to prove the falsity of the invisible."

"Lost his temper and let go, I can understand a thing like that. Whose side are *you* on?"

I was astonished. It was a question no graduate student would think to ask; I had never before considered it. But wasn't *A Theory of Literature* on the side of the invisible?

"I guess I'm with Berkeley," I said.

"Well, I'm the Berkeley who's with the fellow who did the kicking. Is that what that book you're studying's about?"

"No, it isn't," I said. Here was an embarrassment: how to explain Wellek-and-Warren to the man who bore the name of a classical idealist, yet was deaf to the cry of eternals and univer-sals? "It's about a way of reading and analyzing what you read. It's called the New Criticism. You're supposed to read with-out being influenced by history or biography or psychology. As if the words were immutable. You're supposed to . . . well, you just concentrate on the language, and leave out everything to do with . . . I don't know, external entanglements. Human relations."

"The New Criticism," George Berkeley repeated. The white tract of his forehead slowly flooded pink. "Seems to me they're teaching the wrong things in the colleges nowadays. You'll never get ahead based on that kind of idea. You'd do a lot better, believe me, with Dale Carnegie and Mrs. Margate."

Though I was careful to set Dale Carnegie and Mrs. Margate on top of Wellek-and-Warren on the corner of my desk next to the typewriter, I did not do well the rest of that day.

Wednesday was the same. And again Mr. Haroulian slid silently out, circling and circling the narrow space in which I toiled and failed, toiled and failed. Again he looked into my wastebasket—that wild surf, all those ruined and wrinkled forms, those smudged and spoiled and torn tropisms of my despair.

At noon I left Wellek-and-Warren behind and took Mrs. Margate, along with my salami sandwich, to Bryant Park. The midtown heat sizzled in the path. Even the pigeons confined their pecking to random blots of shade eked out by a few dangling dry leaves, or the edge of a bench, or a knot of men with briefcases standing fixed in conversation, sweltering in their puckered seersucker jackets. The brightness dazzled and dazed; pinpoints of painful light glanced out of the necklaces and wristwatches of passers-by. George Berkeley had warned that the sun would trouble my nerves; or perhaps it was Mrs. Margate who was endangering the motionless sticky air. A dread fell over me. I could never live up to her ardor:

Chapter Nine

WHAT IS EXPECTED OF YOUNG WOMEN IN BUSINESS

When the Psalmist saith, "Judge me, O Lord, for I have walked in my integrity," surely he is looking ahead to the conduct of young women in business offices today. When we speak of integrity in this connection, we must always remember that it behooves young women to be accommodating, never condescending; to accept the meanest drudgery of paperwork with humble mien, for this is the instrument of your future ascent; and to treat with superintendents and superiors as with representatives of the power of aspiration. I well recall the case of Miss M.W., an attractive girl of twenty, who considered herself "spunky," and who consistently contradicted her employers, until one day she learned to her dismay that what *she* regarded as "courageous" was viewed by others as "impudent." Woe to the pert young woman in a busy office! (Young men, do not suppose that this advice does not apply to YOU!)

I noticed that Mrs. Margate's handbook was dated 1933, and was self-published. Probably Mr. Margate himself had footed the bill.

On Thursday morning George Berkeley approached my desk. The shallow cheeriness was drained out of him. It was as if the engines of Margate, Haroulian had without warning changed course; he looked like a man dizzied by a wheeling horizon. Two thin streams of sweat voyaged down the immaculate gullies that lay between his little tight nostrils and the flat string that was his mouth. I saw the throb of his throat. On the broad window-sills a pair of electric fans turned sluggishly against an overcast cityscape; it was going to rain.

"Mr. Haroulian wants to see you right away," he said. He did not ask me how I was doing; he did not egg me on to loftier achievement.

"I'll just finish this sheet," I said. I was close to the bottom of the page, and was afraid of losing my place in the march of numbers.

"Right away! Get into Mr. Haroulian's office this minute, will you? I've had enough chewing out from Mr. Haroulian over the likes of you."

Mr. Haroulian began at once to tell me about Lillian, his daughter. Since I had never heard him speak, his voice was a surprise: it ran loud and fast, like a motorcycle. Lillian, he boomed, was twenty-two; a student at Juilliard; a superlative violinist. When Lillian wasn't at school she was practicing—she hardly had a minute, not even to pick up her music. All her time was admirably occupied.

"Schirmer's on East Forty-third Street. Shake a leg and get over there," Mr. Haroulian growled. He handed me his daughter's shopping list; fleetingly, I took in flashes of Mozart, Beethoven, Sibelius. Lillian's photograph was on Mr. Haroulian's desk. A bony royal snippet, heir to the throne, eyes as round as coins—just like Mr. Haroulian himself. All that was missing was Mr. Haroulian's gray imperious mustache, which at that moment appeared to be sweeping me out of his sight like a diminutive but efficient broom. I understood that in Mr. Haroulian's opinion, my time was not so admirably occupied.

Walking uptown to Schirmer's in the thick late-June air, with big raindrops darkening the pavement, I thought of "The Changeling," a story by Mary Lamb that I remembered from childhood. A nurse, ambitious for her offspring, switches two infants in their cradles. One is her own; the other is the daughter of her aristocratic employers. The nurse's natural child, dull and with no talent at all, is lovingly reared by the cultivated aristocratic family, though they are quietly disappointed in the undistinguished girl. Meanwhile their real child, brought up by the nurse, is deprived for years of the development of her innate musical gifts. When the ruse is discovered and the musical daughter is at last restored to her rightful parents, she is showered with music lessons and flourishes. Mr. Haroulian, I felt, in sending me on this humiliating errand, could not recognize that his daughter—exactly my age, after all—might be the inauthentic one, while I, plodding onward in rain-soaked shoes in service to *her*, might secretly be the genuine article. It hardly lessened my bitterness that Wellek-and-Warren was a thousand times more to me than any violin.

That was Thursday. On Friday morning my work on the forms unexpectedly improved. As George Berkeley had promised—before the great wave of his disappointment in the New Criticism—I was starting to get the hang of it, and the rows of digits were finally jumping into their proper boxes. Not all of them, to be sure; for every form I struggled to complete, two or three ruined ones went into the wastebasket. Yet even this minor accomplishment depended on my mastery of the type-writer eraser; I had learned, for example, to erase each carbon separately.

Ten minutes before the lunch hour George Berkeley came to collect Dale Carnegie and Mrs. Margate. "You won't be needing these," he said, and swooped them away. That left Wellek-and-Warren exposed on the corner of my desk; he rested his palm on it. "Dale Carnegie may be a bit more famous, but he doesn't hold a candle to Mrs. Margate. I don't suppose you've even looked into her."

"Yes, I have," I said.

"And what did you think?"

I hesitated: my "spunky" might just turn out to be his "pert." The best answer, I speculated, would be to return diligently to the typewriter.

"Well, never mind. No one here cares *what* you think. Stop typing," he ordered.

I stopped.

"I've always had Mr. Haroulian's perfect confidence—I've had it right along. It's your sort of thinking that's put me in trouble with him. I've been on the telephone with Mr. Haroulian, and we've both decided that you ought to spend the rest of the afternoon just as you please. And you don't need to come back on Monday. Mr. Haroulian's attending his daughter's concert today, or he would be telling you this himself."

I knew he felt betrayed; he had put his trust in higher education.

Then, as if he were handling an unfamiliar and possibly harmful small animal, George Berkeley picked up Wellek-and-Warren and carefully placed it on the floor. He loosened his tie, something I had never seen him do. His damp neck glowed. "And by the way," he said politely, "here's what we here at Margate, Haroulian think of the New Criticism."

With one crisp thwack of his foot he sent *A Theory of Literature* hurtling against the wall.

I crossed the room, retrieved the sacred text, and escaped into the somnolent molasses sunlight of a New York summer afternoon—a failure and an incompetent, and not a changeling at all.

The Synthetic Sublime

More than any other metropolis of the Western world, New York disappears. It disappears and then it disappears again; or say that it metamorphoses between disappearances, so that every seventy-five years or so another city bursts out, as if against nature—new shapes, new pursuits, new immigrants with their unfamiliar tongues and worried uneasy bustle. In nature, the daffodil blooms, withers, vanishes, and in the spring returns— always a daffodil, always indistinguishable from its precursor. Not so New York, preternatural New York! Go to Twenty-third Street and Eighth Avenue: where is the Grand Opera House, with its statuary and carvings, its awnings and Roman-style cornices? Or reconnoiter Thirteenth Street and Broadway: who can find Wallack's Theatre, where the acclaimed Mrs. Jennings, Miss Plessy Mordaunt, and Mr. J. H. Stoddart once starred, and where, it was said, "even a mean play will be a success"? One hundred years ago, no one imagined the dissolution of these dazzling landmarks; they seemed as inevitable, and as permanent, as our Lincoln Center, with its opera and concerts and plays, and its lively streaming crowds.

In Archaeology 101 they tell a New York joke. It is the year 3000. Archaeologists are sifting through the rubble of overgrown mounds, searching for relics of the lost city that once flourished on this brambly wild site. They dig here and there without reason for excitement (beer cans, a plastic sherd or two, unbiodegradable grocery bags), until a: last they uncover what appears to be a primitive concourse of some kind, along which is placed, at surprisingly even intervals, a row of barbaric-looking poles. The poles are molded of an enduring ancient alloy, and each one is topped by a head with a single glass eye and an inch of crude mouth. "Identical sacrificial cultic stands in homage to the city's divinity-king," the archaeologists conclude. What they have found are Second Avenue parking meters: the Ozymandias of the late twentieth century.

The joke may apply to other modern societies (no contemporaneous city, after all, was as modern as Nebuchadnezzar's Babylon), but New York eludes such ironies. New York will never leave town. It will never sink into a desert waste. Catapult us forward a thousand years, and we won't recognize the place; yet it is certain to be, uninterruptedly, New York, populous, evolving, faithfully inconstant, magnetic, man-made, unnatural—the synthetic sublime. If you walk along Lexington Avenue, say, it isn't easy to be reminded that Manhattan is an island, or even that it lies, like everything else, under an infinitude of sky. New York's sky is jigsawed, cut into geometric pieces glimpsed between towers or caught slantwise across a granite-and-glass ravine. There is no horizon; the lucky penthouses and fifteenth-floor apartments and offices may have long views, but the streets have almost none. At night the white glow that fizzes upward from the city—an inverted electric Niagara—obscures the stars, and except for the Planetarium's windowless mimicry, New York is oblivious of the cosmos. It is nearly as indifferent, by and large, to its marine surround. Walt Whitman once sang of the "tall masts of Mannahatta" and of the "crested and scallop-edg'd waves," but the Staten Island ferry and the Circle Line beat on mastless, and the drumming ribbon of the West Side Highway bars us from the sound and smell of waters rushing or lapping.

New York pretends that it is inland and keeps dry indoors and feels shoreless; New York water means faucets and hidden pipes and, now and then, a ceiling leak or the crisis of a burst main. Almost in spite of itself, Riverside Drive looks out on the Hudson, and can, if it likes, remember water. On Manhattan's other flank, the F.D.R. Drive swims alongside the East River like a heavy-chuffing landlubber crocodile, unmindful of the moving water nearby. And here come the bridges, the Queensboro, the Manhattan, the Williamsburg, and finally the Brooklyn, Hart Crane's fabled "harp and altar." These varied spans, squat or spidery—together with the grand George Washington to the north and west—may cry out their poetry of arch and tide and steely ingenuity; but when you ride across in car or bus they are only, again, urban roadways. The tunnels are the same, with their line of lights perpetually alert under the river's tonnage. New York domesticates whatever smacks of sea. And when the two rivers, the Hudson and the East, converge and swallow each other at the Battery's feet, it is the bays alone, the Upper and the Lower, that hurry out to meet the true deep. New York turns its back on the Atlantic. The power and the roar New York looks to are its own.

And if New York is to be misinterpreted and misunderstood, it will not be by future antiquarians, but by its present-day citizens. The Village stymies Wall Street. Chinatown is Greek to Washington Heights. Harlem and Tribeca are mutual enigmas. Neighborhoods are sealed off from one another by the border police of habit and mindset and need and purpose. And there is another border, even more rigid, and surely more disconsolate, than geography: the divide between then and now, a gash that can occur in a single lifetime. Fourth Avenue, masquerading as Park Avenue South, has lost its venerable name; Sixth Avenue—despite its rebirth, half a century ago, as Avenue of the Americas—has not. Where are the hotels of yesteryear? The

Astor, the Chatham, the Savoy-Plaza? The Biltmore and its legendary clock? Where are the rows and rows of second-hand book stores that crept northward from Astor Place to Fourteenth Street? Where are Klein's and Wanamaker's and Gimbel's and Ohrbach's? Where are those urban walkers and scribes—Joseph Mitchell, Meyer Berger, Kate Simon, Alfred Kazin? Where is that cloud of gray fedoras that made men in crowds resemble dandelions gone to seed? When, and why, did New York hats give up the ghost? And who was the last to dance in the Rainbow Room?

The Russian poet Joseph Brodsky—born in Leningrad, exiled to New York, buried in Venice—used to say that he wrote to please his predecessors, not his contemporaries. Often enough New York works toward the opposite: it means to impress the here-and-now, which it autographs with an insouciant wrecking ball. Gone is the cleaner-and-dyer; gone is the shoe-repair man. In their stead, a stylish boutique and a fancy-cookie shop. To see—close at hand—how the present is displaced by a newer present, how streets long confident of their particularity can rapidly molt into streets of a startlingly unexpected character, is to be a bit of a god: what is Time, what is Change, to the gods? For New Yorkers, a millennium's worth of difference can be encompassed in six months. Downtown lofts on spooky dark blocks that once creaked under the weight and thunder and grime of industrial machinery are suddenly filled with sofas upholstered in white linen and oak bars on wheels and paintings under track lighting and polyurethaned coffee tables heaped with European magazines. Bryant Park, notorious shady hangout, blossoms into a cherished noonday amenity. Or else the deserted tenements along the Metro-North line, staring out eyeless and shamefaced at the commuters' train down from Stamford, will, overnight, have had their burnt-out hollows covered over with painted plywood—trompe l'oeil windows and flower pots pretending, Potemkin-like, and by municipal decree, that human habitation has resumed.

Yet despite New York's sleight-of-hand transmutations and fool-the-eye pranks, the lady isn't really sawed in half; she leaps up, alive and smiling. If physical excision is the city's ongoing principle, there are, anyhow, certain surprising tenacities and keepsake intuitions. Wait, for instance, for the downtown No. 104 at the bus stop on Broadway and Seventy-second Street, look across the way, and be amazed—what Renaissance palazzo is this? A tall facade with draped female sculptures on either side, arched cornices, patterned polychrome bricks: ornamental flourish vying with ornamental flourish. And then gaze down the road to your right: one vast slab after another, the uncompromising severity of straight lines, brilliantly winking windows climbing and climbing, not a curve or entablature or parapet or embrasure ruffling the sleek skin of these new residential monoliths. In sharp winter light, a dazzling juxtaposition, filigreed cheek by modernist jowl. The paradox of New York is that its disappearances contain constancies—and not only because some buildings from an earlier generation survive to prod us toward historical self-consciousness. What is most steadfast in New York has the fleet look of the mercurial: the city's persistent daring, vivacity, enchantment, experiment; the marvel of new forms fired by old passions, the rekindling of the snuffed.

The Lower East Side, those tenement-and-pushcart streets of a century ago, once the venue of synagogues and succahs and religious-goods stores and a painful density of population, and later the habitat of creeps and druggies, is now the neighborhood of choice for the great-grandchildren of earlier tenants who were only too happy to escape to the Bronx. The talismanic old Rainbow Room has shut its doors? Never mind: its drama and urgent charm have migrated south. The downtown bands and their girl singers have a different sound, but the bands are there, and the girl singers too. At the Knitting Factory and other clubs—with names like Arlene Grocery, Luna Lounge, Baby Jupiter—you may catch up with Motel Girl, a band specializing in "Las Vegas stripper noir": avant-garde jazz described as jarring, seedy, sexy, Movietone-violent, dark. Even Ratner's on Delancey, the destination of senior citizens with an appetite for potato pancakes and blintzes, has succumbed to bands and poetry readings. Many of the singers and musicians live in the old tenement flats (toilet down the hall) on Avenue B, with monthly rents as high as a thousand dollars. Broadway and Prince, where Dean & DeLuca boasts three hundred varieties of cheese, was home to a notions shop two generations ago; not far away, on Orchard Street, the Tenement Museum stands as an emblem of nostalgic consecration, ignored by its trendy neighbors. You can still buy pickles out of the barrel at Guss's, but the cutting-edge young who come down to Ludlow and Stanton for the music or the glitz rarely find those legendary greenhorn warrens of much historic interest; their turf is the East Village. The Lower East Side's current inhabitants, despite their fascination with the louche, are educated and middle-class, with mothers back on Long Island wishing their guitar-playing daughters had gone to medical school. What these seekers on A, B, and C are after—like Scott and Zelda plunging into fountains to jump-start the Jazz Age—is New York's insuperable constant: the sense of belonging to the glamorous marrow of one's own time.

Uptown's glamour drive is more domestic. On the Upper West Side, the bodegas and the little appetizing and hardware stores on Amsterdam, Columbus, and Broadway are long gone, and the great style emporia dominate, behemoths of food, cooking devices, leather accessories, "natural" cosmetics, no-color cotton sheets, Mission furniture. Zabar's, the Fairway, Barney

Greengrass, Citarella, H & H Bagels—dizzyingly flooded with epicurean getters and spenders—harbor prodigalities of dimpled breads, gourmet coffees, the right kind of polenta, the right kind of rice and salsa, the right kind of coffeemaker and salad-spinner. Body Works offers soaps and lotions and oils, Godiva's chocolates are set out like jewels, Gracious Home dazes with kitchenware chic. There is something of a puzzle in all this exuberant fashionableness and household seductiveness, this bean-grinding, face-creaming, bed-making: where are the political and literary intellectuals the Upper West Side is famous for, why are the conversations about olives and fish?

Across town, the Upper East Side seems, in contrast, staid, reserved, nearly quiet. The streets are less peopled. The wind is colder. A hauteur lurks in the limestone. If the West Side is a roiling marketplace, the East Side is a marble lobby presided over by a monarchical doorman. Fifth Avenue can be tacky here and there, but Madison grows more and more burnished, New York's version of the Rue du Faubourg St. Honoré. Here march the proud shops of the élite European designers, whose names make tailors' music: Yves St. Laurent, Versace, Gucci, Valentino, Giorgio Armani, Prada, Missoni, Dolce & Gabbana. Here is the Tiffany's of greengrocers, where Mozart is played and a couple of tomatoes will cost as much as a movie ticket. Here are L'Occitane for perfumes and Bulgari for diamonds. On Park and Madison affluence reigns, and with it a certain neighborhood serenity—a privacy, a regal seclusion. (Over on Lexington and Third, the city's rush begins again.)

Posh East and extravagant West dislike each other, with the ingrained antipathy of restraint and profusion, calm and bustle; nor are they likely, except for an audacious handful of crosstown adventurers, to rub elbows in the shops. A silent cold war chills Manhattan. Its weapons are Zabar's in the West, Versace in the East. There is no hot line between them.

2.

Who lives in New York? E. B. White, mulling the question fifty years ago, imagined "a farmer arriving from Italy to set up a small grocery in a slum, or a young girl arriving from a small town in Mississippi to escape the indignity of being observed by her neighbors, or a boy arriving from the Corn Belt with a manuscript in his suitcase and a pain in his heart." This has a musty if sweetish scent for us now—eau de Jimmy Stewart, perhaps. The circumstances of the arrivals were generally not so benign; nor was their reception. In a 1922 address before the New York–based American Academy of Arts and Letters, Owen Wister, the author of *The Virginian,* said of the newcomers, "Recent arrivals pollute the original spring. . . . It would be well for us if many recent arrivals would become departures." He meant the immigrants who were just then flooding Castle Garden; but the children of those immigrants would soon be sorting out the dilemmas of welcome and unwelcome by other means.

I remember a ferocious street game that was played in the northeast Bronx long ago, in the neighborhood known as Pelham Bay. It was called "War," and it was exclusively a girls' game. With a piece of colored chalk you drew a small circle, in which you placed a pink rubber ball. Then you drew a second circle around it, concentric but far larger. This second circle you divided into as many pie-slices as there were players. Each player was assigned a pie-slice as her designated territory and wrote in it the name of a country she felt to be her own. So it went like this: Peggy Scanlon chose Ireland; Dorothy Wilson, Scotland; Hilda Weber, Germany; Carolyn Johnson, Sweden; Maria Viggiano (whose Sicilian grandmothers yearly wrapped their fig trees in winter canvas), Italy; Allegra Sadacca (of a Sephardic family recently from Turkey, a remnant of the Spanish Jews exiled by Ferdinand and Isabella in 1492), Spain; Madge Taylor (an immigrant from Iowa), America; and I (whose forebears had endured the despots of Russia for nearly a thousand years), Palestine. So much for the local demographics. Immediately after these self-defining allegiances were declared, someone would shriek "War!" and the asphalt mayhem of racing and tackling and tumbling would begin, with the pink rubber globe as prize. I don't suppose little girls anywhere in New York's boroughs nowadays play this disunited nations game; but if they do, surely the pie-slices are chalked up with preferences for Trinidad, Jamaica, Haiti, Puerto Rico, the Dominican Republic, Colombia, Mexico, Peru, Greece, Lebanon, Albania, Pakistan, India, China, and of course—for antecedents who were never willing immigrants—Africa. In New York, origins still count, and not always benevolently.

3.

The poor of New York occupy streets only blocks away from the palaces. There are cities where such matters are handled otherwise. In Paris some time ago, heading for the Louvre—a row of former royal palaces—I passed a pitiful maternal scene: a dark-eyed young woman half-reclining on the pavement, with a baby in the crook of her arm and a sad-faced little girl huddled against her. The infant's only covering was a newspaper. "Gypsies," someone explained, in a tone that dismissed concern. "By the end of the day, when she's collected her hoard of francs, her husband comes to fetch her in a white limousine." Behind this cynicism lay a social reality. The woman and her children had to be taken, however sardonically, for canny entrepreneurs, not outcasts begging for pennies. The outcasts were elsewhere. They were not in the shadow of the Louvre; they were in the suburbs. In New York lingo, "suburbs" evokes green lawns and commuters of middling affluence. But the great European cities—Paris, Stockholm—have cordoned off their needy, their indigent, their laboring classes. The habitations of the poor are out of town, away from the central brilliance, shunted off and invisible. In New York you cannot lose sight of the poor—the workfare leaf-rakers in the parks, the ragged and piebald homeless, who appear on nearly every corner, some to importune, some to harass, and the pressing mass of the tenement poor, whose eager children fill (as they always have) the public schools. The vivid, hectic, noisily dense barrio, bouncy and bedraggled, that is West 155th Street leads straight across northern Broadway to that austerely resplendent Venetian palace, designed by McKim, Mead, and White, where Owen Wister inveighed against the intruders. But New York, like the stories of O. Henry (one of its early chroniclers), is pleased to spring ironic endings—so there stands the noble Academy, far uptown's distinguished monument to Arts and Letters, surrounded now by poor immigrants, an emerald's throw from the buzz and dust of Broadway's bazaar, where rugs and pots and plastic gewgaws clutter the teeming sidewalks. In New York, proletarian and patrician are neighbors.

4.

As for the upper crust in general, it is known to run New York. This stratum of the social order was once dubbed the Four Hundred, but New York's current patriciate, however it may have multiplied, escapes being counted—though it counts as heavily as ever and remains as conscientiously invisible. Elitism of this kind is rarely political; it almost never becomes mayor. In a democratic ambiance New York's potentates and nabobs have no easy handle; no one names them, not even in tabloid mockery. Then let us call them, collectively, by what they possess: Influence. Influence is financial, corporate, loftily and discreetly legal; Influence is power and planning and money. And money is the armature on which the mammoth superstructure that is New York is sculpted: architecture and philanthropy, art galleries and libraries and foundations, zoos and conservatories and museums, concert halls and universities and houses of worship. The tallest buildings—the Chrysler, the Empire State, the risen polyhedrons of Rockefeller Center, the Twin Towers, assorted old spires—all have their ankles in money. Influence *means* money, whether in the making of it, the spending, or the giving. Influence is usually private and guarded; it may shun celebrity; it needs no public face; its precincts are often reclusive. You are not likely to follow Influence in its daily maneuvers—though you can, all week long, observe the subway riders as they patiently swarm, intent on getting in and getting out and getting there. The jerky cars grind out their wild sawing clamor; locked inside the racket, the passengers display a Buddhist self-forgetfulness. Noiseless Influence, meanwhile, is driven in smoked-glass limousines, hidden, reserved, arcane. If all the rest of the citizenry were carted off, and only Influence were left, the city would be silent. But if Influence were spirited away in some grand and ghostly yacht, a kind of Flying Dutchman, say, the men in their dinner jackets, the women in their gowns, what would happen to New York? The mysterious and mazy coursings of money would dry up. The city would come to a halt.

Old money (old for us, though it was new then) made the palaces. Here is James D. McCabe, Jr., writing in 1872 of the transport cathedral, in Second Empire style, that was the brain-child of Cornelius Vanderbilt, the railway magnate:

> One of the most imposing buildings in the city is the new Grand Central Depot, on Forty-second street and Fourth Avenue. It is constructed of red brick, with iron trimmings painted white, in imitation of marble. The south front is adorned with three and the west front with two massive pavilions. The central pavilion of each front contains an illuminated dock. . . . The car-shed is covered with an immense circular roof of iron and glass. . . . It is lighted from the roof by day, and at night large reflectors, lighted by an electrical apparatus, illuminate the vast interior.

And here again, in 1948, is E. B. White (a man who knew how to catch the beat of what he called "Manhattan's breathing"), describing his own encounter with the Depot's successor, built in 1913 on the same site:

> Grand Central has become honky-tonk, with its extradimensional advertising displays and its tendency to adopt the tactics of a travel broker. I practically lived in Grand Central Terminal at one period (it has all the conveniences and I had no other place to stay) and the great hall seemed to me one of the more inspiring interiors in New York, until Lastex and Coca-Cola got into the temple.

Kodak got in, too, and honky-tonk turned into logo. Like some painted colossus, Kodak's gargantuan sign, in flaming color (it was named the Colorama), presided for years over the criss-crossing rush-hour flow—a fixture of the terminal's contemporary identity. The gilded constellations on the vaulted horizon dimmed to an undifferentiated gray; no one troubled to look up at blinded Orion. A gluey grime thickened the interstices of the marble balustrades. Frankfurter wrappings and sticky paper soda cups littered the public telephones. Commuters in need of a toilet knew what to avoid and went next door to the Grand Hyatt. The temple had become a routinely seedy train station.

And then New York, the Eraser and the Renewer, with a sweep of its resuscitating will, cleansed the temple's degradation. What old money brought into being, new money, along with civic determination, has refurbished. The theme is artful mirroring: the existing grand stair engenders an answering grand stair on the opposite end of the great concourse. The gawky advertising signs are banished and the heavens scrubbed until their stars glitter. Below and behind, the secret ganglia of high-tech engineering and up-to-date lighting may snake and throb, but all across the shining hall it is Commodore Vanderbilt's ghost who walks. Grand Central has no fear of the ornamental; it revels in breadth and unstinting scale; it *intends* to inspire. The idea of the publicly palatial—unashamed lavishness—has returned.

And not only here. Follow Forty-second Street westward to Fifth Avenue and enter the most illustrious temple of all, the lion-sentried Library, where the famed third-floor Reading Room has just undergone its own rebirth—both in homage to, and in dissent from, the modern. Card catalogues have descended into the dustbin of antiquated conveniences. Electrical outlets accommodate laptops; rows of computers parade across the vast polished tables under a gilded rococo ceiling, a Beaux-Arts confection frosted with floral arabesques. Whatever the mavens may say, and however the critics may scowl, New York (in at least one of its multiple manifestations) thirsts for intimations of what the Victorians did not hesitate to invoke: Noble Beauty. New York has learned to value—though never to venerate—its old robber-baron muses, not for their pre-income-tax devourings, but for their appetite for the baronial: the Frick

Collection, the Morgan Library, the Cooper-Hewitt (housed in Andrew Carnegie's sixty-four-room mansion). The vanished Pennsylvania Station, the original—razed a generation ago as an elaborate eyesore, now regretted, its bargain-basement replacement a daily discouragement—will soon rise again, in the nearby body of the superannuated General Post Office (Roman, kingly, columned). Fancy, then, a soaring apparition of the Metropolitan Museum of Art, that prototype of urban palace, and of its philosophical rival, the Museum of Modern Art, hovering over the city, scanning it for symptoms of majesty—the Met and MOMA, joined by spectral flights of the City Ballet, the serious little theaters, and Carnegie Hall, all whispering "Aspire, aspire!"

Susurrations of grandeur.

5.

But grandeur on this style is a neighborhood of the mind, and a narrow one at that. Real neighborhoods and psychological neighborhoods may, in fact, overlap—literary Greenwich Village being the most storied case in point. In the Village of the psyche, the outré is always in, and it is safely conventional to be bizarre. Writers once looked for cheap rent in these streets, after which it began to *feel* writerly to live in the Village, within walking distance of the fountain in Washington Square. The earlier luminaries who resided here are the more enshrined— Washington Irving, James Fenimore Cooper, Louisa May Alcott, Mark Twain, Edgar Allan Poe, O. Henry, Horace Greeley, Walt Whitman, Theodore Dreiser, Bret Harte, Sinclair Lewis, Sherwood Anderson, Upton Sinclair, Willa Cather; and, in a later generation, Thomas Wolfe, E. E. Cummings, Richard Wright,

Djuna Barnes, Edmund Wilson, Elinor Wylie, Hart Crane, James Agee, Marianne Moore, W. H. Auden! Yet fame re-enacted can become parody as well as homage, and there was a touch of in-your-face déjà vu in the nineteen-fifties, when Allen Ginsberg, Jack Kerouac, and LeRoi Jones (afterward known as Amiri Baraka) established the then newborn East Village as a beatnik redoubt. Nowadays it would be hard to discover a writers' roster equal to those of the past, and West Village literariness hangs as a kind of tattered nimbus not over the old (mostly temporary) residences of the celebrated but over the bars, cellars, and cafés they once frequented. The Saturday night hordes that flow through Bleecker Street are mostly from New Jersey. ("The bridge-and-tunnel crowd," sniffs the East Village of the hour.)

Neighborhoods of the mind, though, are rarely so solidly placed in a single location. Of actual neighborhoods (or "sections," in moribund New Yorkese)—Soho, Little Italy, Chelsea, Gramercy Park, Murray Hill, South Street Seaport, and all the rest—only a few are as determinedly self-defined as the Village. But a courageous denizen of any of them (despite home-grown inhibitions of boundary and habit) can venture out to a collectivity of taste and imagination and familiarity unconstrained by geography. Jazz and blues and nightlife aficionados, movie buffs, gays, rap artists, boxing and wrestling zealots, singles, esoteric-restaurant habitués, Central Park joggers, marathon runners, museum addicts, lovers of music or theater or dance, lonely-hearts, shoppers, hotel weekenders, barflies, churchgoers, Talmud enthusiasts, Bronx-born Tibetan Buddhists, students of Sufism, kabbalists, theosophists, voice or ski coaches, SAT and LSAT crammers, amateur painters, union members, members of boards and trustees, Internet devotees, fans of the Yankees or the Mets or the Jets or the Knicks, believers in psychics and tea-leaves readers, streetwalkers and their pimps, antiques fanciers, art collectors, philanthropists, professors of linguistics, lexicog-

raphers, copy editors, librarians, kindergarten teachers, cross-
ing guards, wine votaries, storefront chiropractors, Chinese or
Hebrew or Arabic calligraphers—all these, and inconceivably
more, can emerge from any locality to live, if only for a few
hours, in a sympathetic neighborhood of affinity. Expertise and
idiosyncrasy and bursting desire burn and burn in New York: a
conflagration of manifold, insatiable, tumultuous will.

6.

I was born in a brownstone on East Eighty-eighth Street,
between First and York Avenues—but both the latter avenue
and the area have since altered their designations and their character. York was once Avenue A, and the neighborhood, populated
largely by German immigrants, was called Yorkville. It was in
Yorkville before my birth that my infant brother was kidnapped
by a madwoman. The story as it was told to me is set in a certain
year, but not in any special weather; it seems to me that it must
have been summer. I see my mother, hot, sleeveless, breathless,
frantic, running through the night streets of Yorkville to find the
kidnapper and snatch her baby back. He had been sleeping in his
wicker carriage in a nook among rows of brown bottles and
drawers filled with maple-flavored rock candy on strings, not
four yards from where my young father in his pharmacist's
jacket, a fountain pen always in its pocket, stood tending to his
mortar and pestle, working up a medicinal paste. Into my parents' drug store the madwoman flew, seizing baby and carriage
and all, and out into the dark she fled, only to be discovered some
hours later in nearby Carl Schurz Park, disheveled and undone
by furious infantile howls, and grateful to relinquish the captive
screamer.
    In my half-dreaming re-creation of this long-ago scene—the

stolen child, the fleeing madwoman—why must it be summertime? I think I know why. New York in summer is another sort
of city; in mood and weight it has nothing in common with wintry New York. A New York summer is frenetic, syncopated, blis-
tered, frayed, dusty. There is a desperation in its heat, and a sense
of letdown, despite relief, in its air-conditioned indoors. Melting
squads of tourists, in shorts and open shirts or halters, sweat
pooling under their camera straps, their heads swiveling from
one gaudy carnival sight to the next, push through Times Square
in anxious quick-march. Smells of perspiring hot dogs under
venders' grease-lined umbrellas mingle with the exhaust fumes
of heaving buses. There is nothing relaxed about the summer
city. New York's noise is louder, New York's toughness is
brasher, New York's velocity is speedier. Everything—stores,
offices, schedules, vacations, traffic—demands full steam ahead;
no one can say that the livin' is easy. New York in July is out
of synch, not quite itself, hoping for ransom, kidnapped by
midsummer frolicking: picnickers awaiting free twilight perfor-
mances of Shakespeare in Central Park; street parades of night-
time swelterers along Museum Mile, where tappers and clappers
gather before the Jewish Museum to salute the tootling klezmer
players; breakdancers down from Harlem, twelve-year-olds
effortless and expert and little and lithe, who spin on their heels
across from the hive of Madison Square Garden. In the American heartland in summer, babies fall down wells and pipes, and
that is news. In New York—fidgety, frittering, frenzied, boiling
New York—summer itself is news.

   The true city is the winter city. The woolly enchantment of a
population swaddled and muffled, women and men in long coats,
eccentric boots, winding scarves; steam sculptures forming out
of human breath; hushed streets; tiny white electric points on
skeletal trees! The icy air like a scratch across a sheet of silver,

the smoky chestnut carts, the foggy odor of hot coffee when you open a door, a bakery's sweet mist swirling through its transom, a glimpse of rosy-nosed skaters in the well of the Rockefeller stelae, the rescuing warmth of public lobbies—New York in January is a city of grateful small shocks. And just as in an antiquated English novel of manners, New York has its "season"—lectures, readings, rallies, dinner parties, chamber music in someone's living room. While in summer you cannot rely on the taxis to turn on their air-conditioning, in winter each yellow capsule is a hot little bullet; the driver in his turban remembers his subcontinental home. There is no dusk like a New York winter dusk: the blurry gray of early evening, when the lone walker, ferried between day and night, jostled by strangers in packs, feels most desolate, and when the privacy of burrowing into a coat collar brings on a nameless loss. At such a moment the forest of flowering lights (a brilliance suddenly apprehended) makes its cheering claim: that here, right *here*, is importance, achievement, delight in the work of the world; that here, right here, is the hope of connection, and life in its fulfillment. In a gregarious New York winter, especially in restaurants at eight o'clock, you will hear jokes, stories with amazing climaxes, futures plotted out, jealousies retailed, gossip above all: who's up, who's down, what's in, what's out. Central heating never abolished the theory and practice of the fireside.

7.

What Manhattan talks about, obliquely or openly—what it thinks about, whatever the season—is ambition. Europeans always make much of this: how *hard* New Yorkers work, the long days, the paltry vacations, the single-minded avarice for status, the obsessiveness, the terrible drive. What? No *dolce far niente*? But only an outsider would remark on the city's striving; for New Yorkers it is ingrained, taken for granted, valued. Unlike Bartleby, downtown's most distinctive imaginary inhabitant, New York never prefers not to. New York prefers and prefers and prefers—it prefers power and scope to tranquility and intimacy, it prefers struggle and steel to acquiescence and cushions. New York is where you go to seize the day, to leave your mark, to live within the nerve of your generation. Some might say that there is nothing new in this—why else did Willa Cather begin in Red Cloud, Nebraska, and end on Bank Street? Why else did Jackson Pollock, born in Cody, Wyoming, land in New York?

Yet there is a difference. New York ambition has changed its face. Fifty years ago, when postal clerks and bank tellers wearing vests were what was still called "family men," the hankering young were on the lowest rung of any hierarchy. Their patience was commanded; their deference was expected. It was understood that power and position were the sovereign right of middle age, and that a twenty-three-year-old would have to wait and wait. Opportunity and recognition were light-years away. A few—writers mostly—broke out early: Mary McCarthy at twenty-two, Norman Mailer at twenty-five, Philip Roth and John Updike at twenty-six. Leonard Bernstein and Bobby Fischer were youthful stars. Still, these were all prodigies and exceptions. In the run-of-the-mill world of getting ahead, the young were at the bottom, and stayed there until judged—by their elders at the top—to be sufficiently ripe. The Information Age, with its ear to the ground, reverses all that. The old ways are undone. A twenty-something young woman in publishing keeps a television set on in her office all day, monitoring possible acquisitions: what sells, who's cool. The auditory and the visual, in whatever mode, belong almost exclusively to the newest generation. Everywhere in New York the knowledgeable young are in charge of the sound, the image, the latest word; ambition need no longer stand in line and wait its graying turn. (Fifty-somethings, their passion still unspent, and recalling the slower passages of long ago, may be a little wistful.)

In a city always relinquishing, always replacing, always on the wing, mores close down and expectations alter; milestones fade away; landmarks vanish. In its shifting primordial constancy, New York is faithful to loss and faithful to change. After the hullabaloo over the demise of Books & Company on Madison and Shakespeare & Company on upper Broadway, some still mourn those small principalities of letters. But does anyone born since the Second World War miss the intellectual newsstand next to the Chock Full O' Nuts across from Washington Square, or the Forty-second Street Automat, where you could linger over your teacup and read your paper all afternoon?

Now and then, heartstruck, I pass the crenellated quasi-Gothic building that once housed my high school, where latecomers, myself among them, would tremble before its great arched doorway, fearing reprimand; but the reprimanders are all dead. My Latin teacher is dead. My German teacher is dead. My biology teacher is dead. It is only the city itself that lives on, half-amnesiac, hardly ever glancing back, re-inventing its fabric, insisting on being noticed for what it is now. There is no grief for what precedes the common memory, and ultimately the fickle urban tide, as immutable as the Nile, accommodates every disappearance.

8.

In May of 1860, when Frederick Law Olmsted's Central Park was just in the making, a forty-year-old Wall Street lawyer named George Templeton Strong recorded in his diary his own preference:

> The park below the reservoir begins to look intelligible. Unfinished still, and in process of manufacture, but shewing the outline now of what it is to be. Many points are already beautiful. What will they be when their trees are grown and I'm dead and forgotten?
>
> One thinks sometimes that one would like re-juvenescence, or a new birth. One would prefer, if he could, to annihilate his past and commence life, say in this A.D. 1860, and so enjoy longer acquaintance with this era of special development and material progress, watch the splendid march of science on earth, share the benefits of the steam engine and the electric telegraph, and grow up with this park—which is to be so great a fact for the young men and maidens of New York in 1880, if all goes well and we do not decompose into anarchy meanwhile. . . . Central Park and Astor Library and a developed Columbia University promise to make the city twenty years hence a real center of culture and civilization, furnishing privileges to youth far beyond what it gave me in my boyhood.

A century and a half on, Strong's "era of special development and material progress" may seem quaint to us, for whom fax and e-mail and jets and microwaves are everyday devices, and whose moonwalkers are already old men. By now the park below the reservoir, the library on Fifth Avenue, and the university on Morningside Heights are seasoned inheritances—established components of the city's culture and civilization. But even standing as we do on the lip of the new millennium, who can resist falling into George Templeton Strong's wishful dream of a new birth and a longer acquaintance? His New York of steam engine and telegraph, as ephemeral as the May clouds of 1860, has ceased to be. Our New York, too, will disappear, and a renewed and clarified city will lift out of the breathing breast of the one we know. New York, Enemy of the Merely Picturesque, Headquarters of Misery and Marvel, Eraser and Renewer, Brain and Capital of the Continent!

The immigrants will come—what language will they speak? The towers will climb to the sky—what shapes will they have? The crowds will stream in the streets—what thoughts will they think? Will they think our outworn thoughts, or imaginings we cannot imagine?

A Note About the Author

CYNTHIA OZICK is a novelist, essayist, playwright, and short story writer whose work has won numerous awards, including the American Academy of Arts and Letters Strauss Living Award, four O. Henry First Prizes, the Rea Award for the Short Story, and a Guggenheim Fellowship. Her books have been nominated for both the National Book Critics Circle Award and the National Book Award. She lives with her husband in Westchester County, New York.

A Note on the Type

The text of this book was set in a typeface called Aldus, designed by the celebrated typographer Hermann Zapf in 1952–1953. Based on the classical proportion of the popular Palatino type family, Aldus was originally adapted for Linotype composition as a sightly lighter version that would read better in smaller sizes. Hermann Zapf was born in Nuremberg, Germany, in 1918. He has created many other well-known typefaces, including Comenius, Hunt Roman, Marconi, Melior, Michelangelo, Optima, Saphir, Sistina, Zapf Book, and Zapf Chancery.

Composed by Creative Graphics, Allentown, Pennsylvania
Printed and bound by Quebecor Printing,
Fairfield, Pennsylvania
Designed by Anthea Lingeman